# RADICAL
## TRADITIONS

**THEOLOGY IN A POSTCRITICAL KEY**

### SERIES EDITORS

*Stanley M. Hauerwas, Duke University,*
*and Peter Ochs, University of Virginia*

RADICAL TRADITIONS cuts new lines of inquiry across a confused array of debates concerning the place of theology in modernity and, more generally, the status and role of scriptural faith in contemporary life. Charged with a rejuvenated confidence, spawned in part by the rediscovery of reason as inescapably tradition constituted, a new generation of theologians and religious scholars is returning to scriptural traditions with the hope of retrieving resources long ignored, depreciated, and in many cases ideologically suppressed by modern habits of thought. RADICAL TRADITIONS assembles a promising matrix of strategies, disciplines, and lines of thought that invites Jewish, Christian, and Islamic theologians back to the word, recovering and articulating modes of scriptural reasoning as that which always underlies modernist reasoning and therefore has the capacity — and authority — to correct it.

Far from despairing over modernity's failings, postcritical theologies rediscover resources for renewal and self-correction within the disciplines of academic study themselves. Postcritical theologies open up the possibility of participating once again in the living relationship that binds together God, text, and community of interpretation. RADICAL TRADITIONS thus advocates a "return to the text," which means a commitment to displaying the richness and wisdom of traditions that are at once text based, hermeneutical, and oriented to communal practice.

Books in this series offer the opportunity to speak openly with practitioners of other faiths or even with those who profess no (or limited) faith, both academics and nonacademics, about the ways religious traditions address pivotal issues of the day. Unfettered by foundationalist preoccupations, these books represent a call for new paradigms of reason — a thinking and rationality that are more responsive than originative. By embracing a postcritical posture, they are able to speak unapologetically out of scriptural traditions manifest in the practices of believing communities (Jewish, Christian, and others); articulate those practices through disciplines of philosophic, textual, and cultural criticism; and engage intellectual, social, and political practices that for too long have been insulated from theological evaluation. RADICAL TRADITIONS is radical not only in its confidence in non-apologetic theological speech but also in how the practice of such speech challenges the current social and political arrangements of modernity.

# ABRAHAM'S PROMISE

## Judaism and Jewish-Christian Relations

MICHAEL WYSCHOGROD

*Edited and introduced by*

R. Kendall Soulen

WILLIAM B. EERDMANS PUBLISHING COMPANY
GRAND RAPIDS, MICHIGAN / CAMBRIDGE, U.K.

Published jointly 2004
in the United States of America by
Wm. B. Eerdmans Publishing Co.
255 Jefferson Ave. S.E., Grand Rapids, Michigan 49503 /
P.O. Box 163, Cambridge CB3 9PU U.K.
www.eerdmans.com

and in the United Kingdom by
SCM Press
9-17 St. Alban's Place, London N1 0NX

Printed in the United States of America

09  08  07  06  05  04      7  6  5  4  3  2  1

Library of Congress Cataloging-in-Publication Data

Wyschogrod, Michael, 1928-
Abraham's promise: Judaism and Jewish-Christian relations /
Michael Wyschogrod; edited by R. Kendall Soulen.
        p.        cm. — (Radical traditions)
Includes bibliographical references and index.
ISBN 0-8028-1355-0 (pbk.: alk. paper)
1. Judaism.  2. Judaism — Relations — Christianity.
3. Christianity and other religions — Judaism.
I. Soulen, R. Kendall, 1959-   II. Title.   III. Series.
                BM45.W97   2004
296.3 — dc22

                                            2004042521

FOR MY GRANDCHILDREN

*Margaret Hannah,*

*Ezra Akiva,*

*Aaron Samuel,*

*Paul Morris,*

*and*

*Tracy Elizabeth*

— MW

# Contents

# CONTENTS

## JEWISH-CHRISTIAN RELATIONS

# Acknowledgments

The author and publisher gratefully acknowledge permission to include the following:

"Divine Election and Commandments." Originally published in *Judaism* 10:4 (Fall 1961): 350-352. Used by permission.

"A Theology of Jewish Unity." Originally published in *L'Eylah Journal* 21 (1986): 26-30. Used by permission.

"Sin and Atonement in Judaism." Originally published in *The Human Condition in the Jewish and Christian Traditions*, ed. Frederick Greenspahn (New York: Ktav Publishing House, 1986), pp. 103-128. Used by permission.

"Judaism and Conscience." Originally published in *Standing before God: Studies on Prayer in Scripture and in Tradition with Essays in Honor of John M. Oesterreicher*, ed. Asher Finkel and Lawrence Frizzell (New York: Ktav Publishing House, 1981), pp. 313-328. Used by permission.

"Reflections on the Six Day War after a Quarter Century." Originally published in *Tradition* 26:4 (Summer 1992): 24-25. Used by permission. *Tradition* is published by the Rabbinical Council of America.

"The Revenge of the Animals." Originally published in *Hören und Lernen in der Schule des Namens: Mit der Tradition zum Aufbruch*, Festschrift für Berthold Klappert zum 60. Geburtstag, ed. Jochen Denker et al. (Neukirchen-Vluyn: Neukirchener, 1999), pp. 23-25. Used by permission.

"Faith and the Holocaust." Originally published in *Judaism* 20:3 (Summer 1971): 286-294. Used by permission.

"Franz Rosenzweig's *The Star of Redemption*." Originally published in *Man and World* 6:1 (February 1973): 100-107. Used with kind permission of Kluwer Academic Publishers.

"A Jewish View of Christianity." Originally published in *Toward a Theological En-*

counter: *Jewish Understandings of Christianity,* ed. Leon Klenicki (New York: Paulist Press, 1991), pp. 104-119. Used by permission of Paulist Press (www.paulistpress.com).

"Incarnation and God's Indwelling in Israel." Originally published in *Archivio di Filosofia* 67:1-3 (1999): 147-157. Used by permission of CEDAM.

"A Letter to Cardinal Lustiger." Originally published as "A Letter to a Friend" in *Modern Theology* 11:2 (April 1995): 165-171. Used by permission of Blackwell Publishing Ltd.

"Why Was and Is the Theology of Karl Barth of Interest to a Jewish Theologian?" Originally published in *Footnotes to a Theology: The Karl Barth Colloquium of 1972,* ed. Martin Rumscheidt (Waterloo, Ont.: Corporation for the Publication of Academic Religious Studies in Canada, 1974), pp. 95-111. Supplement to *Studies in Religion/Sciences Religieuses* (1974). Used by permission.

"The Impact of Dialogue with Christianity on My Self-Understanding as a Jew." Originally published in *Die Hebraeische Bibel und ihre zweifache Nachgeschichte,* ed. Erhard Blum, Christian Macholz, and Ekkehard W. Stegemann (Neukirchen-Vluyn: Neukirchener, 1990), pp. 725-736. Used by permission.

# A Biographical Sketch
## of Michael Wyschogrod

MICHAEL WYSCHOGROD was born on September 28, 1928, in Berlin, Germany, the younger of two sons of his parents, Paul Wyschogrod and his wife Margaret, born Ungar. Paul was an internationally recognized chessmaster who had moved in the mid-twenties from Budapest, Hungary, to Berlin with his wife and first son, Marcel, in response to deteriorating economic conditions resulting from the breakup of the Austro-Hungarian monarchy after World War I. Paul earned a marginal living for his family by manufacturing waterproof aprons in the family apartment; these he sold to small stores and at outdoor markets in the city. His real love remained chess, which he counseled his son Michael to avoid. The intellectual effort required, he thought, did not produce proportionate spiritual and financial rewards.

Wyschogrod's earliest memories go back to the years in Berlin just before Hitler's coming to power. His parents sent him to the *Adas Yisroel* school, an Orthodox Jewish institution that combined excellent Jewish and secular instruction. By 1936, the Jewish emigration from Berlin put significant stress on the educational system as teachers and pupils departed. A brother of Margaret lived in the U.S. and he sent the necessary papers, which made emigration to the U.S. possible. They received their visa early in 1939 and departed for New York by way of Warsaw. The three weeks in Warsaw made a very deep impression on the ten-year-old Michael who was a witness to the last moments of pre-war Jewish life in Poland.

After settling in Brooklyn, New York, in 1939, Michael was enrolled in *Yeshiva Torah Vodaath*, a Yiddish-speaking, Eastern European–style Orthodox day school. There his father believed Michael would receive the best possible Talmudic education.

> At the *Mesivta Torah Vodaath* I studied with several men whose spiritual presence will remain with me for the rest of my life. Of these, I would mention only one: Rabbi Schlomo Heiman, of blessed memory, with whom I studied no more than three months before his death. By sheer accident, we also spent several weeks of a summer vacation together. Through him I came to appreciate that part of the Torah that cannot be written down but transmitted only in the being of the person whose everyday conduct exemplifies it. There were others, some now dead, others alive; they all taught generations of Yeshiva students most of whom, I dare say, remained observant Jews.[1]

After graduating from *Yeshiva Torah Vodaath's* high school in 1945, Michael spent the 1945-46 academic year in Talmudic studies, and began his college career at the City College of New York in the fall of 1946.

> As an undergraduate in a philosophy of religion course, I was introduced to Søren Kierkegaard and while at first I had great difficulty in making out what he was driving at (the first book I read was *Either/Or*, whose pseudonyms confused me no end), I knew from the beginning that here was someone of decisive importance to me. . . . Through Kierkegaard I was drawn into Christian theology.[2]

Concurrently, he enrolled at Yeshiva University as a student of Rabbi Joseph B. Soloveitchik, one of the leading Talmudists of the postwar era, with whom he studied Talmud and Jewish philosophy until 1953.

After earning his B.S.S. at City College in 1949, he enrolled as a graduate student in the Philosophy Department of Columbia University, earning his Ph.D. in 1953 with a dissertation later published as *Kierkegaard and Heidegger: The Ontology of Existence.*

From 1953 to 1992, Wyschogrod taught philosophy at several colleges of the City University of New York: City College, Hunter College, and Baruch College, rising in rank from Lecturer to Professor of Philosophy and Chairman of the Department of Philosophy at Baruch College. In 1992, Wyschogrod was appointed Professor of Religious Studies at the University of Houston, a post from which he retired in 2002. He also taught at Bar-Ilan University (Israel), the Graduate Faculty of the New School (New York), Dropsie University (Philadelphia), Heidelberg College for Jewish Studies

---

1. "Divine Election and Commandments," pp. 25-26.
2. "A Jewish Perspective on Karl Barth," in *How Karl Barth Changed My Mind*, ed. Donald M. McKim (Grand Rapids: Eerdmans Publishing Co., 1986), pp. 156-166, p. 157.

(Germany), Theological Faculty Lucerne (Switzerland), the University of Berne (Switzerland), Kirchliche Hochschule Wuppertal (Germany), Princeton Theological Seminary (Princeton, New Jersey), and Rice University (Houston).

Beginning in the mid-fifties, Wyschogrod became active in the national and international Jewish-Christian dialogue, serving as Senior Consultant on Interreligious Affairs of the Synagogue Council of America and Director of the Institute for Jewish-Christian Relations of the American Jewish Congress. In these capacities he worked closely with the Vatican, the World Council of Churches, and various Christian bodies in the U.S. and Europe.

Wyschogrod's writing has focused on contemporary continental philosophy, philosophy of religion, Jewish thought, and Jewish-Christian relations. His major work, *The Body of Faith: God and the People Israel*, has appeared in a number of editions and was translated into German as *Gott und Volk Israel*. He identifies with modern Orthodoxy, the branch of Orthodox Judaism that combines fidelity to rabbinic Judaism with respect for Western culture. He is married to Edith Wyschogrod, a well-known philosopher of religion. They have two children and five grandchildren.

# An Introduction
# to Michael Wyschogrod

I FIRST READ Michael Wyschogrod when I was in graduate school studying Christian theology. The experience was electrifying. I was taking a seminar on the theological interpretation of Paul's letter to the Romans, and my classmates and I had come to the part of the letter in which Paul discusses the relation between the gospel and Israel "after the flesh" (Rom. 9–11). Here, we soon agreed, was a side of the apostle that resisted his interpreters, where the ready categories of Christian theology couldn't absorb the full shock of Paul's pell-mell, ricocheting argument. But we had difficulty expressing just what it was that Augustine, Luther, and the rest failed to see. Someone suggested that we read Michael Wyschogrod, a name then unknown to me. Wyschogrod, apparently, was an orthodox Jewish thinker, already well known and highly respected in Jewish circles, who was increasingly coming to the attention of Christian readers.

As I sat in the library finishing Wyschogrod's essay "Israel, the Church, and Election," I remember being overcome by an almost physical sense of discovery, as though I had bumped into a hitherto invisible rock. What I had just read was undoubtedly the most unapologetic statement of Jewish faith I had ever encountered. Yet instantly I knew that Wyschogrod had helped me to see something in Paul that his Christian commentators had not. It was the theological relevance of the distinction between gentile and Jew. Of course, the distinction was not wholly unfamiliar to me; far from it. I was accustomed to writers who treated the distinction as a useful bit of historical, sociological, or religious description. Above all, I was familiar with the traditional Christian view that held that since Christ's coming the distinction between Jew and gentile had lost whatever theological significance it may once have had. This, after all, was Paul's own view, at least according to his commentators. But Wyschogrod treated the difference differently. For Wyschogrod, the distinction was the indelible mark of an irrevocable divine choice: God's choice to

1

enter history as the God of Israel. The distinction therefore mattered, not only in the past, but also in the present and future. What is more, Wyschogrod treated the distinction as something that mattered not just to Jews, but also to Christians. He addressed Christians not merely as Christians but quite specifically as *gentile Christians*. With a shock of discovery, I realized that in this respect Wyschogrod was closer to Paul than were his Christian interpreters. By addressing me as a gentile in light of God's irrevocable election of Israel, Wyschogrod had helped me to understand Paul better. And, I believe, he had helped me understand myself as a Christian better, too.

*         *         *

Michael Wyschogrod is a singular figure among his generation of Jewish religious thinkers. He cannot easily be assigned to any school or movement or even style of Jewish thought. A generation younger than Joseph Soloveitchik, Martin Buber, and Emmanuel Levinas, he calls each of them to mind in a certain way.

Like his teacher the philosopher and Talmudist Joseph Soloveitchik (1903-1993), Wyschogrod identifies with the branch of Judaism known as modern Orthodoxy, which combines commitment to Torah faithfulness with openness to modern culture and thought. Indeed, Wyschogrod is perhaps modern Orthodoxy's most significant religious thinker since Soloveitchik, who is remembered for having championed *halakhic existence* as a uniquely successful form of intellectual life in the modern world. But while equally convinced of the value of halakhic life, Wyschogrod early on came to differ sharply from Soloveitchik on the subject of interreligious dialogue. Soloveitchik held that Jews can fruitfully engage in dialogue with Christians and others on secular matters, but not on matters of faith, which he believed remained permanently inaccessible to the outsider. According to Wyschogrod, however, Soloveitchik's rule assumes the validity of a distinction between the secular and the sacred, a point that Judaism can never concede. For Wyschogrod,

All Jewish values are ultimately rooted in revelation and to pretend otherwise is to play a charade which will convince no one. The option is whether to talk with Christians or not to talk with them. If we refuse to talk with them, we can keep theology and everything else out of the dialogue. If we do not refuse to talk with them, we cannot keep what is most precious to us out of the discussion.[1]

1. "Orthodox Judaism and Jewish-Christian Dialogue," unpublished essay. Wyschogrod

In this respect, Wyschogrod's stance more nearly recalls that of Martin Buber (1878-1965). Like the great liberal thinker, Wyschogrod is primarily an interpreter of Judaism who is not merely respectful of Christian faith but eager to communicate with Christians on theological matters of the first importance. And Wyschogrod's thought is in fact primarily biblical rather than halakhic in orientation, focusing chiefly on the Bible rather than the oral Torah, another similarity with Buber. Wyschogrod even suggests that he shares with Buber a temperament that feels somewhat closer to Abraham than to Moses.

> Martin Buber, who was not a halachically observant Jew, once told me that he had an Abrahamic and pre-Sinaitic soul. Unlike Buber, I did not completely miss Sinai. But like Buber, my Judaism did not begin at Sinai but rather with Abraham, whom I have always felt a bit closer to than I do to Moses.[2]

Yet as this passage hints, Wyschogrod has never shared Buber's practical distance from the life of the synagogue, nor is he at all persuaded by Buber's interpretation of Torah obedience. "For Buber, the essence of the Torah is the direction of the human heart. If that direction is proper, then the Torah has been satisfied."[3] In Buber's eyes, Torah binds the spirit but not the body, a view quite congenial to a certain Christian temperament as well. For Wyschogrod, in contrast, God's commandments claim all of Jewish life, including its body. That is the truth signified by the rite of circumcision. Because God's claim on Israel is all-encompassing, Torah obedience cannot be reduced to inward disposition in favor of outward action, nor to ethical conduct in favor of ritual observance.

Finally, there is a certain respect in which Wyschogrod invites comparison with the French philosopher Emmanuel Levinas (1906-1995). Both men in their own ways are deeply engaged with the thought of Martin Heidegger and with Heidegger's attempt to restore the question of being to the center of philosophy. More to the point, perhaps, both men are persuaded that Heidegger's path leads ultimately and ineluctably to horror, that man cannot live by being alone. But whereas Levinas sought to counter the sovereignty of being by turning to the ethical, Wyschogrod has become progressively more

---

describes his disagreement with Soloveitchik in this volume in "A Jewish View of Christianity," pp. 155-57.

    2. "The Impact of Dialogue with Christianity on My Self-Understanding as a Jew," p. 235.

    3. "Buber's Evaluation of Christianity: A Jewish Perspective," in *Martin Buber: A Centenary Volume,* ed. Haim Gordon and Jochanan Bloch (Ktav, 1984), pp. 457-472, p. 468.

convinced over his career that the genuine alternative to Heidegger is a different and more radical one.

> At the outset of my career I was far more interested in the philosophy of religion than I am now. By the philosophy of religion I understand the philosophical enterprise that investigates a broad range of religious issues from a philosophical perspective without tying the investigation to any particular tradition of revelation. In the course of the years I have developed considerable skepticism toward this enterprise because I have come to see it as lacking an anchor in the soil of faith. What God does the philosophy of religion deal with? If it is the biblical God, then it is doing biblical theology and not the philosophy of religion. And if the God it deals with is not the biblical God, then what is it, in which philosophical laboratory was it created?[4]

Wyschogrod does not think that the totalizing claims of being can be checked by philosophical inquiry, not even by one that is rigorously ethical in orientation. Indeed, Wyschogrod notes that in modern times the ethical has frequently been the road by which Judaism has been abandoned. Rather, if human life has been delivered from the sovereignty of being, then this is so for one reason only: the God of Abraham, Isaac, and Jacob is the lord of being.

In the end, the Jewish thinker to whom Wyschogrod stands closest is Franz Rosenzweig (1886-1929), the first great herald of what Peter Ochs has called a post-critical Judaism.[5] Raised in a secular home and as a young adult nearly a convert to Christianity, Rosenzweig came to believe that "the ethicization and universalization of Judaism which had become the specialty of Western-oriented, German liberal Judaism had outlived its usefulness and that a time had come for a new beginning."[6] Rosenzweig called for a fundamental reorientation of Jewish thought in light of revelation and the carnal reality of the Jewish people. These are the central themes that Wyschogrod takes up and deepens in all his work. Since Rosenzweig's premature death, many can be said to have learned from him, but only a smaller number have chosen to travel farther down the path that he opened up. Of those that have, Michael Wyschogrod is preeminent.[7]

---

4. "The Impact of Dialogue with Christianity on My Self-Understanding as a Jew," p. 229.

5. See, for example, Peter Ochs, "Returning to Scripture: Trends in Postcritical Interpretation," *Cross Currents* 44:4 (Winter 1994/95): 437-453.

6. See "Franz Rosenzweig's *The Star of Redemption*," pp. 129-130.

7. Other Jewish thinkers who might be classed among Rosenzweig's post-critical heirs include Abraham Heschel, David Weiss Halivni, Eugene Borowitz, Michael Fishbane, Jon Levenson, David Novak, and Peter Ochs.

Yet here too there is a crucial difference. Rosenzweig still hoped to build a bridge between the philosophy of religion and the reality of Judaism, even if a dialectical and in part negative bridge. Wyschogrod does not believe that such a bridge can be built. In this respect, Wyschogrod is often correctly associated with Karl Barth, the Christian theologian whom Wyschogrod most admires and resembles. Indeed, what Wyschogrod writes of Barth applies equally, *mutatis mutandis,* to himself.

> He plunges his reader into the world of faith without defensive introductions, which would necessarily have to begin by taking the standpoint of unbelief seriously and which therefore might end in unbelief. Reading a page of Barth is something like shock therapy because it introduces the reader or the listener to a frame of reference that attempts only to be true to itself and its sources and not to external demands that can be satisfied only by fitting the Church's message into their mold, a mold foreign to it and therefore necessarily distorting.[8]

This does not mean that Wyschogrod perceives no connections joining revelation to its environment, Israel to the nations, faith to reason. The world is full of such connections. But the connections are not preparatory to revelation. They are given in and with the reality of revelation itself. Hence they are apt to be surprising and unpredictable, as movingly evoked in Wyschogrod's autobiographical essay "A Jewish Death in Heidelberg." Above all, the connections cannot be separated from their source: the love by which God chooses to be the God of Israel, and so also the God of the world.

Unencumbered by anxious preliminaries and methodological complexities, Wyschogrod's style is supremely economical and lucid. There is no naïveté, as if he were unaware of his perspective and tools — far from it! Rather there is an eagerness to go directly to questions of substance, rather than circle around them inconclusively. The effect is a bit like the work of the American realist painter Edward Hopper, whose uncluttered, brightly lit canvases quickly draw the viewer into the subject at hand. Wyschogrod's style is characterized, too, by a certain balance, even a kind of equanimity. Partly, I think, this reflects his devotion to his subject matter, a determination to state the truth clearly as he sees it, to let the chips fall where they may. More basically, I think it reflects a habit of mind rooted in faith. In Wyschogrod, we sense that speech about God emerges from a deeper source, from the knowledge that it is possible to live in the presence of God, and to do so gladly.

---

8. Wyschogrod, *The Body of Faith: God and the People Israel* (Northvale, N.J.: Jason Aronson, 1996), p. 79.

* * *

Although Wyschogrod is best known for his book *The Body of Faith*, a comprehensive interpretation of Judaism, his primary mode of literary activity over the years has been the short article and essay, of which he has published several score, many of them in books and journals not easily accessible to the general public. A bibliography of his work can be found at the back of this book. The pieces collected in this volume span nearly four decades of Wyschogrod's life and offer a representative sampling of his thought in two major areas: Judaism and Jewish-Christian relations. Readers familiar only with *The Body of Faith* will find much that is new and stimulating on topics from the Holocaust to the theology of Karl Barth, as well as several previously unpublished works on such subjects as the apostle Paul and Judaism's relation to the land. Since the individual works are prefaced by brief introductory remarks, I will not attempt to describe them in detail here. Nevertheless, I think it may be useful to trace some prominent contours that characterize Wyschogrod's theology as a whole.

Whatever the topic at hand, Wyschogrod's thought orbits a single center of gravity: God's free yet irrevocable love for the people Israel, and in connection with Israel, for the world as a whole. Wyschogrod frequently orients the reader on this reality with a deceptively simple affirmation, and then traces its consequences in a way that combines intellectual rigor with originality and an eagerness to address hard and uncomfortable questions.

A first theme that draws Wyschogrod's attention is that God's election of Israel is based solely on God's unalterable love for Israel, and hence cannot be abrogated from the human side.

> Now it is the proclamation of biblical faith that God chose this people and loves it as no other, unto the end of time.[9]

God did not choose Israel because it was superior in any way to other peoples; indeed, in some respects it may even possess slightly more negative characteristics than other groups. Nor is God's election conditional upon Israel's obedience to the commands that God imposes on Israel as the expression of God's will for Israel's conduct. God's election brings with it God's command and the threat of severe punishment should Israel fail to live up to its election. Yet in spite of the fact that the Jewish people have struggled endlessly against their election, with the most disastrous consequences for themselves and for

9. "Divine Election and Commandments," pp. 27-28.

the rest of humankind, the Divine election remains unaffected because it is an unconditional one, based solely on God's love. Ultimately, God's anger is a passing phase that can only temporarily obscure God's overwhelming love for Israel. Israel can be confident of its election and of God's special love for it amid all the families of the earth.[10]

But these affirmations lead to difficult questions. Why should God be a God of election at all? Why should God love one people as no other? Wyschogrod's understanding of God's freedom prohibits him from arguing that God *had* to be a God of election, since this could be shown only by submitting God to a higher principle of justice or rationality. Yet it is possible, as a way of expressing praise, to seek reasons for what God has done, in order to display God's will as the basis for human gratitude.

Wyschogrod notes that it is common to distinguish between two kinds of love, *agape* and *eros*.[11] *Agape* is charity in the purest sense, without superiority or condescension, while *eros* is sensual love, in which desire and jealousy are possible. The distinction corresponds to some degree to that between soul and body. *Agape* is disinterested and impartial, without regard to persons, while *eros* is interested love, concerned with this person rather than that and desirous of the body of the other. Wyschogrod notes that God's love for the human creature is usually said to resemble *agape* rather than *eros*. As *agape*, God's love cannot exclude.

For Wyschogrod, this account of *agape* is doubly suspect. It is untrue to the human condition because it overlooks the fact that genuine human charity can be truly directed to particular persons only when it concerns itself with their particular identities.

> Undifferentiated love, love that is dispensed equally to all must be love that does not meet the individual in his individuality but sees him as a member of a species, whether that species be the working class, the poor, those created in the image of God, or whatnot. . . . In the name of these abstractions men have committed the most heinous crimes against real, concrete, existing human beings.[12]

What is more, this account of love is untrue to the character of God's love as depicted by the Bible. It fails to see that the glory and dignity of the biblical God consists in God's freedom to engage humanity in a human way. That is to say, God has chosen in favor of genuine encounter with the human crea-

10. "Sin and Atonement in Judaism," p. 68.
11. *The Body of Faith*, pp. 58-65.
12. *The Body of Faith*, p. 61.

ture in his or her individuality. For this reason, God's love is not undifferentiated, having the same quality toward all God's children. Precisely because God is so deeply concerned with human creation, God loves it with a differentiated love, and it comes about that there are those whom God loves especially, with whom one can only say that God has fallen in love. This is what has happened in God's election of Abraham and his seed. God's love for Abraham is more than an impartial, disinterested love, but includes an element of eros. God loves the descendants of Abraham above all the nations of the earth, and desires their response in return. That is why God reacts with wounded fury when God is rejected by Israel.

But this brings us back to our previous question with renewed force: what of those who are not elected? Wyschogrod admits that it is painful to recognize that one is not the specially chosen child. As a result of God's joining the redemption of the world to Israel's election, difficult roles have fallen to Jew and to gentile. All too frequently, both have acted their respective roles poorly.

> Uncannily expert in the failings of the nations, often remembering only its faithfulness and rarely its unfaithfulness, turned inward by the hostility of the peoples among whom it lives, Israel tends to forget that its election is for service, that it is a sign of the infinite and unwarranted gift of God rather than any inherent superiority of the people.[13]

But just as Israel's record is mixed, so is that of the nations.

> Instead of accepting Israel's election with humility, [the nations] rail against it, mocking the God of the Jews, gleefully pointing out the shortcomings of the people he chose, and crucifying it whenever an opportunity presents itself. Israel's presence is a constant reminder to them that they were not chosen but that this people was, and that this people remains in their midst as a thorn in the flesh. Minute by minute, the existence of Israel mocks the pagan gods, the divine beings who rise out of the consciousness of all peoples but which are gentile gods because they are deifications of humanity and the forces of nature rather than the true, living God of Abraham.[14]

Israel and the nations each fall victim to characteristic distortions of their respective identities: Israel to vain pride in its own election, and the nations to envy and rage at Israel. As a consequence, they place obstacles in the path of

---

13. "Israel, the Church, and Election," p. 181.
14. "Israel, the Church, and Election," p. 182.

God's plan to consummate creation through Israel's election. Still, in the end, there is a limit to what human freedom can do. This limit consists in humanity's inability to nullify God's purpose: the election and redemption of Israel and through Israel of humankind as a whole.[15]

Moreover, according to Wyschogrod, the most important consolation still remains. By allowing room for God's freedom to fall in love with Abraham, the gentiles gain a heavenly Father who is also concretely concerned with them, and not just with humanity in the abstract. Wyschogrod develops this point with reference to the story of Esau and Jacob.

> The Bible is, after all, the history of Israel and could therefore be expected to be partial to the Jewish cause. And yet, in recounting the blessing of Jacob and the exclusion of Esau, no careful reader can fail to notice that the sympathy shown Esau is greater than that for Jacob. God shows Esau compassion even if Jacob does not. The consolation of the gentiles is the knowledge that God also stands in relationship with them in the recognition and affirmation of their uniqueness.[16]

In the end, then, the uniqueness and unsubstitutability of God's love for Israel turns out to be the guarantee of God's Fatherhood toward all persons, elect and non-elect. "If Abraham was especially loved by God, it is because God is a Father who does not stand in a legal relationship to his children, which by its nature requires impartiality and objectivity. As a Father, God loves his children and knows each one as who he is with his strengths and weaknesses, his virtues and vices."[17]

Another theme that attracts Wyschogrod's attention is that God's election of Israel is a *carnal* election, the election of the people descended from Abraham. To be sure, Judaism involves a whole complex of ideas, beliefs, values, and obligations, the most important of which is the obligation to observe the commandments of the Torah. Yet essential though these aspects of Jewish life are, they are not the foundation of Judaism.[18] Even the Torah, for many interpreters Judaism's center of gravity, arises from the prior reality of God's election of the Jewish people. Israel is not the accidental bearer of the Torah. Rather, the Torah grows out of Israel's election and God's saving acts performed for his people. The essence of Judaism, then, is God's election and sanctification of a human family. For this reason, Juda-

---

15. "Sin and Atonement in Judaism," pp. 63-68.
16. *The Body of Faith,* p. 64.
17. *The Body of Faith,* p. 64.
18. "The Impact of Dialogue on My Self-Understanding as a Jew," pp. 226-228.

ism cannot be dissolved into ethical teaching, as nineteenth-century Jewish liberalism hoped.

Wyschogrod acknowledges that joining the divine election to the corporeal reality of a particular people invites the most serious objections.[19] In many respects, a divine election based on religious sensibility or moral accomplishment would seem more reasonable than a carnal election that is transmitted through the body. As Judaism itself teaches, God's nature is spiritual. It would appear only natural, therefore, that God should be concerned especially with those features of human existence that most closely resemble God. The true elect would then consist of all those who are spiritually akin to God, from whatever people or nation they descend.

Yet had God proceeded in this fashion, Wyschogrod suggests, the cost would have been great. It is the nature of the human creature to be not only spiritual but material. Had God chosen to engage the human creature only in the spiritual aspect of its being, then the greater portion of what constitutes humanity would have been left out of the relation with God. By electing Israel, God chose to embrace a people in the fullness of its humanity, and in this way to confirm the human creature as it was created to live in the material cosmos. Just this is the mystery of Israel's election.

> Here we are at the heart of God's election of Israel. He loved Abraham, Isaac, and Jacob and therefore he loves their descendants. And he loves not only their souls but also their bodies. This is so because, from the first, God knew that man was an ensouled body. He is not a disembodied spirit temporarily connected to a body. Because man is his soul and his body, he brings his body into the relationship with God. And when God relates to a family, he is not unaware of the corporeality of this family. He confirms this corporeality by not ignoring it but by including it in the covenant.[20]

The comprehensiveness of God's love, in turn, demands an equally comprehensive response. God's election creates a people that is in God's service in the totality of its human being, and not just in its moral and spiritual existence. God requires the sanctification of human existence in all of its aspects, including the recalcitrant realities of family and national life.

The comprehensive character of God's claim on Israel provides the necessary context for understanding Israel's relationship to the land. Viewed apart from the reality of election, Israel's connection to the land of Israel is largely incomprehensible. Unlike other peoples and nations, Israel's memory extends

19. "A Theology of Jewish Unity," pp. 43-52.
20. "A Theology of Jewish Unity," pp. 49-50.

back behind its entrance into the land: it remembers that the land was originally possessed by others. Moreover, Israel has repeatedly experienced expulsion from the land. It has therefore learned that its existence as God's people is not dependent on dwelling in the land. Yet for all of that, the land that God promised to Abraham's descendants is an indispensable part of Israel's life with God. Because God wills to have a people that is holy in every aspect of its existence, God provides a land in which it may dwell, so that even this most elementary dimension of human existence may be brought within the compass of relationship to God. But this also means, in Wyschogrod's view, that dangers of failure are especially great whenever the Jewish people inhabits the promised land.

> The Divine Word is unmistakably clear concerning the Land of Israel. It is *the* soil which above all demands the faithfulness of the people of Israel to its election. Whenever the people of Israel have attempted to constitute a national life on this soil in disregard of its election, the soil has rejected them under the most catastrophic circumstances.[21]

That Israel possesses a right to the land cannot be doubted by those who accept the reality and trustworthiness of the God whose Word is found in the Scriptures. But whether that right is rightly exercised in a particular set of circumstances is far more difficult to say. Wyschogrod is therefore unwilling to claim divine warrant for the State of Israel or for specific territorial claims in the present day.

> To tie the fate of Judaism to the fortunes of the State of Israel, for whose preservation and prosperity we all fervently pray, is simply unauthorized and therefore irresponsible. Along this path could lurk, God forbid, a catastrophe similar to those that was the fate of other messianic claims.[22]

In the present circumstances, therefore, Wyschogrod holds that the deepest layer of Jewish messianism calls for an attitude that combines love of the land with love for all of its inhabitants in the present day, and therefore a practical posture that eschews violence.

> I do not preach absolute non-violence under all circumstances. But I preach a high degree of non-violence, a hatred of violence, a love of the land combined with a high degree of non-violence, a largely non-violent Zionism, a messianic Judaism that keeps alive the living expectation of

21. "Divine Election and Commandments," p. 26.
22. "The Religious Meaning of the Six Day War: A Symposium," *Tradition* 10:1 (Summer 1968): 5-20, p. 15.

the Messiah but also the messianic repudiation of violence, a love of all human beings whether Jewish or non-Jewish, a willingness to wait and even temporarily yield territory if this will save us from bloodshed.[23]

Wyschogrod notes one other important consequence that flows from the fact that God chose to elect a human family rather than a spiritual or ethical elite. By making election a matter of descent, God has made it very difficult for members of the elect community to escape their special identity. Were election based on faith or ethics, Wyschogrod argues, then a change in belief or conduct would terminate membership in the election and the responsibilities connected with it. A Jew, in contrast, cannot resign his or her election. At the most, it is possible for Jewish identity to disappear for all practical purposes after several generations of intermarriage, but this happens only in certain instances and even then may not be entirely successful. For most Jews, a disavowal of Jewish identity is simply not possible, whatever attitude they may take toward this identity. In general, then, one can say God has established a people that cannot leave him. By electing the seed of Abraham, God has bound the world to himself in a way that cannot be dissolved.[24]

What remains to be said about God's free election of Israel? Chiefly this: that God also desires to be Redeemer of the world as the One whose first love is the people Israel.

> Because he said: "I will bless those who bless you, and curse him that curses you; in you shall all the families of the earth be blessed" (Gen. 12:3), he has tied his saving and redemptive concern for the welfare of all humankind to his love for the people of Israel.[25]

Negatively expressed, this means that there are no "general" or "universal" paths that lead to redemption. Without a relationship to the people of the election, no relationship to God's redemptive purpose is possible. Even the rabbinic teaching of the Noachide law, which specifies the minimum standard of conduct that God demands of all persons, is not an exception to this rule. In Wyschogrod's view, the Noachide law is not simply identical with the concept of the natural law. Linked to the story of the Noah covenant, the Noachide law is part of the Torah, and therefore cannot be separated from the Jewish people. Although God is both creator and ruler of the universe, God is revealed to humankind not as the conclusion of the cosmological or teleolog-

23. "Reflections on the Six Day War after a Quarter Century," p. 106.
24. "Theology of Jewish Unity," pp. 43-52.
25. "Israel, the Church, and Election," p. 180.

ical proofs, but as the God of Abraham who took the people of Israel out of the land of Egypt and whose people this nation remains to the end of time. Thus God remains inaccessible to all those who wish to reach God while at the same time seeking to circumvent his people.[26]

But Wyschogrod can also put the same point in positive fashion: Israel is God's dwelling-place in the world.[27] God's presence is not equally diffused throughout creation, but is concentrated at the point of God's love. Because God loves the Jewish people, God is present among them in a special way, and in connection with them, present in the world as a whole. God is also present in a special way in the land of Israel and above all in the Temple, in the Holy of Holies. Even since the destruction of the Temple in 70 C.E., God's presence has not entirely departed from the Temple. Yet Wyschogrod holds that the people of Israel remain the primary abode of God's presence in the world. Christians, Wyschogrod acknowledges, may find themselves recoiling at these affirmations. Is not God the transcendent Creator of all whom no space can contain? Yes, Wyschogrod agrees, God is. Yet this truth must not be so emphasized that it ends up exchanging the biblical God for the abstract Absolute of the philosophers. If God cannot condescend to dwell among humans in a concrete space, then the Christian confession of God's incarnation in Jesus is also baseless. In the end, Judaism and Christianity converge in the conviction that God's presence and saving purpose in the world is concentrated in the flesh of Abraham's seed.

In the light of God's promise to Abraham, the distinction between Jew and gentile is a sign of hope, not a wall of separation. The promise points toward a future when God's covenant with Israel will redound to the benefit of Jew and gentile alike. In the meantime, the Jew cannot afford to be indifferent to the life of the nations. To the contrary, "Israel must therefore work, hope, and expect the day when many peoples shall go and say: 'Come! Let us go up to the mountain of the Lord, to the house of the God of Jacob, that He may teach us His ways and that we may walk in His paths (Isa. 2:3).'"[28] For their part, gentiles who seek the God of Israel can learn to anticipate the blessing that comes to them through Israel's election. They may meditate on the mystery of non-election, remembering that non-election does not equal rejection. "Is it not possible," Wyschogrod asks, "that those who love God so much that, even in their non-election, they submit with love and serenity to the destiny chosen for them by God, are very dear to him indeed?"[29]

26. "Israel, the Church, and Election," pp. 180, 185-186.
27. In this volume see especially the essays "Incarnation and God's Indwelling in Israel," pp. 165-178, and "Judaism and the Land," pp. 110-111.
28. "Israel, the Church, and Election," p. 186.
29. "Israel, the Church, and Election," p. 186.

In the end of days, there will be a reconciliation of all the families of the earth without division. To foreshadow that day, the Jew must speak humbly of his election, the gentile with love of his non-election, both waiting together for the final redemption of creation.[30]

*     *     *

As the previous discussion suggests, it is not possible to separate Wyschogrod's theology of Judaism and his essays explicitly engaging Christianity and Jewish-Christian relations. For Wyschogrod, theologically significant conversation between Jews and Christians is possible because both Christianity and Judaism acknowledge "a movement of God toward humankind as witnessed in Scripture," a movement that engages humankind in God's election of Israel.[31] To be sure, the two communities understand this movement in ways that unmistakably diverge, at least at certain points. Yet the gulf that results is not so wide that understanding is impossible. Indeed, Wyschogrod holds that because the two traditions share certain common premises, it is possible for "each side to summon the other to a better understanding of its own tradition."[32] For Wyschogrod, Jewish-Christian relations concern something more important than "dialogue." They concern a common search for truth in light of the Word of God.

Two topics regularly recur in Wyschogrod's discussions of Christianity: Christology and the church, especially the church's relation to Mosaic law. Surprisingly enough, it is in the former that Wyschogrod perceives a certain crucial convergence between Judaism and Christianity. To be sure, Wyschogrod makes clear that Christian claims on behalf of Jesus of Nazareth are problematic from the perspective of Jewish faith. The claim that Jesus was the Messiah is difficult for Jews to accept because Jesus did not perform a key Messianic function: he did not usher in the Messianic Kingdom. More difficult by far, however, is the Christian claim that God was incarnate in Jesus. For a Jew to be mistaken in this belief would mean a grave violation of the prohibition against idolatry.[33]

---

30. "Israel, the Church, and Election," pp. 186-87.

31. "Why Was and Is the Theology of Karl Barth of Interest to a Jewish Theologian?" p. 215.

32. "Judaism and Evangelical Christianity," in *Evangelicals and Jews in Conversation*, ed. Marc H. Tanenbaum, Marvin R. Wilson, and A. James Rudin (Grand Rapids, Mich.: Baker, 1978), pp. 34-52, p. 34.

33. "A Jewish View of Christianity," pp. 156-157. See also David Berger and Michael Wyschogrod, *Jews and "Jewish Christianity"* (New York: Ktav, 1978).

Nevertheless, Wyschogrod does not think that Jews are entitled to dismiss the Christian claim about God's incarnation in Jesus out of hand. To reject the incarnation on purportedly *a priori* grounds would be to impose external constraints on God's freedom, a notion fundamentally foreign to Judaism. According to Wyschogrod, there is only one condition under which Israel would be entitled to reject the church's claims about Jesus out of hand, and that is if these claims were to imply that God had repudiated God's promises to Israel. For that is something that Israel can safely trust that God will never do, not because God is unable, but because God honors God's promises.[34]

The question, then, is whether the church's Christology entails or implies the abrogation of God's promises to Israel. Wyschogrod does not believe that this is necessarily the case. Indeed, Wyschogrod suggests that the doctrine of God's incarnation could be understood as a kind of intensification of God's covenant with Israel. Although the incarnation is not foreseeable on the basis of the Hebrew Bible, once the fact of the incarnation is assumed (as it is by Christians), it can be regarded as an extension of the Bible's basic thrust.

> The covenant between God and Israel . . . depicts a drawing together of God and Israel. . . . [I]n some sense . . . it can also be said to involve a certain indwelling of God in the people of Israel whose status as a holy people may be said to derive from this indwelling. Understood in this sense, the divinity of Jesus is not radically different — though perhaps more concentrated — than the holiness of the Jewish people.[35]

Seen from this perspective, the Christian doctrine of the incarnation can be understood as a development of the Bible's account of God's movement toward human creation in the people Israel. Christology, Wyschogrod maintains, "is the intensification of the teaching of the indwelling of God in Israel by concentrating that indwelling in one Jew rather than leaving it diffused in the people of Jesus as a whole."[36] So long as Christians do not forget the Jewishness of Jesus or remove him from his Jewish context, the disagreement between Christianity and Judaism on this score may be understood, Wyschogrod believes, as more one of degree than of kind.[37]

---

34. "Why Was and Is the Theology of Karl Barth of Interest to a Jewish Theologian?" p. 218.

35. "Christology: The Immovable Object," *Religion and Intellectual Life* 3:4 (1986): 79.

36. "Incarnation and God's Indwelling in Israel," p. 178.

37. "Why Was and Is the Theology of Karl Barth of Interest to a Jewish Theologian?" p. 223.

None of this means that Wyschogrod regards the christological impasse between Judaism and Christianity as overcome, for Christology remains in a certain sense the "most difficult" issue the Jew faces in dialogue with Christianity.[38] But it does imply the following:

> [T]he disagreement between Judaism and Christianity [with respect to the incarnation], when understood in this light, while not reconcilable, can be brought into the context within which it is a difference of faith regarding the free and sovereign act of the God of Israel.[39]

In contrast to Wyschogrod's cautiously conciliatory tone with respect to the issue of Christology, he seems to view the church with a mixture of wonder and ambivalence. Here is a community of persons assembled from all the nations who are united not by common descent or language but by a common desire to worship the God of Abraham. What should Israel make of this astonishing phenomenon?

For Wyschogrod, it is evident that Israel should approach the church with hopeful respect. As we saw, Wyschogrod holds that Israel's own hope for redemption leads it to expect a day when the nations will join Israel in the praise of God's name. To this extent, at least, the church appears to fit into Israel's own pattern of expectations, since the church has helped to spread the knowledge of God to the ends of the earth.

> The wonder is that nations not of the stock of Abraham have come within the orbit of the faith of Israel, experiencing humankind and history with Jewish categories deeply rooted in Jewish experience and sensibility. How can a Jewish theologian not perceive that something wonderful is at work here, something that must in some way be connected with the love of the God of Israel for all his children, Isaac as well as Ishmael, Jacob as well as Esau?[40]

Ultimately, however, the question of whether Israel can see in the church a sign that is fundamentally congruent with God's plan of salvation for the world depends upon the church's attitude toward the Jewish people. Will the nations be content to receive God's blessings if these are attached to God's

---

38. "A Jewish View of Christianity," p. 157.
39. "Why Was and Is the Theology of Karl Barth of Interest to a Jewish Theologian?" p. 216.
40. "Why Was and Is the Theology of Karl Barth of Interest to a Jewish Theologian?" p. 213.

covenant with Israel? Or will they seek to do away with the beloved child in order to usurp the favored place in the Parent's affection?

Unfortunately, on this point the phenomenon of the church threatens to turn from a reflection of God's promise to another dark token of the nations' rage and envy of Israel. Traditionally, the church has not understood itself in terms of its relation to God's ongoing covenant with the Jewish people. Instead it has proclaimed itself to be the true Israel, comprising the faithful of all nations, in relation to which the old carnal Israel existed as a temporary foreshadowing.

For Wyschogrod, the acid test of Christian supersessionism — the belief that the church has replaced Israel as the bearer of God's election — appears in the church's conduct towards Jews in its own midst, i.e., towards Jews who are baptized. As Wyschogrod argues in his letter to Cardinal Jean-Marie Lustiger, the Jewish-born archbishop of Paris, it is precisely at this point that the church demonstrates in an ultimate way whether it understands itself in terms of God's covenant with the Jewish people. If the church acknowledges the permanence and centrality of Israel's election as central to its own identity, it will expect baptized Jews to continue to affirm their Jewish identity and continue to observe Torah. But if the church truly believes that it has fundamentally superseded God's covenant with Israel, it will prohibit baptized Jews from obeying Torah and maintaining a distinct identity within the church.

> Were all Jews to recognize the truth, they would cease their stubborn insistence on continuing to exist as an identifiable people and become an integral part of the new Israel — the Church — which is God's new covenant partner in the world. The disappearance of the Jews from the world would be no theological loss because their place would have been taken by the new people of God.[41]

In sum, Wyschogrod believes that the problem of supersessionism turns on the church's capacity to understand its own identity in terms of the abiding religious significance of the distinction between Jew and gentile. On this crucial issue Wyschogrod carefully distinguishes between what he believes was the church's original view and what later became its standard position.[42]

Originally, Wyschogrod argues, early Christians envisioned a fellowship with two branches, the Jewish and the gentile (cf. Acts 15). They had in com-

41. "A Letter to Cardinal Lustiger," p. 208.
42. See "A Jewish View of Christianity," pp. 160-164; "A Letter to Cardinal Lustiger," pp. 207-209.

mon their faith in Jesus, but differed in that Jews remained under the commandments of the Torah while gentiles were bound only by the Noachide laws. This understanding of Christian existence still presupposed the reality of God's covenant with the stock of Abraham while adding to this the belief that in Jesus of Nazareth, the blessings of the covenant had begun to accrue to the gentiles as gentiles, i.e., apart from circumcision and observance of the Torah. Through faith in Christ, gentiles became — not Jews — but associate members of Israel's covenant.[43]

Gradually, however, this view of the church was replaced by a very different one. According to this second view, Christ's coming meant that the difference between Jews and gentiles has been erased. As a consequence, the practice of the Torah was formally forbidden among baptized Jews, and baptized Jews typically lost their Jewish identity within two or three generations. This shift in practice, together with the judgment that it reflects regarding the significance of the corporeal body of Israel, is the heart and soul of supersessionism. Since the church did not insist that Jews retain their identity even in the church, it can be inferred that the church seriously holds that its election supersedes that of the old Israel.[44] The church's posture demonstrates its belief that God's relation to the world no longer entails God's covenant with the Jewish people. Now the church views itself as the true spiritual community that was the goal of God's purpose all along.

That Wyschogrod would seem to argue *in favor* of Torah observance among baptized Jews might strike some as quite incredible. It presupposes a level of concern for the Jewish Christian and for the church's theological integrity that might appear quixotic — to put it mildly — in light of the historic relation of Judaism and Christianity. Yet the position flows quite inevitably from Wyschogrod's first principles — above all, from his understanding of Jewish identity as participation in the family of God's irrevocable election. Writing early in his career on the case of "Brother Daniel," a Jewish convert to Christianity who sought to immigrate to the State of Israel under the Israeli law of return, Wyschogrod explained:

> I would like to be understood well. I have no intention of minimizing the seriousness of apostasy, which is a break with a legacy of martyrdom that every Jew carries in his flesh. But I am not prepared to write any Jew off, whether he wears a grey flannel suit or a cassock. The God Who found Jonah in the belly of the fish and Who dwells with Israel in the midst of

43. "Paul, Jews, and Gentiles," pp. 188-201.
44. "Israel, the Church, and Election," p. 184.

their impurity can find Brother Daniel on the slopes of the Carmel and bring him back, on the wings of eagles, to the Jewish fraternity.[45]

The question that Wyschogrod presses time and again is whether on this particular point the proper *Jewish* understanding is not also the proper *Christian* understanding as well. To be sure, of the two views identified above regarding the church's posture toward Jewish followers of Jesus, it is the second that has determined the church's practice for most of its history, a development that Wyschogrod regrets. The basis of what eventually became the church's dominant self-understanding, he believes, is the redefinition of God's true covenant in terms of an exclusively spiritual relation between God and the faithful. The church declares that what matters is not one's corporeal identity as either Jew or gentile, but one's inward spiritual identity as one who believes. In this way, the church separates membership in the church, the New Israel, from membership in a natural human family, and thereby makes the covenant open and accessible to persons from every nation. But it does so at the cost of discarding the bond that joins God's covenant to the natural seed of Abraham, thereby casting off the carnal anchor joining God to creation.

At this point, Wyschogrod believes that Judaism can no longer meet the church's teaching with firm but respectful dissent, as it could its christological claims. By claiming to be God's new people, the church directly assaults the trustworthiness of God's promise to Israel and the world. From the Jewish point of view, the church's claim is one more example of the nations' protest against the election of the stock of Abraham, which Israel must repudiate as a rebellion against God's word. When the church affirms that the true bearer of God's election is the community of the faithful, it obliterates the religious significance of the distinction between Jew and gentile and denies Israel's identity as God's uniquely beloved.

> In a sense, the Christian doctrine of election is a demythologization of the Jewish doctrine of election, which Christianity interprets as the concrete symbol of a possibility open to all people.[46]

Wyschogrod fears that this primary "demythologization" inaugurates a further process of abstraction that extends throughout Christian thought. If the new, spiritual Israel replaces the old in the course of God's plan for creation, then it is only natural to believe that God's relation to humanity is primarily

---

45. Comment on Aharon Lichtenstein's "Brother Daniel and the Jewish Fraternity," *Judaism* 13:1 (Winter 1964): 107-110.

46. "Israel, the Church, and Election," p. 184.

oriented on the spiritual dimension of human being from the outset. At the end of this path of generalization, Wyschogrod believes, stands the long history of Christianity's deep involvement in philosophy.

> The substitution of a universal election of faith for the national election of the seed of Abraham lays the groundwork for a universalization that must, in due course, look to philosophy with its even more universal structures. . . . For this reason, the Christian mind was driven to an ever greater concern with philosophy, a tendency that, while not totally absent in the history of Judaism, never reaches the proportions it does in Christianity.[47]

In light of the church's initial demythologization of Israel's election, the philosophical component of Christian thought is no mere accident of intellectual history, but rooted in the church's supersessionistic understanding of the Christian kerygma. The problem, according to Wyschogrod, is that the church cannot "go behind" God's election of Israel to a more general, spiritual plane of God's relationship to humanity without paying a heavy price. That price is an inevitable estrangement from the concreteness of God's identity as the God of Abraham, Isaac, and Jacob, and a numbness to the mystery and blessing of one's own identity as either Jew or gentile.

*　　*　　*

Yet clearly Wyschogrod does not believe that Christianity is doomed to estrangement from the God of Israel and from the Jewish people. For one thing, he sees impressive evidence to the contrary in the prominent (if not entirely unproblematic) place of Israel in the theology of Karl Barth. For another, Wyschogrod acknowledges the (re)emergence in recent decades of a form of Christianity that seeks to understand its relationship to the Jewish people in ways that are not supersessionist. As Wyschogrod writes in his letter to Cardinal Lustiger,

> An increasing number of Christians are no longer comfortable with the old theology. If "the gracious gifts of God and his calling are irrevocable" (Rom. 11:29), then it would seem that God's election of Israel is not just an historical curiosity but a contemporary reality. According to Pope John XXIII, God's covenant with the Jewish people has never been re-

---

46. "Israel, the Church, and Election," p. 184. See also "Why Was and Is the Theology of Karl Barth of Interest to a Jewish Theologian?" p. 214.

voked. However the Catholic Church today interprets its identity as the new Israel, it no longer seems possible to view the election of Israel as having been superseded by that of the Church, leaving Israel out in the cold. But if, from the Christian point of view, Israel's election remains a contemporary reality, then the disappearance of the Jewish people from the world cannot be an acceptable development.[48]

Wyschogrod makes no effort to trace the contours of a non-supersessionist Christianity in detail; to do so would go beyond his vocation as a theologian of Judaism. But at different points he does suggest at least three features that would likely characterize it. First, a post- or non-supersessionist Christianity will not play off against each other God's incarnation in Jesus Christ and God's dwelling in the midst of the Jewish people. On the contrary, it will recognize God's love for Jesus' people as the indispensable context of Jesus himself and of all that God brings about in and through him. Second, a non-supersessionist Christianity will no longer teach that Israel has forfeited its election on account of its rejection of the gospel. On the contrary, it will attend more carefully to Paul's climactic warning to his gentile audience in Romans 11 and affirm "that Israel has not lost its election in spite of its rejection of its Messiah, decisive as that event had been."[49] In contrast to a Christianity that stresses "Israel's transgressions and its remoteness from God," a post-supersessionist Christianity will be characterized by Christians "who — without overlooking Israel's failures — sense the overwhelming love with which God relates to this people and who find it possible to participate in that love."[50] Finally, a post-supersessionist Christianity will seriously consider the example of the early church as reported in Acts 15 and begin to recover an understanding of the abiding theological relevance of the distinction between Jew and gentile *within the fellowship of the church itself.* On the one hand, this means that in those cases in which Jews are baptized, the church will not *deny* but *presuppose* the continued validity of that person's Jewish identity and the obligations that accompany it, including Torah observance. On the other hand, it will mean that Gentile Christians will understand themselves as

> the gathering of peoples around the people of Israel, the entry of the adopted sons and daughters into the household of God. Through the Jew Jesus, when properly interpreted, the gentile enters into the covenant and

48. "A Letter to Cardinal Lustiger," p. 208.
49. "A Jewish Perspective on Incarnation," *Modern Theology* 12:2 (April 1996): 195-209, p. 207.
50. "Incarnation and God's Indwelling in Israel," p. 175.

becomes a member of the household, as long as he or she does not claim that his or her entrance replaces the original children.[51]

Speaking of the emergence of a post-supersessionist Christianity, Wyschogrod writes, "The existence of this Christianity has helped me shape a Jewish identity that can live in deep appreciation of this new Christianity."[52] I believe that readers, both gentile and Jew, who wrestle with the essays collected in this volume will come away from them with a deep appreciation for Wyschogrod's rigorous theological vision, even when they cannot share it at every point. But be warned: the experience can be electrifying.

R. Kendall Soulen

---

51. "Incarnation," *Pro Ecclesia* 2:2 (Spring 1993): 208-215, p. 215.
52. "The Impact of Dialogue with Christianity on My Self-Understanding as a Jew," p. 236.

# JUDAISM

# Divine Election and Commandments

In 1961 Michael Wyschogrod together with some twenty other writers contributed to a symposium sponsored by the journal *Judaism* on the topic "My Jewish Affirmation." The questions posed to the participants included: What do you regard as centrally significant in Jewish tradition and presently viable? By what lines of force do you consider yourself linked to the American Jewish community, the State of Israel and the Jewish people generally? and What, in your own background and experience, do you judge to have been decisive in your present Jewish engagement? Wyschogrod's contribution to the symposium economically introduces many of the themes that occupy him in his later work. Originally published in *Judaism* 10:4 (Fall 1961): 350-352.

—◦◦◦—

IN ACCOUNTING for my commitment to Orthodox Judaism, the first consideration that comes to my mind is that I was raised in a fairly Orthodox home and that my education, first in Germany and then here, was imparted in schools that devoted at least as much effort to Torah subjects as to secular ones. At the *Mesivta Torah Vodaath* I studied with several men whose spiritual presence will remain with me for the rest of my life. Of these, I would mention only one: Rabbi Schlomo Heiman, of blessed memory, with whom I studied no more than three months before his death. By sheer accident, we also spent several weeks of a summer vacation together. Through him I came to appreciate that part of the Torah that cannot be written down but transmitted only in the being of the person whose everyday conduct exemplifies it.

There were others, some now dead, others alive; they all taught generations of Yeshiva students most of whom, I dare say, remained observant Jews. I no longer see these people as often as I should, what with my involvement in academic work and related projects. Nevertheless, in the kind of stock-taking demanded by this symposium, I find myself thinking of them first.

Judaism means to me the election of the seed of Abraham as the nation of God, the imposition upon this people of a series of commandments which express God's will for the conduct of his people and the endless struggle by this people against its election, with the most disastrous consequences to itself as well as the rest of mankind. In spite of all this, the Divine election remains unaffected because it is an unconditional one, but subject to revocation. Lest all this sound inexcusably arrogant, I can only say that indeed it would be, were it the self-election of a people. As it is, it is a sign of God's absolute sovereignty which is not bound by human conceptions of fairness. Israel's election has meant that this people must observe a code of conduct far more difficult than that of any other people and that, when it does not live up to its election, it is visited by punishments so terrible that no human justice could ever warrant them. From this it follows that I view the establishment of the State of Israel with the greatest trepidation. The Divine Word is unmistakably clear concerning the Land of Israel. It is *the* soil which above all demands the faithfulness of the people of Israel to its election. Whenever the people of Israel have attempted to constitute a national life on this soil in disregard of its election, the soil has rejected them under the most catastrophic circumstances. The last thirty years have shown under what judgment the people of Israel live even on soil less sacred than that of the Holy Land; how much more perilous is it in the Land of Israel! I am therefore filled with the deepest fear when I view the optimistic, self-reliant cheerfulness with which the bulk of Jewish opinion, both Israel and other, views the State of Israel. And I shudder when I think of the responsibility devolving on the shoulders of the leaders of this state, some of whom give the Bible the place of prominence on their desks, cluttered with the affairs of a modern state.

When I look at the American Jewish scene, I find much that is heartening. We are witnessing the maturing of a generation at home in this country in all but the deepest sense (no believing Jew can dispense with the reality of the exile, and America is spiritually secure enough not to demand our dispensing with it), deeply faithful to the Covenant whose level of Jewish literacy would have been inconceivable thirty years ago. An example of this is the coming into being of *Yavneh*, a national organization of religious Jewish students with chapters at leading campuses across the nation. This has been an entirely spontaneous development; while professional Jewish organizations pour millions and millions of dollars into activities kept alive artificially and with the greatest of effort, *Yavneh* came into being by itself when Orthodox students at various universities were drawn together by the need to pray, to observe *kashruth* and have regular sessions of Torah study. Before anyone realized what was going on, a national organization came into being, financed by members' dues. While less than two years old, *Yavneh* has already conducted a series of summer courses in various fields of Jewish learning. These courses grant no credit and award no degrees; they serve only to deepen the Torah education of the participants. At the second annual convention, held during the past Labor Day weekend, close to four hundred students attended and participated in a series of lectures and seminars second to none in their intellectual rigor and religious sensitivity. All this is evidence of the fruits of Yeshiva education whose effects are just now beginning to be felt on the American Jewish scene.

Side by side with such manifestations I also observe the "Jewish" organizations, heavy with money and access to the media of public communication that only money can buy, for whom the Jew's relationship to God is a topic of very little interest. Instead, they are busy with such projects as the eradication of all manifestations of Christianity from American public life, manifestations to which they object, it can be suspected, not so much because they are Christian as because they are religious and take seriously the Word of God as a genuine event in human history. They issue pronouncements on public issues, such as the birth control controversy, without even mentioning the rabbinic view of the matter, as if the Jewish point of view were self-evidently identical with the ideology of the social sciences or the liberalism of the *New York Post.* One's first and most natural reaction is to declare the word "Jewish" an equivocal one: on the one hand stands the community of believers, those faithful to the Sinaitic Covenant, while on the other we group all interpretations of the "Jewish" in national, ethnic and essentially secular terms. While the greatest temptation for a Jewish Barthianism is to perform just this separation and emphasize the ensuing gulf, traversable only by Divine grace, a reverent faithfulness to the biblical Word precludes such a "solution" for the believing Jew. The trouble is that the election of Israel is an election of the seed of Abraham which is an election of the flesh. To our human religious consciousness, an election by religious sensibility rather than by birth would seem more reasonable. But the Divine election, in its sovereignty, is of a people of the flesh, a people having its share, if not slightly more, of negative national characteristics, characteristics accentuated by a harrowing history of suffering.

Now it is the proclamation of biblical faith that God chose this people and loves it as no other, unto the end of time. Consequently, even the hardly disguised self-hatred of the new *Commentary* and Prof. Mordecai Kaplan's re-interpretation of Judaism in the spirit of John Dewey is a part of Israel's history of redemption which the believing theologian cannot ignore, if only because he, like every other Jew, is held accountable for them in Divine judgment. And, as the transgressions of the people he loves, these manifestations may even be dear to God as the misdeeds of a child are to his parents.

There is no doubt in my mind that American Jewry is living through a period of decision. Those segments of the community whose interest is primarily a secular one, will, within a relatively few generations, lose their interest in any form of Jewish life and thereby make unnecessary the diverse "reinterpretations" so prevalent today. To those who remain, the Covenant and its obligations will remain real.

# The One God of Abraham and the Unity of the God of Jewish Philosophy

Wyschogrod argues that the biblical conception of the one God must be carefully distinguished from the metaphysical concept of divine unity in Parmenides, Plato, and Maimonides. The biblical confession of the oneness of God is not a statement about the nature of God or even about the non-reality of gods other than YHWH. Rather, it concerns the relationship of the God of Israel to Israel and the nations, and the relationship of Israel and the nations to each other. Previously published in German as "Der eine Gott Abrahams und die Einheit des Gottes der jüdischen Philosophie," in *Das Reden vom einen Gott bei Juden und Christen*, ed. Clemens Thoma and Michael Wyschogrod (Bern: Peter Lang, 1984), pp. 29-48. First publication in English.

THE CLASSIFICATION of Judaism, Christianity, and Islam as monotheistic religions is one of the best-established axioms of religious scholarship. The historical relationship of Christianity and Islam to Judaism makes this classification plausible. The monotheism of Christianity and Islam is related to their origins in Judaism whose monotheism is thus fundamental. This picture is not without its difficulties. In the case of Christianity, its trinitarian teaching has seemed — at least to some Jewish and Muslim critics — to compromise its monotheism to some degree. And in the case of Judaism, the question is raised as to when monotheism appeared in the development of Judaism. The traditional view was that it is simultaneous with the election of Abraham which is depicted in rabbinic literature as a function of Abraham's discovery of the one, true God, maker of heaven and earth. But classical biblical criticism as represented by the school of Wellhausen rejected this view as far too simplistic. For it, monotheism is a highly advanced form of religious consciousness which, for that very reason, could not have been there from the very beginning. "According to the prevailing view," writes Yehezkel Kaufmann, "it was under the influence of the literary prophets that Israelite religion slowly evolved its monotheistic character."[1] Kaufmann rejects this view and connects the monotheistic revolution in Judaism with the person of Moses. In spite of these problems and a number of others, the classification of mature Judaism as monotheistic and the tracing of the monotheism of Christianity and Islam to their origins in Judaism is widely accepted.

Yet there is no concept in Judaism which requires as much careful analysis as the oneness of God. Properly understood, the biblical texts which speak of the oneness of God uncover the very center of the Jewish encounter with God. Improperly understood, they turn the God of Abraham, Isaac, and Jacob into a metaphysical Absolute that has very little relationship to the God who entered into covenant with Abraham and who brought the children of Israel out of Egypt. Curiously enough, much in this question hinges on the simple interpretation or translation of verses, particularly Deuteronomy 6:4: *Sh'ma Yisrael Adonai Elohaynu Adonai echad*. This verse, which for the moment we will leave untranslated, is undoubtedly the most significant verse of the whole Bible in popular Jewish consciousness and probably also for rabbinic Judaism. The rabbis ordained the recitation of this verse together with Deuteronomy 6:5-9, Deuteronomy 11:13-21, and Numbers 15:37-41 twice daily in the morning and evening services. The recitation of these passages is considered by the rabbis as biblically ordained, though there is some disagreement about whether this applies to all of the above-mentioned passages or only to some of them. In any case, it certainly applies to Deuteronomy 6:4. Rabbinic prayer thus consists of the recitation of the biblical passages referred to together with the Eighteen Benedictions, a text composed by the rabbis and containing no biblical quotations. The religious preeminence of Deuteronomy 6:4 for the rabbis and for Judaism as it has existed since the end of the Talmudic period is thus established.

For this very reason, it becomes most important to understand what it is that Deuteronomy 6:4 is asserting. Of the six words in the verse, the one that has naturally attracted most attention is the last, the word *echad*. In the Babylonian Talmud (*Berakoth* 13b) we read "It has been taught. Symmachus

---

1. Yehezkel Kaufmann, *The Religion of Israel*, trans. Moshe Greenberg (Chicago: University of Chicago Press, 1960), p. 153.

says: Whoever prolongs the word has his days and years prolonged. R. Ahab. Jacob said, [He must dwell] on the *echad*." Since the word *echad* is usually translated as "one," the verse has been read to attribute to God a particular quality, namely oneness. And this is how the verse has usually been translated: "Hear, O Israel, the Lord our God, the Lord is one." Translated and interpreted in this sense, the problem is one of understanding. What does it mean to assert that God is one? What does it mean to assert that anything is one? Is God one in the same sense in which a tree is one tree and not two trees? And if not, then how does the sense in which God is one differ from the sense in which the tree is one? These are questions which demand answers because without them the meaning of Deuteronomy 6:4 remains unclear.

Our inquiry has now taken a metaphysical turn. This is inevitable because for the Western mind, the topic of oneness or "the one" rests on two foundations: the Deuteronomic text (6:4) to which we have already referred and the Greek metaphysical tradition originating with the pre-Socratics and particularly Parmenides whose influence is paramount in all future discussions of oneness or "the one." To understand Parmenides' contribution to this problem, we must enter the domain of metaphysical thinking. Parmenides' (c. 475 B.C.E.) basic vision can be summarized in terms of a thought that he considered unthinkable, the thought of non-being. He writes:

> Come, I will tell you — and you must accept my word when you have heard it — the ways of inquiry which alone are to be thought: the one that *it is,* and it is not possible for *it not to be,* is the way of credibility, for it follows Truth; the other, that *it is not,* and that *it is bound not to be;* this I tell you is a path that cannot be explored; for you could neither recognize that which *is not,* nor express it.[2]

Parmenides here asserts the non-thinkability of non-being. Being can be thought because it is. But non-being cannot be thought because when we think of non-being we are not thinking or we convert non-being into being in order to think about it. Similarly, we cannot speak about non-being because all propositions consist of a subject and a predicate which is attributed to the subject. The form of propositions is S is P where S is the subject and P the predicate. But such a proposition asserts that something is something else and were we to speak of non-being, we would in effect be saying that non-being is which is self-contradictory since it would be saying that non-being is being.

2. Kathleen Freeman, *Ancilla to the Pre-Socratic Philosophers* (Oxford: Basil Blackwell, 1952), p. 42.

Once non-being is eliminated from our metaphysical vocabulary, difference is no longer tenable. A is different from B only because A *is not* B. But if there is no non-being, then A cannot not be B. It then follows that A is B and C and D and everything else. In short, with the elimination of non-being, an undifferentiated Absolute Being emerges in which no distinctions can be made and in which no change is possible. The reason for this is that change also presupposes non-being. Change occurs when something which previously lacked a certain characteristic acquires that characteristic. But to lack a characteristic is not to be something and that is not possible if there is no non-being. The Absolute of Parmenides is thus without change, time, difference, or otherness. It is an Absolute undifferentiated unity which is the reality behind the apparent world of change, time, otherness, and difference.

Plato, the neo-Platonists, and to some extent even Aristotle accepted Parmenides' views on absolute being. At times, attempts were made to dilute Parmenides' views without rejecting them completely. Plato develops a metaphysics of levels according to which Parmenides is right on the level of ultimate reality but the phenomenal world of change is assigned a lower level of being. But in the final analysis, ultimate reality consists of an undifferentiated one that knows nothing of time and change, not to speak of the hopes and disappointments of human beings. The metaphysical orientation originating with Parmenides is reflected in Jewish thinking as early as the Gaonic period. Treatise II of Saadia Gaon's (882-942 C.E.) *Book of Beliefs and Opinions*[3] deals with the oneness of God. Saadia focuses on three aspects of the oneness of God: that there does not exist another God beside the one God, that the one God is not corporeal, and that by referring to God as "living," "omnipotent," and "omniscient," we are not introducing mutability into his essence. These three aspects of the oneness of God can be divided into two aspects of oneness: the external and the internal. The external is coextensive with the claim that there are not two but only one God. Here the oneness eliminates another, external God who is the equal of the first God. Saadia's two other aspects — that God is not corporeal and that there is no mutability (or multiplicity) in his essence refers to an internal interpretation of the oneness of God. Here oneness is not applied to the elimination of outside competitors but to the characterization of the being of God as non-corporeal and lacking a multiplicity of attributes. External oneness is biblically rooted and we will return to it soon. But internal oneness is philosophically motivated, resulting from

3. Saadia Gaon, *The Book of Beliefs and Opinions*, trans. S. Rosenblatt (New Haven: Yale University Press, 1948). Saadia Gaon al-Fayyumi was the first systematic philosopher of Judaism and a pioneering exegete, grammarian, liturgist, and chronologist.

Parmenidian metaphysics mediated to Saadia through the Greek philosophic tradition.

What is particularly noteworthy in Saadia is the conflation of the polemic against corporeality with the polemic against a multiplicity of attributes. For Saadia, the "allegation of the existence within His essence of distinction" is "equivalent to an allegation . . . that He [God] is really a physical being."[4] "For," he concludes, "anything that harbors distinction within itself is unquestionably a physical being." Here we have penetrated to the root of Saadia's and later Maimonides' anticorporeality. The root is metaphysical. There is the realm of distinction which is the corporeal. That is, in the words of Parmenides, "a path that cannot be explored" for it grants being to non-being. As we read Saadia's polemic against causing any increase or mutability in God's essence, we hear passages such as the following from Parmenides:

> . . . Being has no coming-into-being and no destruction, for it is whole of limb, without motion, and without end. And it never Was, nor Will Be, because it Is without end. And it never Was, nor Will Be, because it Is now, a whole all together. . . . Nor is Being divisible, since it is all alike. Nor is there anything there which could prevent it from holding together, nor any lesser thing, but all is full of being.[5]

The noncorporeality and non-mutability of God results from the need to identify the God of the Bible with the Being of Parmenides.

For Maimonides, as for Saadia, the absolute internal oneness of God is critical. He writes:

> For this reason, we, the community of those who profess the Unity by virtue of a knowledge of the truth — just as we do not say that there is in His essence a superadded notion by virtue of which He has created the heavens, and another one by virtue of which He has created the elements, and a third one by virtue of which He has created the intellects — so we do not say that there is in Him a superadded notion by virtue of which He possesses power, and another by virtue of which He possesses will, and a third one by virtue of which He knows the things created by Him. His essence is, on the contrary, one and simple, having no notion that is superadded to it in any respect.[6]

---

4. Saadiah Gaon, *Beliefs and Opinions*, p. 103.

5. Freeman, *Ancilla*, pp. 43, 44.

6. Maimonides, *Guide of the Perplexed*, trans. Shlomo Pines (Chicago: University of Chicago Press, 1969), Part I, chap. 53, p. 122.

The difficulties associated with this point of view are numerous. If no attributes can be predicated of God, then we simply cannot say anything about him, not even that he exists and that he is one, for existence and oneness are also attributes. Maimonides concedes this. Speaking of God, he writes that "His essence does not have an accident attaching to it when it exists, in which case its existence would be a notion that is superadded to it."[7] Similarly, he is one without possessing the attribute of unity. Pushed to its logical conclusion, we arrive at a position that denies the possibility of any speech about God.

It is at this point that we encounter the deepest paradox of Maimonides' position. Maimonides saves himself from agnosticism by advancing the view that while it is not possible to say what God is, it is possible to say what he is not. He interprets all positive statements about God in the negative sense. When we say that he is living, we mean that he is not dead and when we say that he is eternal, we mean that there is no cause that has brought him into being. Our purpose here is not to evaluate the viability of this solution. It is obvious that it is not without problems. From the logical point of view, the judgment that S *is not* P can be expressed as S is non-P, turning the negative into a positive copula. The paradox, from our point of view, is that Maimonides uses non-being to rescue him from a problem originally generated by the Parmenidian claim that non-being cannot be thought and therefore cannot be. With non-being eliminated, Parmenides is left with an undifferentiated plenum of being from which all change, temporality, and differentiation is eliminated. Maimonides applies this to God whose total undifferentiation expresses itself in his absolute unity which precludes all attributes since the possession of any attributes beyond God's simple essence would contradict his absolute unity. But because this reasoning drives Maimonides to the edge of agnosticism, he modifies his viewpoint by resorting to a negative theology according to which only statements that assert what God is not are theologically admissible. But because discourse reflects ontology, negative statements about God are possible only because non-being in some way intersects with the being of God. And if that were so, the absolutely undifferentiated nature of the divine being would not have to be assumed.

I can only conclude that Maimonides was not altogether clear about the Parmenidian roots of his metaphysics and the underlying ontology which fed his theology of an absolute divine unity. Had he been more aware of these issues, he could not have ultimately staked his Judaism on a negative theology which refused to notice the Bible's lack of interest in the problem so central to Maimonides, the problem of anthropomorphism.

7. Maimonides, *Guide*, p. 132.

The interpretation of Deuteronomy 6:4 in light of the Parmenidian problematic is therefore fundamentally mistaken. Deuteronomy 6:4 is not making a metaphysical statement. It is not asserting that there is no multiplicity in the being of God, that nothing is superadded to his essence or that the being of God consists of a non-differentiated unity to which no attributes can be applied. Deuteronomy 6:4 is not asserting any of these things because these assertions come out of a metaphysical frame of mind that is completely foreign to the Bible. What Deuteronomy 6:4 does assert is that the Jewish people is loyal to and recognizes as God only J. and no other God. It is really an expression of loyalty to J., of everlasting obligation to serve him and no one else. The correct translation of Deuteronomy 6:4 is therefore: "Hear, O Israel! The Lord is Our God, the Lord alone." This is how Deuteronomy 6:4 reads in the most recent Jewish Publication Society[8] translation of the Bible and it is the correct reading.

How can we prove this? First and foremost, from the context. The context is the speech of Moses in which he exhorts the people of Israel to obey God's commandments. That emphasis starts with the first verse of Deuteronomy 5 and the recitation of the Ten Commandments in that chapter. Moses is not sanguine that the people of Israel will keep the commandments. One can detect a great fear that the people will turn away from them, neglect them and bring disaster on themselves. Moses points out that the people heard the commandments spoken by God (6:19). True, they did not hear all of them because they were unable to bear the direct presence of God (6:22) and begged Moses to mediate so they would not have to hear the direct word of God. And God had pity on them and let them go, depending on Moses to communicate the commandments to them. But we get the distinct impression that while God acquiesced in this arrangement, he is not happy about it. Since he fears that the Israelites will not obey his commandments, he seems to feel that the danger of this is increased under the new arrangement since the people will not have heard all of the commandments from God directly but only the first words. For this reason, Moses points out that they did hear the opening words and if they did not hear all of them directly from God, it is because they begged off and God agreed. But the fear that they will not obey remains with God and Moses.

It is in this context that 6:4 is spoken. It is spoken in the context of a great fear, the fear that the people will be disobedient. And why will they be disobedient? Because J. will not be their only God. Their loyalty will be divided. They will probably not simply forget J. Too much has happened between J. and the people of Israel for them simply to forget J. But J. will not be

8. *The Torah* (Philadelphia: Jewish Publication Society of America, 1962).

their only God. Together with J., they will serve "the gods of the people that are around you" (6:14). And this J. will not tolerate because he is a "jealous" (6:15) God who will not share the people of Israel with another god. And that is what 6:4 asserts: J. is to be your only God, not one of two or three or four gods, all of whom you wish to appease. You either worship me completely, says J., or you do not worship me at all. That is the meaning of the verse that follows immediately after 6:4: "And you shall love the Lord your God with all your heart, and with all your soul, and with all your might." The emphasis on "all" in this verse is designed to rule out precisely the possibility that God fears: a partial service, combined with service of another god or of other gods. This is not possible. Either J. is served completely as the only God, or he is not served at all. Service of J. cannot be combined with some degree of loyalty to another God, even if that loyalty is of lesser degree than the loyalty to J. J. can only be served with "all" the heart, and "all" the soul, and "all" the might of which humankind is capable. And if "all" is devoted to J., then there is nothing left with which to worship any other God, to any degree whatsoever.

It is worth noting that in these chapters of Deuteronomy the emphasis is not on the truth that there is no other God beside J. "It is commonly assumed," writes Yehezkel Kaufmann, "that the religion of YHWH began as henotheism or monolatry, recognizing him as sole legitimate god in Israel, but acknowledging the existence of other national gods."[9] It is not necessary for us to take a position on this question. Whether there exist other divine beings whom non-Israelites may legitimately worship or whether, in fact, there are no such beings and there are only nations who mistakenly think that there are, the important fact is that Israel may not worship any other god than J. Deuteronomy recognizes that there are peoples who worship other gods and who clearly believe that these other gods are not simply figments of people's imaginations but real, divine beings who have the power to reward and punish those who please or displease them. If J. demands total loyalty ("all your heart"), then this demand is not based on default as if J. must be worshiped because there are no other gods who can be worshiped, but irrespective of whether there are other gods. If all the heart is given to J., then the issue of whether there are other gods does not arise since there is nothing left with which to worship these other gods.

It is clear that the rabbis understood Deuteronomy 6:4 in the context in which we have placed it. This can be inferred without difficulty from the passages they connected with 6:4 and the recitation of which they prescribed twice daily. As we have already said, they connected 6:5-9 with 6:4. This is justi-

---

9. Kaufmann, *Religion of Israel*, p. 8.

fied both by its contiguity to 6:4 and for the reasons we have already discussed. But they also added Deuteronomy 11:13-21 and Numbers 15:37-41. In 11:13-21, we again hear of the danger of worshiping other gods and of the punishment that will befall Israel if it does so. Numbers 11:13-21 speaks of the fringes on Israelite garments which are to remind the people of the commandments and of the dire consequences of disobeying them. The three passages together spell out the rabbinic interpretation of the meaning of 6:4. 6:4 is not a proposition designed to provide us with metaphysical information about God. It is, as we have seen, a declaration that only J. is to be worshiped coupled with the conviction that the proper worship of J. consists of obeying his commandments as set forth in the ten commandments and in the Torah as a whole.

If any further evidence of the rabbinic reading is required, we need only turn to the Mishnah:

> R. Joshua b. Korha said: Why was the section of "Hear" [Deut. 6:4] placed before that of "And it shall come to pass" [Deut. 11:13]? So that one should first accept upon himself the yoke of the kingdom of heaven and then take upon himself the yoke of the commandments.[10]

Throughout the Talmud, the recitation of the *Shema* is referred to as "the acceptance of the yoke of the kingdom of heaven." This expression would be quite inappropriate if Deuteronomy 6:4 were read as a metaphysical statement about the nature of God. Instead, it is read as a declaration of total and unconditional loyalty to God's sovereign rule and the acceptance of what follows from that loyalty: obedience to his divine will as expressed in the Torah.

While it is true that theoretically it is possible to believe that the Jewish people are obligated to serve J. only and that other nations are entitled to worship other gods, it is not difficult to understand that a strong conviction that the Jewish people may only worship J. tends to lead to the corollary belief that he is the only god who should be worshiped by anyone. This is precisely the development we observe in rabbinic thought. We have already pointed out that the heart of rabbinic prayer is the recitation of Deuteronomy 6:4 with its concomitant passages and of the so-called Eighteen Benedictions, also known as the standing prayer. This prayer assumes various forms on the holidays, the most interesting and longest version being that on the Rosh Hashanah, the Jewish New Year. The Rosh Hashanah *Amidah* (standing prayer) is built on three themes: God's kingship, God's remembrance, and the blowing of the Shofar.

Each of these themes is elaborated in a rabbinically composed text and

---

10. B. *Berachoth*, Chap. 2, Mishnah 2.

supported by extensive quotations from the Bible. The section of the Rosh Hashanah *Amidah* of particular interest to us is the one dealing with the kingship of God. It is of interest to us for two reasons: it quotes Deuteronomy 6:4 and it focuses its complete attention on the future unification of humankind under the one God. It reads:

> We hope therefore, Lord our God, soon to behold thy majestic glory, when the abominations shall be removed from the earth, and the false gods exterminated; when the world shall be perfected under the reign of the Almighty, and all mankind will call upon thy name, and all the wicked of the earth will turn to thee. May all the inhabitants of the world realize and know that to thee every knee must bend, every tongue must vow allegiance. May they bend the knee and prostrate themselves before thee, Lord our God, and give honor to thy glorious name; may they all accept the yoke of thy kingdom, and do thou reign over them speedily forever and ever. For the kingdom is thine, and to all eternity thou wilt reign in glory, as it is written in thy Torah. . . .

After this, ten verses are quoted, of which Deuteronomy 6:4 is the last, and this section of the *Amidah* concludes:

> Our God and God of our fathers, reign over the whole universe in thy glory; be exalted over all the earth in thy grandeur; shine forth in thy splendid majesty over all the inhabitants of thy world. May every being know that thou hast made it; may every creature realize that thou hast created it; may every breathing thing proclaim: "The Lord God of Israel is King, and his kingdom rules over all."

There is no rabbinic text which expresses more clearly the hope that, in time, all humankind will worship the one true God. This hope is derived from two verses in which the oneness of God is spoken of: Deuteronomy 6:4 and Zechariah 14:9: "And the Lord shall be king over all the earth: in that day shall the Lord be one, and his name one." These two verses — Deuteronomy 6:4 and Zechariah 14:9 — are connected by the word *echad*. In both instances, the word has the same meaning. God is *echad* when he alone is king, when he alone is worshiped. Kabalists and metaphysicians had a very exciting time with Zechariah 14:9. How can God and his name become one? Either God always was one or he is not one, but how can anything, particularly God, become one, particularly absolutely one? But these questions do not arise if the verse is properly understood. *Echad* here means "the only one." If other Gods are worshiped, then God is not the only one, and if God alone is worshiped then he is the only one. In this sense, God can become the only one if at first J. and other gods are worshiped and then only J. is worshiped, not only by Israel but by all of humanity. The issue is not God becoming metaphysically one when he was not metaphysically one at an earlier point. The hope is that God will become the only one worshiped anywhere in the world.

Our investigation has thus taken a decisive turn. Whereas we started with the impression that the oneness of God is a statement about the nature of God (internal oneness) or about the non-reality of gods other than J. (external oneness), we now find through the juxtaposition of Deuteronomy 6:4 and Zechariah 14:9 that the issue of the oneness of God really deals with the relationship of Israel and the nations to the God of Israel and of Israel and the nations to each other. In the first instance, the oneness of God means that Israel is to worship no other God but J. Secondly, it means that the day will come when the God of Israel will be recognized as the only God by all of humanity. And thirdly — though this is not as explicit as the previous two — the impact that the above-mentioned hope has on Israel's relation with the nations. If the God worshiped currently by Israel is destined to become the God of all, then some kind of educational task seems to devolve on Israel. It can be argued, of course, that the future loyalty of the nations to J. will come about by itself, without Israel playing any mediating role. But that does not sound very plausible. The history of God's relationship with Israel must in some way lay the groundwork for the nations drawing to God. More precisely, the nations drawing to God is not unrelated to their drawing to God's first people, Israel. Zechariah 8:23 makes this clear:

> Thus saith the Lord of hosts; In those days it shall come to pass, that ten men, out of all the languages of the nations, shall take hold, yea they shall take hold of the skirt of him that is a Jew, saying, We will go with you: for we have heard that God is with you.

The movement to the God of Israel is thus seen as continuous with a cleaving to the Jews, the people who have carried God's name in the world since Abraham. It is, after all, not accidental that through Christianity many segments of the nations have bound themselves to a particular Jew to whom they have been able to say: "God is with you." And it is for this reason that Maimonides was able to characterize Christianity and Islam as religions which "served to clear the way for King Messiah, to prepare the whole world to worship God with one accord. . . ."[11] The process that will culminate in the

---

11. *The Code of Maimonides*, Book 14, trans. Abraham M. Hershman (New Haven: Yale University Press, 1949), p. xxiii.

state of affairs described in Zechariah 14:9 is at work in the process of history and characterizes Israel's interaction with the nations.

The task of Israel is to retain its relationship to the specific person who is its God. In this context, the word "monotheism" does not do the job. It is a word with which I have long been uncomfortable. Two persons can both be monotheists — believe that there is only one God — and worship different gods. If one believes that only Baal is God and worships him and the other believes that only Zeus is God and worships him, then both are "monotheists" but, in fact, they have very little in common. It is like two monarchists who disagree about who the rightful ruler is, though they are both monarchists and both believe that there is only one king. The issue is therefore not monotheism in the abstract. The issue is whether J. is God or whether someone else is.

The task of Israel is to proclaim that only J. is God. J. is thus identified by a proper name not by the noun God. "Only J. is God" asserts that the one specific person described in the Bible is God. And the specificity of J. can only be expressed through the stories recorded in the Bible. He is the God who created heaven and earth, chose Abraham, brought the children of Israel out of Egypt. This is the reason that the history of the Jewish people plays such an essential role in the definition of J. While, in one sense, "creator of heaven and earth" alone defines him uniquely, in the broader sense only a relatively adequate recounting of his deeds determines that we are speaking about the particular J. who is the only God. Without such a recounting, we are likely to be referring to God as an abstract noun rather than to the God who does not hesitate to assume a proper name. When the proper name of God recedes into the background, we move into the realm of first causes and unmoved movers, the God of pure reason rather than the covenant partner of Israel.

We must return to the theme with which we started: the three monotheistic religions. In the light of what we have said, this concept now appears somewhat more problematic. If belief that there is only one God characterizes a religion as monotheistic, then Judaism, Christianity, and Islam are monotheistic religions (though, in the case of Christianity, the doctrine of the Trinity raises some problems). But if the question is not primarily whether there is one or more gods but whether the one God who exists is J. or someone else, then the different stories told in the three faiths become far more important. While the three faiths have many common stories, they also have different ones. I think they all agree on the story of Noah and the exodus from Egypt. But they do not all agree that God became human in Jesus or that he chose Mohammed as one of his prophets. Some degree of disagreement is to be expected. But how much of that is possible before it becomes clear that the three religions in question actually have different Gods? To take a mundane example, suppose we have a mutual friend about whom we both know very much and yet may disagree about whether he vacationed last summer on the French Riviera or not. At this stage, we are both clearly referring to the same person but disagreeing about a detail. But if these details increase, after a while we may begin to wonder whether we are talking of the same Henry. Translated into the realm of Judaism, Christianity, and Islam, that is the danger that lurks in our different stories.

What unites the three faiths is that they agree about much of the story and much of the teaching that communicates God's will for the conduct of humankind. Some of the disagreement is a result of the individuality of all personal encounters. Even on the human level, a different aspect of our personalities finds expression in different relationships. Each one of our faiths has its own, unique relationship with God and there is perhaps even something illicit in comparing relationships. Nevertheless, it is very significant that we all look forward to the unification of the human family in the common service of the God of Abraham, Isaac, and Jacob, because only then will God and God's name be one.

The oneness of the biblical God is therefore not the oneness of Parmenides, Plato, and the neo-Platonic tradition. Biblical oneness is essentially a hope for the human family: that all of humanity will serve the one and only God. But there is one other aspect of this God to which we must refer because it lies at the heart of the distinction between the God of Abraham, Isaac, and Jacob and the God of the philosophers as well as the Gods of the pagan. I can best express this distinction by saying that the biblical God is not placed in any framework more all-encompassing than he while the pagan gods and the God of the philosophers (e.g., Aristotle and Hegel) are always placed in an all-embracing framework of some sort. In mythology, this is expressed in some story recounting the origin of the gods. The gods are beings who have some kind of birth and who are subject to fate. They appear from a background that enables us to classify them and to understand them psychologically and metaphysically. From the philosophical perspective, being reigns over the Gods and even over the God of monotheism. Both God and his creatures have being so that being unites God and his creatures, thereby reducing God to one being among others, even if God is the mightiest of beings. In our time, it was Martin Heidegger[12] who rediscovered the ontological basis of philosophy and distinguished ontology and the ontic sciences that dealt with beings rather than being itself, with theology counted among the ontic sci-

12. Martin Heidegger, *Being and Time*, trans. John Macquarrie and Edward Robinson (London: SCM Press, 1962), p. 30.

ences. Where being becomes the highest concept of thought, God becomes one being among others and ontology comes to rule over theology.

The God of the Bible does not enter being because the question of his origin is never posed. When this question is posed, a framework that is broader than God is presupposed and God is made subject to this framework. But the God of Israel is the lord of all frameworks and subject to none. This is the remarkable power of God: the Bible does not hesitate to speak of him in personal and anthropomorphic terms. It shows a God who enters the human world and into relation with humanity by means of speech and command. At the same time, this God transcends the world he has created and is not subject to any power or force. The only being who comes close to having the power to restrict God is the human being whose creation God regrets (Gen. 6:6) but here too we can be certain that God will save humankind and that humanity's disobedience will not prevail.

In the final analysis, then, the Jewish understanding of God is intact as long as no power or structure is posited that is equal to God and that is in a position to oppose successfully the will of God. In spite of all the difficulties Christian trinitarian teaching poses for Judaism, the absence of the theme of conflict among the persons of the Trinity maintains trinitarianism as a problem for rather than a complete break with Judaism.

# A Theology of Jewish Unity

In view of contemporary Judaism's crisis of fragmentation, Michael Wyschogrod argues that the litmus test for any interpretation of Judaism is its capacity to construct a plausible platform for Jewish unity. A Jewish philosophy that cuts off a significant portion of the Jewish people from the house of Israel thereby demonstrates its own Jewish inadequacy. Wyschogrod proposes that traditional believing Judaism possesses the richest and most resilient account of Jewish unity, according to which the foundation of Jewish unity is the nature of Jewish election as the seed of Abraham, Isaac, and Jacob. This election unites all Jews, irrespective of their beliefs. Originally published in *L'Eylah Journal* 21 (1986): 26-30.

—◈◈◈—

## I

THE QUESTION of Jewish unity is one of the most critical issues in Jewish life today. This is hardly surprising. There are few periods of Jewish history which were not characterized by numerous differences of opinion. Both the Bible and the Talmud are essentially records of debate, of the clash of ideas and perspectives. Since the destruction of the Temple, Judaism has not operated under any one centralized authority. From time to time, regional authorities came into being (e.g., the Resh Galutha in Babylonia and the Council of Four Lands in Poland) but these did not evolve into a universal Jewish authority. In short, nothing like a Jewish papacy ever appeared.

Nevertheless, before the advent of modern times, a fundamental Jewish unity was a palpable reality. It is not difficult to formulate the basis of this unity. It consisted of a widely shared interpretation of the nature and purpose of the Jewish people. The Jewish people consisted of the descendants of Abraham, Isaac, and Jacob, whom God had chosen as his special people. He had given the Torah to this people and had demanded that it live up to the Torah's demands. Because the Jewish people did not do so, they were expelled from their land and forced to live in exile. In his own good time, God would redeem Israel from its exile and reestablish Jewish sovereignty under Davidic rule. However widely they were dispersed, Jews felt themselves belonging to one people with a particular origin and a particular destiny in the world. And this unity was not fundamentally diminished by a certain amount of traffic both into and out of Judaism. At all periods, there were Jews who opted to leave the Jewish people and there were gentiles who opted to attach themselves to Judaism. But this traffic was mostly small in numbers so that the self-interpretation of Jews as deriving from the patriarchs was not put in question. The consensus that united Jews was thus one of family continuity as well as shared theology.

This consensus ran into increasing difficulty with the enlightenment and the advent of modernity. The religious foundation of Judaism was severely weakened. The decline of religious faith was not a phenomenon restricted to Jews. Modern times have seen a profound process of secularization whose causes are complex and perhaps not fully understood. But for Jews, secularization took on the quality of a new opportunity. Jews had been excluded from the Christian society of the middle ages. This exclusion seemed solely a religious one. Would the weakening of religious commitment not make it easier for Jews to be accepted into European society? Many Jews saw in secularization the birth of a new order in which each human being would be appreciated in his humanity instead of being subsumed under a religious classification which, in the case of Jews, served to exclude them from mainline society. Unlike other Europeans, Jews had a special reason for embracing the ongoing secularization and the result was that the shedding of religious identity became a matter of some urgency to large numbers of Jews.

What Jews did not and perhaps could not have foreseen was that something else would take the place of religious identity in Europe and that something else was nationalism. As religion lost its altogether preeminent role, it was gradually replaced by the nation and this caused Jews even greater difficulty. At first, this did not seem inevitable. Couldn't national identity include persons of diverse religious faiths? Couldn't Jews be considered Germans or Frenchmen of Jewish faith? Jews did everything possible to make this possible. They outdid all others in their loyalty and devotion to the fatherland or the motherland, as the case may have been. The nationalism thus generated was directly proportional to the degree of insecurity and most often the attempt was unsuccessful. There were two basic reasons for this. In most countries, national and religious identities were closely intertwined. In one country, to be a true national of that country one had to be a Roman Catholic. In another, one had to be Russian Orthodox while in a third it was Lutheranism that was required. In short, too often religion was so closely intertwined with national identity that a Jew was simply not a full-fledged member of the national community irrespective of how easy it was to speak of "Germans of the Mosaic persuasion." Secondly, sooner or later it was noticed both by Jews and gentiles that being Jewish was not just a religious but also a national identity. And if this was so, Jews could not be Germans or Frenchmen because they already belonged to the Jewish nation. However vigorously this was denied by Jews who wished desperately to be included in the non-Jewish, national identity, it somehow proved very difficult to deny that — in spite of the fundamental prominence played by religion in Jewish identity — there was also a significant national dimension to that identity which was quite different from the purely religious understanding of Christian self-definition.

All of which leads us to the contemporary situation. This situation, at least in a preliminary way, can only be characterized as one of unprecedented Jewish fragmentation. It is not necessary to list and explain the many different kinds of Jewishness extant. Suffice it to say that they range from a relatively intact version of pre-modern Jewish self-understanding to a completely secular and almost non-national Yiddishist self-definition. In between are the varieties of Zionist definitions with all their religious and other complexities. With all the many Jewish definitions in existence, they also all overlap each other so that a staggering number of permutations is both theoretically possible and actually realized in Jewish life. It is not surprising that non-Jews are often deeply confused. Proceeding from the assumption that Judaism is a religion, Christians are greatly surprised when they learn that there are non-religious Jews. Christian churches generally define themselves theologically and churches have come apart and new churches founded on — at least to non-Christians — relatively minor nuances of theological interpretation. How then can Jews coexist in a broad Judaism which has place for all interpretations of the faith? Aren't the disagreements between Orthodox and Reform Jewish — not to speak of nonbelieving Jews — too great to be contained in any "church"? What meaning does the word "Jew" have if there are so many different kinds of Jews?

In response to this question, there are two possibilities. We can attempt to formulate some definition which will embrace all the diverse currents to which we have alluded. In order to succeed at this task, we would have to obtain the agreement of all parties concerned to whatever unifying thread is presented as holding together the diverse part of the entity that is Judaism. It is not impossible that such a definition of "Jew" or "Judaism" can be found. When we set aside the teaching of Judaism, the concepts and values that define it in a programmatic way, we are left with a shared historic destiny that embraces many Jews who share that destiny even as they disagree about many things. Such a platform for Jewish unity ought not to be lightly dismissed even if it must also be unsatisfactory for more intellectually demanding Jews. Such a platform would focus on a certain kind of lowest common denominator, leaving out of consideration those aspects of Judaism or Jewishness which are most precious to various segments of Jewry. Among these would be the religious aspect particularly precious to religious Jews, the partiality to justice that particularly concerns some Reform and secular Jews and the national component that is central to Zionist and Israel-oriented Jews. When these "special interests" are bracketed, we are left with the kind of unity that is in the air when Holocaust survivors of many diverse philosophies and ideologies meet. The common experience of the Holocaust is so powerful that normal differences pale into insignificance in the light of the shared catastrophe. In this context, we can observe the gradual emergence of a kind of Jewish civil religion that has made possible a degree of Jewish unity during difficult times in the recent past.

But each segment of the Jewish ideological spectrum needs to develop its own justification for Jewish unity. In so doing, it will draw on ideas and interpretations unique to its own particular orientation and not necessarily shared by other segments of Jewry. Its understanding of Jewish unity will therefore not be shared completely, or perhaps even not at all, by other segments of Jewry. In one sense, then, such a particular platform for Jewish unity could be seen as divisive because it would not hesitate to emphasize aspects of the tradition which other branches of the family would not only not emphasize but even reject. Nevertheless, the exercise must be conducted. The reason for this is that we are here dealing with a litmus test of the viability of various interpretations of Judaism. *No interpretation of Judaism which is unable to construct a plausible platform for Jewish unity is a viable interpretation of Judaism.* Any Jewish philosophy which can cut off a significant portion of the living Jewish people from the house of Israel thereby demonstrates its own Jewish inadequacy. Only a Judaism or Jewishness that is permeated by love for the Jewish people and an almost absolute determination to affirm all Jews even as it disagrees with this or that interpretation of Judaism can today be taken seriously.

And this is particularly applicable to "believing Jewry." As the form of Judaism most continuous with classical Judaism, the temptation for religious

Jewry to read out of the fold nonbelieving Jews or Jews who do not believe exactly what it believes, is particularly strong. But it is particularly believing Jewry which does most damage to itself by embarking on such an exclusionary path. It does so because the deepest unity of the Jewish people is rooted in the relationship of this people to God. Jewish unity is therefore a theological issue of the greatest seriousness. And believing Judaism emerges, I think, as the most authentic interpretation of Judaism for various reasons, one of which is the richness and plausibility of its understanding of Jewish unity. Only a believing Judaism has a theology of Jewish unity.

# II

We must return to what we referred to earlier as the pre-modern basis of Jewish unity. This consisted of the basic story of Judaism. God, the creator of the universe, creates human beings to whom he makes his creation subservient. The human creature finds himself in a situation of great comfort and security. He is thus the recipient of an immense divine gift which he could not have deserved since it is given to him as he is brought into existence, before he could have done anything that would make him deserve it. There is only one demand that is made of him in return for all the favors that have been showered on him. He is asked to refrain from eating the fruit of one of the trees in the garden. As is well known, man does not live up to the one demand that is made of him, starting a process of human war against God which ultimately leads to the destruction of the whole of humanity with the exception of one of the families of man. After these preliminaries, God's attention turns to a particular person, Abraham, whose fate and the fate of whose descendants becomes the almost total preoccupation of the Bible. Whereas God's earlier interest was all of humanity, with the advent of Abraham a certain narrowing of the divine interest is noticeable. While for the first two generations descendants of Abraham appear who are not Jews (i.e., Ishmael and Esau), with Jacob that is no longer possible and all the descendants of Jacob are Jews and the same is true in all subsequent generations. The Jewish people thus understands itself as the continuation of generations that started with Abraham and continue to the present.

This human family, originating with Abraham, is a covenanted family. By saying this, two features must be noticed. The first is widely noticed but incompletely understood. God's relationship with the Jewish people, the seed of Abraham, is deeply connected with a set of demands made by God of the Jewish people. In the case of Abraham, the number of explicit demands is not very great but the smallness of numbers is made up by the archetype of all demands: the sacrifice of his son Isaac. We thus have an interweaving of the selection of a human family such that genealogy, physical descent from the father, plays a critical role together with a relationship of command and obedience. The second point worthy of notice is that the relationship of command coexists with the relationship of covenant. Because we are dealing with God's relationship with man, the appearance of covenant is not without surprise. Covenant seems more appropriate in the relation of equals. Can God not simply command? Instead, from the first, there is a certain symmetry. The obligation of each side is derived from value received. Adam's obligation to refrain from eating the fruit of the designated tree seems related to the gifts that his creator showered on him in his creation, and Abraham's call to sacrifice his son comes to him after God had made binding commitments with respect to the fate of his descendants. In short, the relationship of the Jewish people to God is as much a matter of genealogy as it is a matter of obedience and obedience itself yields to covenant, a more literal relationship than could be expected.

Two questions are crystallizing. First, why covenant rather than command? Why does God not simply command, imposing his demands on man? Why the treaty model, involving a certain degree of equality between the covenant partners? Second, why did God not enter into covenant with a community of faith, defined by adherence to certain tenets of belief and obedience to certain maxims of conduct? In short, why is Judaism what it is and not a church? At a number of places, the New Testament addresses itself to this question. In Luke 3, John the Baptist admonishes his listeners to repent in view of the imminence of the end. He adds (v. 8): "Bear fruits that befit repentance, and do not begin to say to yourselves, 'We have Abraham as our father'; for I tell you, God is able from these stones to raise up children to Abraham." And in Romans (9:6-8), Paul writes: "For not all who are descended from Israel belong to Israel, and not all are children of Abraham because they are his descendants; but 'Through Isaac shall your descendants be named.' This means that it is not the children of the flesh who are the children of God, but the children of the promise are reckoned as descendants." Paul concludes by quoting Hosea 2:23, "And I will say to Not my people, 'You are my people'; and he shall say, 'You are my God,'" and Hosea 1:10, "And in the place where it was said to them, 'You are not my people,' it shall be said to them, 'Sons of the living God.'"

The attitude of the New Testament is quite clear. Jews labor under the illusion that they have some sort of advantage in being descended from Abraham. In so thinking, they are thoroughly mistaken. Being descended from

48

Abraham is no advantage whatsoever. God is able to declare anyone a child of Abraham ("God is able from these stones to raise up children of Abraham"). And Paul confirms this by pointing out that not all of Abraham's children were of Israel. Isaac was of Israel but Esau was not. So being a physical descendant of Abraham does not make one a child of promise. By quoting the verses from Hosea, Paul says that God can take a people who is not chosen and make it chosen. God is not bound by genealogical considerations. He can thus reject those who are of the seed of Abraham and substitute for them as his chosen people another people who were previously not chosen. This is presumably the church which is not a natural family characterized by descent from a common ancestor but an association of persons from many peoples united by a common faith.

The New Testament's and Paul's point of view has a certain plausibility. Isn't physical descent unimportant? Shouldn't people be judged by what they believe and what they do and not by who they are descended from? In the past, nobility was hereditary. But wasn't all that nonsense? Our liberal and rational selves reject hereditary advantages. Didn't even Maimonides teach that the convert to Judaism need have no hesitation in addressing God as the "God of our fathers" even though these fathers are not his physical fathers? By converting to Judaism, Maimonides asserts, the convert becomes a spiritual son of Abraham and that is quite good enough. And perhaps it is even better. God can raise children to Abraham from stones. And in the case of the convert, he has done just that.

And yet, this cannot all be so. Even Paul has to assert (Rom. 11:28) that "they are beloved for the sake of their forefathers." Descent from Abraham is not totally without value. God's love for Israel is rooted in his love for the fathers. It is perhaps like the love of a man for a woman who dies and leaves children behind. When the bereaved lover looks at the woman's children, he sees her face and presence in them and cannot help but love them. They remind him of his beloved. And when they misbehave, he will be prone to forgive them. Not always and not under all circumstances. When their misconduct is particularly outrageous, he may be forced to punish them. But his anger cannot last long. He will look at them and in their faces he will see the face of his beloved. And his anger will subside.

Here we are at the heart of God's election of Israel. He loved Abraham, Isaac, and Jacob and therefore he loves their descendants. And he loves not only their souls but also their bodies. This is so because, from the first, God knew that man was an ensouled body. He is not a disembodied spirit temporarily connected to a body. Because man is his soul and his body, he brings his body into the relationship with God. And when God relates to a family, he is not unaware of the corporeality of this family. He confirms this corporeality by not ignoring it but by including it in the covenant. The collectivity that stands before God is thus the people of Israel as the seed of Abraham, Isaac, and Jacob. It is not an artificial collectivity, constituted as an interest group or a group sharing common ideas. Interests and ideas change. We drift in and out of artificial groups. We belong to many and our degree of involvement in each varies as our inclinations and preferences evolve in time. But a family does not change. We may like or dislike our relatives. We may seek their company or avoid it. But we cannot sever the bond that binds us to our blood relatives. A wife or a husband can be divorced. But a child or a parent cannot and that is the kind of bond that connects the Jewish people with God.

God wanted a people who could not leave him. Had he chosen a community of faith, he could never have counted on the service of any particular member of that community. One can always walk out of a community of faith by changing one's mind. But one cannot change one's face. And with a face, one belongs to a family with which one is associated by all those who recognize the face. The Jewish people is thus God's family in the world. God is present in the world through this family. No relation with their God is possible without a relation with this people. When Jesus says (John 14:6) "No one comes to the Father but by me," he says something that Judaism cannot accept because it concentrates in one Jew something that is true only of the Jewish people as a whole. There is no way to God except through the Jewish people. A gentile who was ready to accept the whole Torah except that he wished to have no relationship to the Jewish people could not enter the covenant. To enter the covenant one must become part of this particular people or family. And even the gentile who wisely chooses to remain in the Noachide covenant cannot do so without the Jewish people. It is through this people that the story of Noah's covenant has been preserved. The story of Noah is part of the Torah and the Torah is not a book that can be separated from the Jewish people, as if it had a life of its own on the shelves of libraries and secondhand bookstores. The Jewish people is the carrier of the Torah as a people in whose life it is embodied.

Having attempted to answer the question as to why God chose a biological family rather than a community of faith, it is now possible to raise the question concerning the covenant. Why does God relate to Israel in covenant with its implication of equality rather than in a relationship of command with the expectation of obedience? I believe that a partial understanding of this becomes possible. A community of faith can be commanded because it consists exclusively of persons who stand in a relationship of faith to the source of the commands. But it is otherwise with a natural family. There is a certain secularization inherent in this concept. However central a role an ideology or a faith plays in the life of a natural community, its being is not constituted by the ideology or faith. It is there in a natural way. Individuals in the family can always reject or only partially accept the ideology or faith without losing membership in the family. But a contract signed by the family binds all members of it. The covenant cannot be shed as easily as a faith can. It is a commitment given for value received. By relating to the Jewish people in the context of covenant, the human integrity of the Jewish people is recognized and it is not turned into a community of faith alone.

## III

The foundation for Jewish unity is the nature of Jewish election as seed of Abraham, Isaac, and Jacob. This is the unshakable foundation that unites all Jews, irrespective of their beliefs. Were Judaism primarily a community of faith, all differences of belief would strike at the foundation of Jewish unity. And given the seriousness of the differences of belief among Jews, no viable unity of the Jewish people would be possible. Understood in the terms outlined above, the existence of the Jewish people becomes the foundation of Jewish unity. Jewish existence imposes a common destiny on Jews. This is a destiny that encompasses all Jews. It is a destiny from which it is substantially impossible to resign. Here and there an individual Jew can disguise his identity, intermarry and in several generations perhaps disappear entirely as a Jew. But this is not a real option for most Jews both because it is inherently difficult for many Jews to do and because it is morally objectionable for most. In general, then, God has succeeded. He has brought into being a people who is tied to him irrevocably and to whom he is tied irrevocably. Nothing can ever change that.

The believing Jew must therefore perceive the sanctity of every Jew. There is no point in minimizing the differences of opinion that separate Jews. It would be folly not to try to diminish those differences, not to try to narrow the ideological gaps that separate Jews into so many factions. To depend on the family bonds of the Jewish people alone is to ignore the rifts that plague families. Families have their share of conflict, even of violence. The recognition of the kind of bond that unites Jews, rather than causing neglect of the search for unity, ought to be the basis for the search. While I have stressed the family-like bonds that unite the Jewish people, we must remember that the Jewish people is a special kind of family, a family born in love of God and obedience to his commandments. We will draw closer to each other and to

God as our family bonds are strengthened by a deepening and widening of those beliefs that have united the Jewish people through the ages.

There remains one final point that I must make. Everything I have said will be proven false once and for all if, God forbid, a war among Jews should ever become possible. War among Christians has been and is a commonplace. The reason for this is, I think, that the Christian divides his identity between a religion and a nation. When at war in his national capacity, the Christian identity is left dormant and the war rages through the other identity. But this is not possible for Jews. Should large-scale violence among Jews ever become real, then Judaism will have ended. But that will never happen.

# Sin and Atonement in Judaism

Wyschogrod believes that Judaism's conceptions of sin and atonement are especially beset by misunderstanding, not least among Jews. Popular Jewish understanding is doubly hampered, on the one side by the uncritical adoption of secular theories of wrongdoing that miss the religious dimension of sin, and on the other by the desire to maximize the difference between Jewish conceptions of sin and atonement and their (also partly misunderstood) Christian counterparts. Over against both tendencies Wyschogrod emphasizes the importance of seeing both sin and redemption in light of God's irrevocable love for Israel. Previously published in *The Human Condition in the Jewish and Christian Traditions*, ed. Frederick Greenspahn (New York: Ktav Publishing House, 1986), pp. 103-128.

———❦❦❦———

ANY CONTEMPORARY analysis of the notions of sin and atonement in Judaism is an exercise conducted, consciously or unconsciously, overtly or covertly, in dialogue with two presences: secularism and Christianity. It is, of course, possible to practice historical scholarship and to attempt an explication of these concepts in the Hebrew Bible and in postbiblical Judaism on their own terms, independently of any hidden contemporary agenda, aiming to learn how these matters were understood "then" and nothing more. But texts do not interpret themselves. The understanding that a text generates results from the interaction of the text with the consciousness of a reader who approaches the text with a frame of reference which is the source of the ques-

53

tions that the reader puts to the text, which, in turn, determine the answers he receives. This insight must not be exaggerated into a relativism that dissolves the text into the consciousness of its readers. There are not as many texts as there are readers. But there is also the situation of the reader, which we ignore at our peril.

Because of these considerations, we cannot ignore the two presences to which I have already referred: secularism and Christianity. Contemporary Jewish folk wisdom has little sympathy for the idea of sin and therefore has relatively little use for the relief of atonement. Any but the most fleeting reference to these ideas sounds strange to many Jewish ears. The accepted teaching is that sin is a Christian preoccupation with which Judaism is not burdened. Judaism, it is asserted, takes a positive view of this world, and this is exemplified in Judaism's positive attitude to sexuality, in contrast to Christianity's preference for celibacy. The more sophisticated version of this attitude then proceeds to explain that condemnation of the material came to Christianity from Platonic and Gnostic sources which were and are in sharp conflict with the life-affirming realism of Judaism, for which celibacy is not only not a virtue but — if the word can be used — a sin. While there is a real difference between the Jewish and Christian evaluations of sin and of the human condition in relationship to sin, I am convinced that the current Jewish folk wisdom with respect to sin is rooted more in secularism than in any justifiable distinction between Judaism and Christianity. It is the secular spirit of our time that finds talk about sin objectionable. And the secular spirit is currently very influential among Jews.

# I

There is no concept in which the contrast between the secular and religious attitudes is more sharply reflected than in the concept of sin. Sin is violation of the command of God. It is this that distinguishes sin from wrongdoing. The wrongdoer feels that he has done something against what is right. Conduct in which he has engaged was bad, immoral, wrong. Or perhaps he has failed to do what was his duty. But the focus is on the act committed or omitted. The analogy is to a wrong mathematical calculation. To add up a column of numbers incorrectly is to get the wrong answer, to have done the problem wrongly. To have done a morally wrong deed is not identical with doing a mathematical problem wrongly. There is a sense of guilt in the moral case which is probably absent in the wrong mathematics, where the sense is more of regret than guilt. The similarity between the two, however, is the sense of violation of a certain objective order which occurred when the wrong was committed. But such violation does not constitute sin.

Sin is possible only when the transgression is a violation of the command of a divine lawgiver. In its pristine form, sin presupposes a command which has no persuasive ingredient other than the authority of him who issues the command. It seems to me possible that this is the meaning of the first prohibition recorded in the Bible: "And the Lord God commanded the man, saying, Of every tree of the garden thou mayest freely eat: but of the tree of the knowledge of good and evil, thou shalt not eat of it: for on the day that thou eatest of it thou shalt surely die" (Gen. 2:16-17). The implication clearly is that eating of the forbidden tree will result in man obtaining knowledge of good and evil. Instead of simply obeying the divine lawgiver, he will then be in a position to know why the good is good and the evil, evil. It seems that God does not wish man to have this knowledge. He is to obey God in order to obey God and for no other reason. And when he disobeys God, he has not violated a law that has an autonomous claim on his conscience and which therefore puts him in the wrong in an objective sense, but he has rebelled against God, whose command he has broken. The violation is, then, directed at God. And because it is directed at God, it constitutes a break in the relationship between God and man which requires remediation.

It is for this reason that sin is so difficult for modern, secular man to accept. He is not convinced that such a being as God exists. And even if, in some sense, such a being exists, he is not convinced that this being issues commands which he is obligated to obey. Contemporary man insists on knowing why the good is good and evil, evil. And once such knowledge is obtained, or the illusion of such knowledge is obtained, the need for a commanding God disappears entirely. For if the commanding God forbids that which is anyhow inherently evil and commands that which is anyhow inherently good, then his forbidding and commanding adds nothing at all to what is essential, namely, that the good is good and the evil, evil. And if God forbids that which is not inherently evil and commands that which is not inherently good, then his forbidding and commanding lacks all authority, since the mere fact that God forbids or commands something cannot by itself make it either evil or good. This discovery, first made by Plato in the *Euthyphro*, substitutes an autonomous moral realm for a commanding God and eliminates the concept of sin from our moral dictionary.

I have already said that this seems to me to be the issue in man's first sin, his eating of the tree of knowledge of good and evil. The argument used by the serpent to persuade Eve to eat the fruit of the forbidden tree almost explicitly makes this point: "Of course," says the serpent to Eve, "you will not die. God knows that as soon as you eat it, your eyes will be opened and you will be like gods knowing good and evil" (Gen. 3:4-5). Man's first sin is thus an act of disobedience whose aim is to obtain a knowledge that will make man God-like. Without this knowledge, man is dependent on God's commands for his knowledge of good and evil. With this knowledge, man is able to make his own moral judgments and thereby become God-like because he no longer needs God's commands. Prior to his having tasted the forbidden fruit, he does not yet have the knowledge in question. Because he is not yet God-like, he only has the divine prohibition. His choice, at that point, is whether to accept God's prohibition of an act which he does not know to be inherently evil or to reject the prohibition because it appears to him to be a capricious exercise of the divine authority. By opting for the latter, man not only disobeys God but signals his determination not to accept permanently the status of a creature of God dependent on God for instruction as to what is permitted and forbidden. He is determined to make his own judgment as to what is good or bad and thus become God-like. The inner meaning of sin is not simply an act of disobedience against God but an attempt to overthrow God by making man into a God-like creature.

The theme under discussion, the threat to God which emanates from the appearance of God-like men, does not disappear with the incidence of man's first sin. Just prior to the flood narrative we read that "the sons of God saw that the daughters of men were beautiful; so they took for themselves such women as they chose" (Gen. 6:2). From this union resulted the Nephilim, heroic figures of somewhat superhuman proportions. However we interpret this disturbing because quasi-mythological interlude, it is clear that in some ways God is threatened by all this. "My spirit," he says, "shall not strive with man forever, for that he is but flesh, and his days shall be a hundred and twenty years" (Gen. 6:3). Here God seems to console himself that in spite of the various dangers posed by the possibility of man acquiring, if not already possessing, divine qualities, he remains a mortal creature of flesh and blood and is therefore not an ultimate threat to God. As if to prove man's vulnerability, God sends the flood, which results in the destruction of all humanity except for Noah and his immediate family. And the tower of Babel (Gen. 11:1-9), whose top was to reach heaven, may indeed be another human attempt in the Bible to elevate man into rivalry with God. Needless to say, all these attempts fail, but they do make clear that the Bible is aware of a strong resistance in man to a resigned acceptance of his humanity and of a desire to challenge the divinity of God.

What is at stake in man's first sin, then, is a morality based on obedience to God versus a morality based on human recognition of what is right and wrong. Having eaten of the forbidden fruit, God concludes that "man has become like one of us, knowing good and evil" (Gen. 3:22). It is interesting that the first immorality man discovers autonomously is sexual in nature: "Then the eyes of both of them were opened and they discovered that they were naked: so they stitched fig-leaves together and made themselves loincloths" (Gen. 3:7). Here Adam and Eve "discover" that nudity is shameful even though they were never commanded by God not to go nude. The opening of the eyes to which the text refers is thus the autonomous human ability to perceive something to be wrong. And when God comes calling on man, he and his wife hide from God. And when challenged by God after their inevitable discovery, Adam explains, "I heard the sound as you were walking in the garden, and I was afraid because I was naked, and I hid myself" (Gen. 3:10). Immediately, God understands what had happened. "Who told you," he asks, "that you were naked? Have you eaten from the tree which I forbade you?" (Gen. 3:11). God immediately recognizes that Adam and Eve are making independent moral judgments that are not derived from any divine command, and that can only mean that man has disobeyed God's command not to eat of the forbidden fruit. He has thus obtained knowledge of good and evil and is no longer dependent on God's command as the exclusive source of guidance in moral matters.

I have stressed this point because I am convinced that without it we cannot understand the notion of sin. Sin is a religious and not an ethical category. To "have knowledge of good and evil" is to be unable to sin. This is so not because those who possess this "knowledge" always act in accordance with it but because, even when they do not, their violation is not an act whose essence is the violation of God's command. It is a violation of the requirements of morality, however those requirements are understood. And here we come to something of a problem in the realm of autonomous morality, that is, morality based on "knowledge" of good and evil and not strictly on divine command. Simply stated, the problem is this: isn't all violation of such autonomous morality to be understood as error rather than willful wrongdoing? And if indeed it is error, then it is really not evil, since evil occurs only when someone knows that something is evil and does it anyway.

In order to clarify this point, we revert to our earlier, mathematical analogy. No one adds 7 and 5 and makes them 11, knowing that they add up to 12. When 7 and 5 are made to equal 11, we are dealing with error. No matter how harmful the consequences of such an error might be — and under some circumstances they could be very harmful — it still remains a fact that we are dealing with error and nothing else. Even if we can accuse the person who committed the error of negligence or laziness, the culpable offense then becomes the negligence, the not paying sufficient attention to the addition rather than the judgment that $7 + 5 = 11$. That is an error that no one can willingly, knowingly make. And the same is true, according to Plato, with morality. All men, he believed, desire the good, and if some men do things that are not good, it must be because they mistakenly thought the not-good to be the good. Subjectively, they were pursuing what to them seemed the good even if, in fact, they were pursuing that which was evil. The solution was therefore a correction of their deficient knowledge. Once able to recognize correctly the real good, they would automatically pursue it, since it is, by definition, not possible to know the good without doing it. The Platonic doctrine is thus a genuine doctrine of the knowledge of good and evil. Man is essentially a knowing being whose conduct is a function of his knowledge. When there is wrong conduct, there is wrong knowledge for the illusion of knowledge, and the cure transpires in the intellectual domain.

It is quite otherwise with the biblical understanding of sin. The Bible is, of course, aware of the possibility of sin being committed "in error" and makes specific provision for it.[1] We read of the sinner in error:

> And when ye shall err, and not observe all these commandments, which the Lord hath spoken unto Moses, even all that the Lord hath commanded you by the hand of Moses, from the day that the Lord gave commandment and onward throughout your generations; then it shall be, if it be done in error by the congregation, it being hid from their eyes, that all the congregation shall offer one young bullock for a burnt-offering, for a sweet savour unto the Lord — with the meal-offering thereof, and the drink-offering thereof, according to the ordinance — and one he-goat for a sin-offering. (Num. 15:22-24)

After several more verses dealing with the sinner in error, the text turns its attention to the more serious case:

> But the soul that doeth aught with a high hand, whether he be homeborn or a stranger, the same blasphemeth the Lord; and that soul shall be cut off from among his people. Because he hath despised the word of the Lord, and hath broken His commandment; that soul shall utterly be cut off, his iniquity shall be upon him. (Num. 15:30-31)

No clearer definition of sin could be given. To sin not in error but "with a high hand" is to blaspheme God by despising his word and breaking his com-

---

1. Leviticus 4–5; Numbers 15:22ff.

mandment. The essence of sin is precisely this break in the relationship with God. The focus of attention is not on the particular nature of the act, its inherent wrongness or immorality. The focus is on the giver of the command and the damage that the sin has done to man's relationship with the being who is behind the command. And if this is true in violation, it is also true in obedience. If to violate God's commandment is to blaspheme him, to reject his authority, and to rebel against his rule, then obeying his command is to honor God, to recognize his authority, and to proclaim oneself dependent on him and subject to his will.

If this is true, then rebellion against God is possible in one of two modes. The obvious one is disobedience, to which the text above addresses itself. But a less obvious though perhaps equally serious form of rebellion is to act in accordance with God's command not because he so commanded but because it is the right thing to do, in and by itself and independently of the will of God. There are those who would argue that this does not constitute rebellion at all. Why does it matter why we do the right thing, as long as we do the right thing? Did not the rabbis attribute to God the wish that the Israelites might fulfill the commandments even if they "abandoned" God?[2] It seems to me that a certain misunderstanding of biblical thinking is here involved. It is easy to get lost in the content of the law and to forget its source. When the rabbis taught that it is better to fulfill the commandments "not for the sake of heaven" than not to fulfill them at all, they did so because they believed that through fulfilling them not for the sake of heaven man will come to fulfill them for the sake of heaven. They knew that the proper way of fulfilling the Torah was as obedience to God's commandment. But when man develops a morality not based on God's commandment — even if coincidentally much of it may coincide with those commandments — an act of expulsion of God has occurred. He is no longer the lawgiver. Now reason or moral intuition or something else performs the function that the Bible can only envisage God as performing. Man thus dethrones God, and this form of rebellion is particularly dangerous because it leaves man morally fulfilled, freed of the guilt that may be experienced — sooner or later — by the rebel who violated God's commands and who might not remain as self-righteous as the moral rebel. The moral rebel finds a relationship with God increasingly irrelevant as his moral convictions deepen and he engages himself more and more in the realization of his moral ideals in the context of the real world.

The reality of sin is therefore a function of the sense of dependence on God. Where this dependence is weakened either because of a loss of belief in

2. *Midrash Rabbah Lamentations,* trans. A. Cohen (London: Soncino, 1939), pp. 2-3.

the reality of God or because of the growth of the conviction that moral values can be autonomously justified without reference to God, the very concept of sin tends to disappear from discourse. In contemporary Judaism, the more liberal the interpretation of Judaism, the less frequent the reference to sin. And when reference to sin does occur, it is almost always in the moral context, whose principles are thought to be self-validating. In more Orthodox circles, where the tendency is to honor the nonethical aspects of the Torah equally with its ethical aspects, reference to sin is more frequent. Here, too, one can observe some reluctance to speak of guilt and punishment, concepts that many today find psychologically unhealthy. Altogether, the widely prevailing influence of secularism on many segments of Jewry has removed sin from the center of most Jewish thought of this century. This was particularly noticeable in the reaction to the Holocaust. The traditional Jewish response to catastrophes through the ages — and they were not particularly infrequent — was to blame them on the sins of Israel. After the Holocaust, this theme was almost totally absent in Jewish responses. Much of this can undoubtedly be explained by the magnitude of the Holocaust, in the light of which explanations in terms of sin become very difficult. But the general secularization of the Jewish community also played a role. Many Jews no longer find it possible to think of actual historical events in this world as "caused" by God in any realistic sense. To ignore this is to ignore the religious crisis of contemporary Judaism.

# II

We must now turn our attention to the other presence with which the problem of sin and atonement in Judaism is intertwined: Christianity. An accurate assessment of Christian teaching about those topics is, of course, not easy, given the lengthy history of Christianity and the diversity of views embraced by that history. But since we are not studying the doctrine of sin and atonement in Christianity but rather in Judaism, we need only examine the Christian attitudes toward these topics to the extent that they influenced Jewish thinking on the subject. That influence made itself felt by way of contrast. It was widely believed by Jews that Christianity attributed to man's first sin almost unlimited importance. Because of that sin, Christianity — as seen by Judaism — saw man as coming into the world as a depraved being without the slightest hope of salvation in the absence of the most extraordinary intervention on the part of God. The intervention in question — God's sacrifice of his only begotten son for the sins of the world — had to take the form it did because there was not the slightest hope of man's salvation in the normal course of things. The normal course of things, given man's totally fallen state after his ancestor's first sin, could lead nowhere but to eternal damnation. Further, it was thought by Jews that Christianity taught an unyielding doctrine of pre-destination according to which God determined who were to be virtuous and saved and who sinful and damned. Seen in this light, the exercise of human freedom was profoundly illusory. Man was in God's hands, and therefore the virtuous could take no credit for their own virtue, since it was the power of God in grace that turned them to faith and to action in accordance with faith. Any other interpretation would ignore man's fatal depravity and put into man's power the ability to extricate himself from the power of sin, which holds total sway over him. While Christianity was thus quite prepared to de-prive the good of credit for their goodness, it was less prepared to exonerate the wrongdoer, on the ground that his wrongdoing was determined by God and was therefore not the fault of the wrongdoer. Inheriting the sin of Adam, man is burdened with the one sin committed by his ancestor who had not yet fallen, and the blame that attaches to post-Adam man is a combination of the blame that attaches to Adam and the sin of the individual who comes after Adam.

Against this at least in part inaccurate summary of "the" Christian posi-tion, popular Jewish wisdom poses an at least in part inaccurate version of Ju-daism. Judaism, it is held, believes in man's totally free will. It is totally within man's free will to obey or disobey God's commandments. In fact, not only is it possible to obey God's commandments, it is not even particularly difficult. In this connection, Deuteronomy is quoted.

> The commandment that I lay on you this day is not too difficult for you, it is not too remote. It is not in heaven, that you should say, "Who will go up to heaven for us to fetch it and tell it to us, so that we can keep it?" Nor is it beyond the sea, that you should say, "Who will cross the sea for us to fetch it and tell it to us, so that we can keep it?" It is a thing very near to you, upon your lips and in your heart ready to be kept. (Deut. 30:11-14)

The text continues, "See, I have set before you this day, the life and the good, and the death and the evil" (v. 15). It concludes with the admonition, "Choose life" (v. 19). Based on this and similar texts, the emphasis on the freedom of the individual is not difficult to understand. Whatever effects the sin of Adam and Eve might have had, it certainly did not revoke man's freedom to choose either to obey or to disobey. All is in man's power, with the right choice, iden-tified with the choice for life, being almost the natural course of action. If anything, it is the choice of evil that requires explanation, just as we do not particularly seek explanations when a living person desires to continue to live but we do seek an explanation when someone desires to take his life. Given this "optimistic" view, one is tempted to ask why there is so much evil in the world, i.e., why so many seem to choose irrationally, for death as against life, for rebellion as against obedience. Nevertheless, this is the teaching attributed frequently to Judaism.

Let us understand that there are two extraneous considerations that push Judaism in this direction. The first is the secular one. We have seen that for the secular attitude the very notion of sin is unacceptable. The secularist is committed to a humanism in which man either creates or recognizes values which govern his conduct. A Judaism which insists on genuine human freedom is thus more compatible with secular humanism than one which diminishes human freedom and makes sin inevitable for all but the elect. Modulated in a certain way, the position I have referred to as the popular Jewish position — though it is inherently a religious rather than a secular one — can end up reading sin out of Judaism altogether. If man has such total freedom of choice and if the good is such a "natural" choice and if repentance is so relatively easy, then there is really not much reason for taking sin very seriously at all. It is easy to see that the atmosphere produced by such optimism with regard to the human situation coalesces with the general attitude of an optimistic secular humanism which may then be the conscious or unconscious driving force behind the popular Jewish position.

The other such driving force is probably the desire of Judaism to distance itself from Christianity. If the sketch we have given of the Christian position is indeed the one many Jews believe to be the Christian position, then it is easy to see that Jews would want to react to it by presenting a Judaism sharply different from this Christianity. If Christianity minimizes free will, Judaism will maximize it. If Christianity is pessimistic, Judaism will be optimistic. If Christianity is otherworldy, Judaism will be this-wordly. If Christianity emphasizes sin, Judaism will de-emphasize it. The list could be extended quite a bit.

At work here is a certain tendency to polarization that is observable as traditions develop. As one group stresses some aspects of truth, other groups will come to stress other and even opposite aspects of the truth in order to define their identities over against the initial, incomplete position. The two resulting positions are often equally incomplete, sometimes even distorted, and the second is clearly the distorted reaction to the original distortion. The two distortions can then very correctly be said to deserve each other, and unless something is done to help each tradition speak out of its resources, serious damage results for all concerned.

In this particular case, the task of Jewish theology is to think about sin and atonement out of the integrity of Judaism and without attempting either to polemicize against or to please any other faith. We must also avoid basing our answer on a small number of quotations one way or the other. It is perfectly clear that when dealing with a tradition as old and complex as Judaism, individual passages will be found to back up almost any position. Our task is to listen to all the instruments in the orchestra, to all the voices of the tradition, to all the texts, and to fashion from them an interpretation that reflects the thrust of the tradition presented in the most insightful way possible. Done in this spirit, how do things look?

It appears to me quite clear that the Hebrew Bible assigns considerable choice to man. From the first commandment addressed to Adam to the end of the Pentateuch, there seems to me to be a clear implication that it is within man's power to accept or reject God's commandments. Given the narrative economy that is characteristic of the biblical style and given the fact that the Bible likes to tell stories far better than to ask second-order, theoretical questions about those stories, it is difficult to escape the conclusion that the Bible understands that, by and large, people do what they do because they want to do it and that they could have done other than what they in fact ended up doing. True, here and there, the Bible does attribute to God intervention in human choices. The best-known example is God's "hardening" of Pharaoh's heart so that he does not permit the children of Israel to depart from Egypt (Exod. 7:33ff.). While it would be irresponsible to ignore this very interesting incident, neither is it possible to build a whole theology on it. There is a very special consideration at work there that is clearly not the usual situation. It is God's intention to "multiply my signs and my wonders" (Exod. 7:3), a goal that is announced in the very same verse which speaks of the hardening of Pharaoh's heart. Since the purpose here is to bring about a situation which will reveal to the whole world the power of God, a very quick agreement by Pharaoh to let the people of Israel go would make it impossible for God to triumph in the kind of confrontation that, in fact, occurs and which is made possible by Pharaoh's stubbornness and refusal to yield to God's demands. But it is hardly proper to generalize from this situation to all human choices and to conclude that man's decisions merely reflect God's control of those decisions. This is especially true in view of the fact that biblical prophecy does not consist of the making of predictions that are certain to come true. While often the prophets speak with a certain assurance of the inevitability of the events they foretell, this must be interpreted in light of the basic mission of the Hebrew prophet, which is to call Israel to repentance. Even when not explicitly stated, there is an implicit "if" in all prophetic messages. The painful events they predict will occur "if" Israel does not repent and can be avoided by repentance. When the prophets seem to be omitting this "if" and speaking with a seeming certainty of future catastrophic events, they do so only to make more vivid those events so as to stimulate the people to mend their ways. But throughout, the belief is that these ways can be mended and the catastrophe averted.

And yet, this is not the whole truth. It is true that in prophetic eschatology the emphasis is on Israel's task to carry out the covenant and thereby to bring redemption about. In fact, Martin Buber has focused on this point in distinguishing between prophetic and apocalyptic eschatology.[3] Prophetic eschatology is dependent on man's turning, while apocalyptic eschatology foretells cataclysmic events in which evil will be vanquished and the good triumph. The magnitude of these extraordinary future events is itself an indication of the cosmic and metahuman aspect of the future events. Without contesting the significance of the distinction and while agreeing with Buber's sympathy for prophetic and deep reserve toward apocalyptic eschatology, it would nevertheless be an error to overlook a basic truth: that it is implicit in the Bible that God remains in control of history, and that in spite of the reality of human freedom, man's ability to frustrate God's plan for his creation is not without limits.

There is no question but that man has, from the first, frustrated God's plan. While the Bible does not quite tell us what the plan was, it is clear that Adam's sin was not in accordance with God's plan. The punishment that is meted out to Adam and Eve (Gen. 3:14-19) brings about a condition of human existence sharply different from the one God had instituted at first. The flood was another stage of interference with God's original plan. After creating man, "God saw everything that he had made and, behold, it was very good" (Gen. 1:31). It does not take long before "it repented God that he had made man on the earth, and it grieved him" (Gen. 6:6). From a creation which included man that God found "very good" to a sense of sorrow for having created man and a decision to kill all of humanity except one family is a long distance indeed, and all this was brought about by nothing else but the sin of man. Clearly this is not what God had expected. The world he had intended for man to live in was a far more pleasant, happy, and harmonious place than the world we know today or the world as it was recreated after Adam's sin and the ravages of the flood. There is therefore little question that it was and is within man's power to seriously interfere with God's plans. But there is an absolute difference between seriously interfering with God's plan and com-

3. Martin Buber, *Israel and the World* (New York: Schocken, 1948), p. 36.

pletely wrecking it. While man has the power to do the former, I do not think he can quite achieve the latter.

The messianic promise that is so prominent in the prophets is, at least in part, a return to man's condition prior to Adam's sin. While this is certainly not stressed or even mentioned in the Bible, the correspondence between the state of affairs prior to the sin and the vision of the future we find, for example, in Isaiah (2:1-4) is too great to be coincidental. Be that as it may, the question is whether the realization of this future is conditional. It is tempting to draw an analogy with the predictions of catastrophe. Just as the catastrophic predictions, as we have seen, are conditional on Israel's lack of repentance, does it not seem sensible that the messianic prophecies, too, are conditional on Israel's repentance? If this were indeed the case, then man's destiny would truly be in his hand, with catastrophe and a messianic future both possible, a function of man's decision to continue sinning or to return to God.

But I do not think that this parallelism, in fact, applies. The negative and the positive are not equally balanced for the God of Israel. His anger lasts but for a moment while his mercy is forever (Ps. 30:6). He visits the iniquity of the fathers upon the children to the third and fourth generation but keeps mercy unto the thousandth generation (Exod. 20:5-6). The messianic promises made to Israel and to all of humanity are therefore not conditional promises. Starting with chapter 40, we read a series of prophecies of redemption in Isaiah which are among the most powerful in all prophetic literature. Drawing a parallel with the redemption from Egypt (Isa. 52:3-6), which is also not attributed to Israel's repentance, these prophecies communicate a tone of certainty that is fundamental to the consolation they offer a suffering people. The general message is clear. Israel's election is irrevocable. If and when Israel sins, it is punished, even severely. The people will be expelled from their land and sent into exile. But this punishment will not destroy Israel, and it will not last forever. God's love for Israel will return, and a reconciliation will take place. God will bring back the exiles from wherever they are and reestablish the kingdom as before. It cannot be denied that Israel's repentance would be very helpful in bringing this about. But in the final analysis it is not completely dependent on such repentance. In the Talmud, too, the desirability of repentance as a means of bringing redemption about is recognized. We read: "Rab said: 'All the predestined dates for redemption have passed and the matter depends only on repentance and good deeds.' But Samuel maintained: 'It is sufficient for a mourner to keep his mourning.'"[4] It is quite clear that Samuel maintained that the suffering of the exile without repentance is not com-

4. B. *Sanhedrin* 97b.

pletely outside of God's control. We read: "R. Eliezer said: 'If Israel repents they will be redeemed; if not, they will not be redeemed.' R. Joshua said to him: 'If they do not repent, they will not be redeemed? The Holy One, blessed be He, will place over them a king whose decrees will be as harsh as Haman's, and the Israelites will repent and return to doing good.'"[5] So even if repentance is essential to the redemption, God can so arrange things that repentance will occur.

I have emphasized the certainty of redemption in order to show that despite the freedom Judaism assigns to man, and despite man's not inconsiderable power to frustrate and sidetrack God's plan, the power of man to wreck things is not ultimate. The achievement of God's plan is certain, and man can, therefore, at most play a role but nothing more. If this is so, then there is a certain truth in predestination. Perhaps it ought not to be applied on the level of the individual. Perhaps it is going too far to say that this person will be virtuous and saved and the other one sinful and damned. But it seems to me also not possible to believe that God has put the destiny of his creation totally in the hands of man and that man could decide on any scenario that he wishes. Could the enemies of Israel succeed in eliminating the last vestiges of the Jewish people from the world? I do not believe so. If that were to happen, it would constitute a clear falsification of biblical faith. And the same would be true if every last Jew decided to assimilate, leaving a world without Jews. My point is not that something like that could not happen, viewed purely from a human point of view. Given the price Jews have paid for remaining Jews in recent times and given the forces of secularization abroad in the world in general, such a termination of Jewish history is by no means inconceivable. My point is that such an end to the long history of the Jewish people is impossible to the person who is committed to the Hebrew Bible as the word of God. And if all this is so, then God retains a firm control over history. Certainly the deeds of human beings can do much to move the world either toward redemption or toward catastrophe. But this is true only within limits. At the critical moment, there is a divine steering of history, and since history is made by human beings, there must also be a certain control by God of human decisions. The hardening of the heart of Pharaoh was a negative manifestation of this control. And there must also be a positive focus of such influence. Man is, after all, in God's hands. And while God has chosen to withdraw his power so as to enable human beings to make their own decisions and to accept the consequences of those decisions, he has not totally left the writing of the script of history to man, with the po-

5. B. *Sanhedrin* 97b-98a.

tential for ultimate disaster completely left to him. Exactly how this divine control is exercised cannot be known. Whether God turns the heart of Israel to repentance or whether he brings suffering on Israel which causes repentance — the view of R. Joshua above — is immaterial. The point is that human free will cannot be the final determinant of the outcome.

If we return for a moment to the simplified summary of the Christian attitude to sin and atonement earlier offered, we will remember that the predestination doctrine was intertwined with the interpretation of man's fall. Since the fall, man is naturally depraved and headed for damnation, from which only faith in Jesus as the messiah can save him. The net effect, at least to the Jewish observer, has been that Christianity seems to have emphasized the sinfulness of man far more than does Judaism. It is a popular view among Jews that Christianity tends, far more than Judaism, to generate feelings of guilt and worthlessness. Much of this is connected with the Jewish conviction that Christianity has a rather unhealthy view of human sexuality. Whereas Judaism requires marriage and the having of children, Christianity considers celibacy the preferred state because of a fundamental distaste for sexuality. While the average Jew expresses his case in such terms, the more sophisticated Jew speaks of Greek pagan and gnostic influences on Christianity which devalue the body by setting up a very sharp dichotomy between the body, which is seen as evil, and the soul, which is the principle of rationality and the aspect of man on which the image of God in man is implanted. In contrast, Jews point to God's declaring the creation — both matter and spirit — to be good. Judaism, it is claimed, rejects the bifurcation of man and creation into the material and the spiritual. While all this must not be taken so far as to deny totally the reality of sin and evil, it is nevertheless argued that sin in Judaism plays a much less central role than it does in Christianity, particularly in view of the ever-present possibility of repentance for the Jew when sin does occur.

I am convinced that to express in the way we just have the Jewish attitude toward sin is to express a serious distortion of Judaism. The dreadful possibilities of sin and the catastrophic consequences of sin are integral and fundamental parts of Judaism, both biblical and rabbinic. If the consciousness of sin has diminished among large masses of Jews, this is to be attributed to secularism and a loss of faith, processes which have had particular impact among the Jews of modernity. And where modernity has had more limited input, such as among Hasidic Jews and other very Orthodox Jews, the consciousness of sin is very pronounced, at present as before. The foundation for this is, of course, biblical. We have already spoken of the record of rebellion that begins with Adam and continues with Cain, the generation of the flood, and the tower of Babel. While sin does not play a critical role with the patriarchs, it attaches itself to the generation of the exodus through the golden calf, the sin of the spies sent by Moses, and many other incidents too numerous to mention. The book of Judges repeats again and again the formula "the Israelites did what was wrong in the eyes of God" (e.g., Judg. 2:11), whereupon they are punished by being subjected to foreign rule. When they cry to God in their suffering, God sends a redeemer who expels the invaders. Soon thereafter the Israelites revert to their evil ways and the cycle starts over again. In short, Jewish history is, de facto, a history of disobedience and sin. The fact that Christian theology has never tired of pointing this out should not tempt the Jewish theologian to pretend that the truth is otherwise. The exhortations of the prophets and their calls to "turning" depend upon their diagnosis of the sinfulness of Israel and the dire consequences that this sin will produce.

And yet this is not the whole truth. It is Jeremiah who has God say, "I remember the unfailing devotion of your youth, the love of your bridal days, when you followed Me in the wilderness, through a land unsown" (2:2). Israel's record is not only one of disobedience. There is also loyalty. The faithfulness of the patriarchs, epitomized by Abraham's willingness to sacrifice his only son at God's command, is also part of the record. So the record is not one of unrelieved depravity. While the fidelity of Israel is no match for that of God, the fidelity of Israel is not non-existent, which proves that obedience, like disobedience, is possible.

And there is the election. Israel's serious and not infrequent sin occurs in the context of its election, of the special love that God has for his people, the seed of Abraham, Isaac, and Jacob. Considered from one point of view, this makes Israel's sin more weighty, since it is the repayment with evil of the endless grace God has shown for his people. While this is true, it also casts Israel's punishment in another light. However dire the prophecies are and however great the suffering of the people, the sense of being enveloped by the eternal love of God for Israel never leaves the awareness of the people. The divine anger is experienced in the context of God's overwhelming love for Israel, which is bound to conquer the anger and lead to reconciliation between Israel and its God. It is for this reason that there can be no question of the ultimate rejection of Israel or of the nonfulfillment of the eschatological promises. So we have here a curious mixture of fear and confidence. There is genuine "fear of heaven," of the punishment that God inflicts for sin. But there is also the confidence of election and a special sense of being loved by God above all the families of the earth. The terror of total damnation, of total rejection by God is thus absent, and it is perhaps this, more than anything else, which enables Jewish optimism to coexist with profound understanding of the sinfulness of man and the reality of punishment.

# III

The concept of atonement, with which we are now ready to deal, is not only related to the concept of sin, but it is the case that the two are intimately interrelated. In the religious context, atonement refers to the correction of sin. While this possibility does not seem particularly unusual to the religious consciousness, it is not generally realized that philosophical ethics almost never deals with the possibility of correcting wrongdoing. The ethical philosopher — of whom Kant is an excellent example — is concerned with establishing a rational ethics. He is usually judged and he judges himself by the degree to which he succeeds in this enterprise. If he does succeed, he has set up a rational structure of value by reference to which we can evaluate ethically past or future actions. But little attention is paid to what happens when a person violates the ethical norms in question. It cannot be said, of course, that the ethical philosopher is unaware of this possibility. He just does not deal with it. He probably believes that this is not part of his task. As a philosopher, he establishes what is rationally normative and since violation is, almost by definition, irrational and contingent, there is no philosophic necessity for dealing with it.

But perhaps even more important is the philosopher's realization that there is not and cannot be any method for erasing wrongdoing. A mathematical error can be corrected in the sense that it can be identified and the calculation or proof can be done again correctly. But what was done is done, and the past cannot be changed. The past can be learned from and the repetition of the mistake can be avoided, but the past mistake cannot be erased. And because this is so, there is no place for a doctrine of atonement in autonomous human ethics. In such ethics it is the moral law itself which makes its demands on the subject. But because the moral law is not a person, it cannot forgive anything, just as mathematics cannot pardon those who add incorrectly or drop an integer in a subtraction. The mathematical law is an objective truth to which reference is constantly made and which determines the correctness or incorrectness of the actual mathematical operations performed. But the laws of mathematics — or of ethics, in the autonomous sense — cannot forgive anyone for anything.

In biblical ethics, the primary source is the command of God. Separated from its source in the will of God, no biblical law has any autonomous validity, from the most "irrational" and cultic to the most "rational" and ethical. It is the fact that God commands or forbids it and not what God commands or forbids that is of central importance in biblical thought. From this it follows, as we have already seen, that all sin is first and foremost an offense against

God, whose authority is contested by sin. But precisely because this is so, forgiveness is possible. If my sin consists of rejecting God's command and thereby incurring his anger, then it must at least be theoretically possible for God to forgive me and to erase the sin as sin. And this is precisely what atonement does. God tells sinning man that, in a sense, the past can be changed. Under the proper circumstances, God will forgive sins and restore things to their state before the sin was committed. Better yet, according to the rabbis, God can restore things to a state better than what they were before the sin.[6] Not only can he wipe the sin off the books, but he can convert the sins into acts of virtue, with the resulting merit equal to the gravity of the sin. The repentant sinner thus emerges with a large accumulation of merit, especially if his sins were particularly weighty and numerous. The rabbis conclude that a repentant sinner stands higher than a righteous person who never sinned.[7] This is possible only because God waits for the sinner to repent and, when he does, receives him in healing reconciliation.

After the destruction of the Temple in 70 c.e., the primary method of reconciliation in rabbinic thought became repentance. This was by no means a revolution in Judaism, since there had been considerable emphasis on repentance in the Pentateuch.[8] But in the Pentateuch there was also cultic atonement, i.e., the sacrificial system of atonement. With the destruction of the Temple, sacrifice was no longer possible, and the emphasis therefore shifted to repentance. Not a few Christian voices have quoted Leviticus 17:11, "the life of a creature is the blood, and I appoint it to make expiation on the altar for yourselves: it is the blood, that is the life, that makes expiation." Because of the absence of sacrifice, Judaism, it was argued, had lost the possibility of expiation. Christianity, on the other hand, was born in the ultimate sacrifice of the Son of God, a sacrifice that was reenacted frequently in the Eucharist. For this reason, atonement of sin was no longer available in Judaism and very much available in Christianity.

The usual Jewish response to this argument was to stress the power of repentance. As we have already noted, in so doing Judaism was basing itself on Pentateuchal passages dealing with repentance, but especially the numerous prophetic texts that spoke with very little admiration of sacrifices unaccompanied by the turning of the heart. While a careful analysis of these prophetic texts will reveal that they were directed at sacrifices without repentance and not at sacrifices as such, the presence of texts directed at repentance with-

6. *Exod. Rabbah* 31:1.
7. *B. Berakot* 34b.
8. Deuteronomy 30:2.

out sacrifices seems to imply the efficacy of repentance without sacrifices and the uselessness of sacrifices without repentance. It was thus not difficult for the rabbis to conclude that, especially under circumstances when sacrifices were no longer possible, sincere repentance was sufficient atonement.

Nevertheless, the rabbis did not lose interest in the Temple and in its sacrificial cult. They carefully preserved the laws governing the cult, and they structured the prayer service largely as a memorial to the sacrifices. "Our lips," they quoted, "will perform the service of the bullocks" (Hos. 14:3).[9] It would therefore be inaccurate to maintain that Judaism does not feel a certain incompleteness in the absence of the sacrifices. This is, of course, not true of liberal Judaism, which has long rejected the hope for the restoration of the sacrifices, which it considers appropriate to a more primitive stage of religion but totally unacceptable to the "higher" religions. But traditional Judaism looks forward to the restoration of the sacrificial cult in a rebuilt Jerusalem Temple.

It is, of course, true that repentance is a more "rational" method of obtaining forgiveness than sacrifice. Repentance is a spiritual act. It consists of the recognition of wrongdoing and of the determination to refrain from further wrongdoing. Sacrifice, on the other hand, seems predicated on crass anthropomorphism. To the rational mind, the notion that God has needs, particularly physical needs, is abhorrent. When connected with the atonement for sin, sacrifice seems to have a magical quality to it which cannot appear attractive to the modern mind. And yet, it is superficial to overlook the limitations of a purely rationalized religion. As the tendency to stress the ethical aspects of religion becomes stronger, religion is gradually transformed into an "ethical culture" from which all traces of the transcendental and the holy have been removed. And when this happens, atonement for sin becomes increasingly difficult because the ethical law becomes autonomous and the personal relationship with the lawgiver, which is an essential precondition for atonement, is lost. The cultic aspect of religion must therefore be kept alive. Religion must make it possible for the holy to appear to the believer, and this cannot be done in a purely ethical and rational context.

Classical Christianity understood this insight and fashioned the sacraments, particularly the Eucharist, as the center of its cultic life. Judaism in its rabbinic form introduced no sacraments to take the place of the discontinued sacrifices. The reason for the failure of the rabbis to develop sacramental substitutes for the sacrifices is not easy to determine. It may have had something to do with a certain continuity between the prophetic attitude of reserve to-

9. *B. Yoma* 86b.

71

ward the sacrifices and the rabbinic attitude. It may also have some connection with the biblical battle against sacrifice outside of Jerusalem, which may have been so deeply rooted in rabbinic consciousness that the notion of sacrament outside of Jerusalem had to be ruled out. Most probable, in my view, is the judgment that for the rabbis the memory of cult was itself a form of the practice of cult. By keeping alive the knowledge of the Temple service and the constant prayer for its reestablishment, the rabbis felt that the cult was, in fact, being practiced. Had they fashioned a substitute sacramental system which could be practiced in the Diaspora, the memory of Jerusalem and its cult might have receded and the ultimate return to Zion would have been considered unnecessary. The ability to accept the memory of cult in the place of cult may then have been an expression of the eternal bond between the cult and the Jewish people and the land of Israel.


# IV


Our discussion of sin and atonement in Judaism has laid primary emphasis on the treatment these topics receive in biblical thought. We have not hesitated to amplify various biblical passages and concepts by drawing on rabbinic writings. In so doing we have followed a rather traditional path, because for traditional Judaism "Torah" is the written biblical text interpreted and elaborated by the rabbis. For the contemporary historical scholar such a blending of biblical and rabbinic literature is problematic. Since the two literatures are separated by at least hundreds of years, the modern scholar almost automatically keeps them apart, reading rabbinic texts not as a very helpful guide to the understanding of biblical texts but for the light they shed on rabbinic rather than biblical thinking. For some, rabbinic Judaism is almost completely discontinuous with biblical Judaism. The rabbis, it is claimed, almost completely recast the Judaism of the Bible to conform to new social and political conditions as well as their more highly developed ethical sensibilities.

If there is any validity to this theory, not much evidence can be found for it in the thinking of the rabbis with respect to sin and atonement. I do not find any sharp break with biblical thinking on these subjects. Sin is seen as a human possibility, but so is abstention from sin. Repentance is interpreted as the primary way of obtaining divine forgiveness, but this thought is also not unknown to the Bible, particularly to the prophets. The one teaching that is rather novel with the rabbis is the teaching of the evil inclination, the *yetzer hara*, to which we now turn our attention.

There is no need here to repeat the surveys about the *yetzer hara*.[10] From the numerous passages dealing with the evil inclination in rabbinic literature it is clear that the evil inclination is a personification of the temptation that faces the human being. The human being is suspended in choice. He can choose good or evil. In order to dramatize this position of choice, the rabbis think of man as a judge who listens to the cases made by two sides, weighs the arguments, and makes a choice. The evil inclination argues the advantages of the choice of evil, while the good inclination *(yetzer hatov)* presents the arguments for the choice of good. As is usually the case in literature (e.g., Lucifer in Milton's *Paradise Lost*), the negative characters receive more attention and emerge more sharply than the positive ones. The evil inclination is thus discussed more thoroughly in rabbinic literature than the good inclination. The evil inclination is depicted as extremely crafty and shrewd, knowing man's weaknesses and the right strategy for inducing him to sin. Furthermore, the evil inclination grows with a person's spiritual stature. "He who is greater than his neighbor," says the Talmud, "his *yetzer* is also greater."[11] No one is therefore safe from temptation, because the evil inclination increases in strength as man's spiritual level rises, so that he is never free from temptation.

The question we must ask ourselves is whether the personification of temptation reflected in the doctrine of the evil and good inclinations represents a substantive change in the rabbis' views of the nature of sin. Without the inclinations, man is faced with temptation and struggles with himself to overcome it. By speaking of the evil inclination which urges man to sin, the evil is, as it were, taken out of man himself and placed on the tempter. We are reminded of the serpent in Genesis 3, who persuades Eve to sin and whom Eve blames for her sin (v. 13). While God does not seem to accept Eve's plea of guilty with an explanation inasmuch as he pronounces sentence on her, the fact that the serpent is also punished proves that he bears his own guilt. And once this is recognized, we are entitled to wonder whether Eve's punishment would have been greater had she sinned without advice of the serpent. The rabbis also recognized that the existence of the evil inclination mitigates the magnitude of Israel's sin.

> God regretted the evil inclination and He said, "What damage have I wrought! I regret that I have created it in My world." In that hour the gate of mercy was opened for the sinners in Israel, so as to receive them in re-

10. See Solomon Schechter, *Aspects of Rabbinic Theology* (New York: Schocken, 1961), pp. 242-292, and C. G. Montefiore and H. Loewe, *A Rabbinic Anthology* (New York: Schocken, 1974), pp. 295-314.

11. *B. Sukkah* 52a.

pentance. They say, "It is revealed and known unto Thee that it was the evil inclination which incited us, in Thy great mercy receive us in perfect repentance before Thee."[12]

While such a passage should not receive excessive emphasis, it does make clear that the rabbis understood the argument that man could not sin if God did not make it possible. In a number of instances rabbinic texts have Israel explicitly blame the *yetzer hara*, and by implication God, for not curbing the *yetzer hara*, and God agrees.[13]

But the most interesting rabbinic contribution to the discussion of sin is the recognition that the energy which goes into sin is not totally negative but is an essential aspect of the human personality. Commenting on God's assessment of creation as "very good" (Gen. 1:31), R. Nachman b. Samuel said:

> That is the evil inclination. But is the evil inclination very good? Yes, for if it were not for the evil inclination, man would not build a house, or take a wife, or beget a child, or engage in business, as it says, "All labour and skillful work comes of a man's rivalry with his neighbor."[14]

From this passage it would therefore seem that the evil inclination becomes evil in the direction it takes and is not inherently evil. Directed at normal human competitive and sexual activity, the energy in question is an essential and good part of God's creation. Directed at illicit ends, these energies become the evil inclination and the source of man's sin.

The doctrine of the evil inclination is not permitted by the rabbis to assume Manichean proportions. The sources of darkness and rebellion are not satanic powers that threaten God. The material world, of which building a house, taking a wife, and begetting children are symbols, is not, as for the Gnostics, the realm that is opposite and antagonistic to spirit. By pronouncing "It was very good," God takes responsibility for the totality of his creation, in which sin, as well as redemption, becomes possible.

12. *Tanna deBe Eliyahu*, ed. M. Friedmann (Vienna, 1902), p. 62.
13. E.g., *Exod. Rabbah* 46:4.
14. *Gen. Rabbah* 9:17.

# Judaism and Conscience

Wyschogrod develops a nuanced assessment of the place and significance of conscience in the Jewish tradition. Because Judaism accords primacy to God's revelation and command, it has traditionally accorded only a relatively small place to the phenomenon of conscience. Nevertheless, Wyschogrod argues that contemporary Judaism can ill afford to neglect the phenomenon of conscience at the present time, when many Jews experience uprootedness from their sacred past and when continued participation in Jewish life often rests on an individual's decision. Whether a Jew hears in Jewish tradition the Voice of Sinai is a matter between that individual, his conscience, and God. But that he ought to try to listen is a dictate of conscience. First published in *Standing before God: Studies on Prayer in Scripture and in Tradition with Essays in Honor of John M. Oesterreicher*, ed. Asher Finkel and Lawrence Frizzell (New York: Ktav Publishing House, 1981), pp. 313-328.

———❦❦❦———

NEVER HAS conscience been in the forefront of human thinking as it is today. A number of convergent influences account for this. There is the emphasis on individuality which is characteristic of Western civilization. The totalitarian states of the twentieth century have perhaps permanently damaged the moral reliability of all authority, thereby forcing greater reliance on individual conscience. The dehumanizing effects of mass society have brought about an attempt toward liberation from the collective by a turning inward in conscience. For these and other reasons, the contemporary religious world places great emphasis on conscience as the source of moral authority.

Judaism has not remained uninfluenced by these developments. As a religion particularly replete with a specific code of conduct, the gradual abandonment by most Jews of the Torah way of life was at least an implicit and mostly unformulated exercise of conscience as an act of dissent from established norms. Most Jews did not put the matter in these terms. Instead, it was seen as a transition into modernity or, in the case of American Jewish immigrants, as a necessary response to the demands of the New World. But somewhere in the soul of the Jews who for the first time partook of forbidden foods or put on an electric light on the Sabbath, there was an exercise of conscience which reassured the individual that what he was doing was not wrong. Gradually, these deviations from the norms of the past were institutionalized into various forms of liberal Judaism. But even here, an explicit doctrine of conscience did not appear. De facto, the reformers were undoubtedly guided by conscience in deciding what in the tradition was to be retained and what discarded. But they did not develop conscience into a doctrine.

In this respect, the reformers were very traditional. The Judaism they set out to reform did not have a doctrine of conscience as such. In fact, there is no classical Hebrew term for the concept nor has it ever figured prominently either in Jewish theology or in Jewish history. No Jewish encyclopedia I could find has an article on conscience. The topic is covered in almost every general encyclopedia, with the *Encyclopedia of Religion and Ethics* devoting part of its general article on conscience to the place of this concept in Judaism. Instead of dealing with conscience in Judaism, however, this article, in spite of its heading, deals with a general exposition of Jewish ethics as if ethics and conscience were the same. And the same is true of Jewish history. No great departures in the development of Judaism can be ascribed to faithfulness to a call of conscience as, for instance, the Reformation to the conscience of Luther. Whatever the dynamics of Jewish history may have been, the proclamation "Here I stand: I can do no other" is not familiar to Jewish ears. The conclusion to which we are forced, then, is that Judaism lacks a doctrine of conscience as it is generally understood from stoicism to scholasticism through the Reformation to the present.

At this point, we have a number of alternatives. We can argue that, appearances to the contrary notwithstanding, there is a notion of conscience in Judaism. Or we can maintain that there neither is nor can be a doctrine of conscience in Judaism because of the primacy of revelation. A third possibility, one closely tied to the second, is to claim that an ethics of conscience, by the inner logic of its case, tends toward the deification of man, as for instance in the case of Heidegger. And, finally, we can take the position that Judaism is indeed the poorer for its lack of a doctrine of conscience because without conscience man never transcends the hegemony of the "Great Beast," the term Simone Weil applied to the collective whose rule she found intolerable in Judaism. Even superficial consideration of these alternatives reveals that they are not totally mutually exclusive, though of course some are more difficult to combine than others. None of them is without an element of the truth, though again there is more truth in some than in others. It is this complexity that makes the problem of conscience so fascinating for Jewish theology.

# I

Is there a notion of conscience in Judaism? We have already found that there is no term for it in classical Hebrew; in contemporary Hebrew the term *Mazpun* is used, the root of which means "hidden or inward." But the absence of a word in itself, while important, is not totally decisive. The idea as such may exist, even if there is no particular word to express it. Are there any instances in classical Jewish literature that might reasonably be interpreted as evidence that the notion of conscience is not totally foreign to the tradition? In the twenty-fourth chapter of the First Book of Samuel we read the very moving episode of David's adventure in the cave of En-Gedi. David's relations with Saul had been going from bad to worse and Saul was determined to capture his erstwhile favorite and kill him. When he is told: "Behold, David is in the wilderness of En-Gedi" (1 Sam. 24:2), he mobilizes three thousand of his best warriors for the search. David and his men seek refuge in a cave, presumably a rather large one. Suddenly, Saul appears in the cave alone, to attend to his natural functions. David's men, seeing in this development the hand of God who had promised David victory over Saul, urge David not to miss his opportunity. But David replies: "The Lord forbid it me, that I should do this thing unto my lord, the Lord's anointed, to put forth my hand against him, seeing he is the Lord's anointed" (24:7). Therefore, instead of killing Saul, he cuts off a piece of the king's garment, without the king being aware of it. But instead of being proud of his restraint, David begins to feel an inner discomfort. "And it came to pass afterward, that David's heart smote him, because he had cut off Saul's skirt" (24:6). It seems rather difficult to avoid the conclusion that we are dealing here with the phenomenon of conscience. Having performed an action, David learns through inner suffering that what he did was not right. Even in the decision not to kill the Lord's anointed, we can detect the voice of conscience, especially since David is urged by his men not to miss his opportunity. We thus seem to have in this incident an example of conscience vetoing a contemplated course of action as well as disapproving of one already committed. In fact, David's pangs of conscience for cutting the king's garment may even have been intensified by the prior victory his conscience had scored over his men's more activist advice. By cutting Saul's garment, David deprives conscience of the total victory it demands even if, from a more balanced point of view, David had more reason to be proud of his restraint than ashamed of the minor transgression.

And then there is the other episode in the life of David when the voice of conscience seems to play a role. David had seduced Bath-Sheba and she had become pregnant. Since her husband was away at war, David summoned him from the front so that it might be supposed that the child she was to bear was his. But Uriah refuses to visit his wife because, he reasons, at a time when his comrades are in battle he cannot "go into my house, to eat and to drink, and to lie with my wife" (2 Sam. 11:11). He returns to his comrades without having seen his wife. David, seeing no other alternative, orders Uriah's death in battle, after which Bath-Sheba becomes his wife. And then the biblical writer continues:

> And the Lord sent Nathan to David. He came to him and said to him, "There were two men in a certain city, the one rich and the other poor. The rich man had very many flocks and herds; but the poor man had nothing but one little ewe lamb, which he had bought. And he brought it up, and it grew up with him and with his children; it used to eat of his morsel, and drink from his cup, and lie in his bosom, and it was like a daughter to him. Now there came a traveler to the rich man, and he was unwilling to take one of his own flock or herd to prepare for the wayfarer who had come to him, but he took the poor man's lamb, and prepared it for the man who had come to him." Then David's anger was greatly kindled against the man; and he said to Nathan, "As the Lord lives, the man who has done this deserves to die; and he shall restore the lamb fourfold, because he did this thing, and because he had no pity."
>
> Nathan said to David, "You are the man. Thus says the Lord, the God of Israel, 'I anointed you king over Israel, and I delivered you out of the hand of Saul; and I gave you your master's house, and your master's wives into your bosom, and gave you the house of Israel and of Judah; and if this were too little, I would add to you as much more. Why have you despised the word of the Lord, to do what is evil in his sight? You have smitten Uriah the Hittite with the sword, and have taken his wife to be your wife, and have slain him with the sword of the Ammonites. Now therefore

the sword shall never depart from your house, because you have despised me, and have taken the wife of Uriah the Hittite to be your wife.' Thus says the Lord, 'Behold, I will raise up evil against you out of your own house; and I will take your wives before your eyes, and give them to your neighbor, and he shall lie with your wives in the sight of this sun. For you did it secretly; but I will do this thing before all Israel, and before the sun.'" David said to Nathan, "I have sinned against the Lord." And Nathan said to David, "The Lord also has put away your sin; you shall not die." (2 Sam 12:1-13)

Particularly significant for our purpose is Nathan's parable. Instead of merely delivering God's condemnation, Nathan's parable draws from David a moral judgment that emanates from his deepest moral self. It is David who condemns himself, who passes judgment over the rich man's outrageous robbery of the poor man's single possession. This outrage is so great that David pronounces the hypothetical culprit worthy of death, even if from the normal legal point of view no capital crime has been committed. And when Nathan thunders his unforgettable "Thou art the man," it is answered by an unequivocal "I have sinned against the Lord," a confession without explanation or mitigation but bold, simple and clear, the usual tone of a guilty conscience. Here again it is difficult to escape the conclusion that we are dealing with the phenomenon of conscience, even if the word is not used.

The third text of interest to our inquiry is drawn from rabbinic literature. Here, of course, the law is central and one would not expect the notion of conscience to play a prominent role since, as almost every writer on this subject correctly insists, from the point of view of the established legal order conscience can be an unsettling and disruptive force that the law cannot handle and toward which, therefore, the law must remain, at the very least, reserved. The law is objective and impartial and excludes, generally speaking, motifs of compassion or pity. "And a poor man," we are told in Exodus (23:3), "thou shalt not favor in his cause." And the Mishnah in *Kethuboth* (9:2) adds: "In legal matters no compassion is shown." This is the attitude one would expect in legal literature; it can come as a surprise only to those who have no feeling for the force of impartiality as a dimension of justice. And yet, this is not the whole story. We read the following in the tractate Baba Meṣi'a of the Babylonian Talmud (83a):

Some porters negligently broke a barrel of wine belonging to Rabbah son of R. Huna. Thereupon he seized their garments; so they went and complained to Rab. "Return them their garments," he ordered. "Is that the law?" he enquired. "Even so," he rejoined: "'That thou mayest walk in the way of good men.'" (Prov. 2:20). Their garments having been returned, they observed, "We are poor men, have worked all day and are in need: are we to get nothing?" "Go and pay them," he ordered. "Is that the law?" he asked. "Even so," was his reply: "'and keep the path of the righteous.'"

Having broken their employer's barrel of wine negligently, the laborers are legally responsible for the damage they caused. But Rab waives this "that thou mayest walk in the way of good men." But this is not sufficient, for he orders the laborers paid for the day's work. Here the law yields to something beyond it, something that cannot be codified but only perceived in the unique situation that presents itself and in which the moral agent must make a judgment taking into account the law but also an inner voice which he cannot suppress. The likelihood is that here we are dealing with something very much akin to conscience even if it is not called that or developed into an explicit doctrine.

And yet, we cannot leave this part of our discussion without giving due weight to the negative moment of the problem. David's feeling of remorse after he had cut Saul's garment is not, after all, a major event of Jewish theology. The difficulty with the theme of conscience in Nathan's exhortation to David is that while classical conscience is a voice that speaks within man, Nathan is the other who addresses David as spokesman of God and therefore, even if we agree that the content of his message is an appeal to conscience, to the extent that Nathan speaks from the outside he represents the heteronomous and not the voice of conscience. It is particularly strange that the same David whose conscience speaks up in defense of Saul's garment remains silent in the Bath-Sheba episode and that it takes a prophet to make David see the magnitude of his transgression. It would not be difficult to invoke psychological explanations for this difference; however successful these may be, they cannot obscure the fact that in the decisive transgression of his life, David's conscience, as the voice that speaks inwardly, remains silent and must be awakened by an outer voice. And finally, the case of the broken barrel of wine, too, is not quite a perfect example of the functioning of conscience. Whose conscience does this episode illustrate? If anyone's, it is Rab's but he is judging another, not himself. Can we speak of conscience when it is the injustice of another instead of the self that is the issue? Traditionally, conscience has been understood as that voice which censures the agent's own misdeeds, either before or after the fact. Whether it is the same conscience which speaks when I wax indignant at the crimes of another or whether there is a fundamental difference between my sense of justice turned outward and my self-condemnation turned inward, is a serious problem of moral phenomenology. That there is a difference between perceiving evil in another and in myself was illustrated by David's readiness to condemn the rich man of Nathan's parable without, at the same time, perceiving the magnitude of his own transgression. We must therefore conclude that Rab's otherwise admirable decision is a problematic illustration of the voice of conscience.

We leave this section then with a mixed verdict. There are examples of conscience in Jewish literature but they are not in clear, bold relief.

## II

Why did the conscience fail to achieve an unequivocally central role in Jewish thought? The question becomes particularly pressing once we realize that no plausible sociological explanation seems to be forthcoming. From the sociological point of view, conscience begins to play a prominent role in situations in which social cohesion is threatened and the individual is thrown into himself. He no longer receives the kind of support that is characteristic of societies in their vitality when value structures are intact, unquestioned, and function to their optimum as instruments of social control. With the relativization of such value structures, with the appearance of competing systems soliciting the loyalty of the individual, choices of a rather fundamental kind have to be made from within the resources available to the individual. The fact that the notion of conscience makes its appearance in the ancient world not at the height of Greek philosophy, with Plato and Aristotle, but rather toward the end in Cicero and Seneca is, of course, a case in point. Can this sort of analysis help us with our problem? It does not seem so. If our problem were only the absence of conscience in biblical Judaism, the case would be different. We could then attempt to argue that biblical Judaism precedes the period of social dissolution during which one would expect to find the appearance of conscience. But the fact is, of course, that conscience fails to become important throughout Jewish history, a history which includes periods of decline and dissolution as well as growth and cohesion. It seems quite clear that the periods immediately following the destruction of the second Temple or the expulsion from Spain were times of serious social dissolution, permeated as they were by the disappearance of age-old institutions. Nevertheless, even at such times, we do not find the appearance to any serious extent of conscience as a motif in Jewish thought and this leads me to believe that the explanation, if any, must be other than sociological.

The explanation is theological. Judaism is based on obedience to God.

In conscience it is not after all God who is being heard but man. The Jew, however, is required to listen to God and not to man.

To make this a bit clearer, we must now focus briefly on the phenomenon of conscience. Here, as so often elsewhere, the phenomenon under discussion is often confused with various theories about the phenomenon so that we no longer remember where theory begins and phenomenon ends. Perhaps it would therefore be better to start with some theories about conscience rather than conscience itself. It would appear that theories of conscience fall into two general categories: the autonomous and the heteronomous. For the autonomous theory of conscience, man recognizes in conscience what is right and what is wrong. This recognition is not a hearing of an external judgment, it is not a yielding to the inscrutable will of God, but an internal act of recognition of the moral truth, somewhat analogous to the recognition of the truth of a mathematical proposition or a principle of logic. The difference, of course, is that even for the autonomous theory of conscience we must distinguish between the general moral sense by means of which we apprehend universal moral principles and conscience which is largely, if not exclusively, particular, passing judgment on specific and concrete situations whether of the past or the proposed future. Whatever problems may lurk in the transition from the universal to the particular, and they are not inconsiderable, it remains true for the autonomous theory that by listening to the voice of conscience we do not simply abdicate our will and our sense of the right to another, but that in the deepest sense, it is our moral judgment that makes itself heard in the specific situation. From this point of view, conscience is an affirmation of our sense of the right, very often in conflict with the judgment of society, the church, or possibly even God if and when his command conflicts with the dictate of conscience. Philosophically, this is an affirmation of an ethical humanism, of the moral self-sufficiency of man who in the final analysis must make his own judgments in his own light in deference to his humanity.

It is not difficult to see that understood in this way, the doctrine of conscience is not easily reconcilable with an ethic that looks to the word of God as its criterion of the right. The divine word is not a projection of, nor is it continuous with, man's moral sense. It is the judge of man's moral sense and as such it is the judge of man's self-deification. We will soon touch on an important contemporary *reductio ad absurdum* of this attitude in Heidegger's interpretation of conscience. But, it may be asked, is this the only possible interpretation of conscience? Can conscience not be thought of as the voice of God speaking to man in solitude and addressing to him the divine command? The answer is of course that it can and has been thought of in this way. Interestingly enough, it is in Karl Barth, the most authentic voice of the Reformation in our time, that we find a definition of conscience that is most sensitive to this aspect of the problem. Barth writes:

> Conscience . . . conscientia . . . , the knowing with God of what God knows, has to be understood strictly as the conscience freed and raised by God . . . and not a universal and always effective human disposition and capacity. Freedom of conscience is not, therefore, the permission, which in the 18th and 19th century sense we all have, to think what we consider fine and desirable. It is rather the power, which God imparts to those who accept His revelation, to think what in His judgment is right, and therefore true and wise.[1]

Barth is fully aware that as an expression of "what we consider fine and desirable," conscience is natural theology in the realm of the ethical and just as the God of natural theology is a humanly constructed idol, so conscience understood as a human faculty will yield only man's view of what is fine and desirable and not God's. Barth therefore sees conscience not as a universal human faculty shared by all men to the extent that they are men and rational, but as a special gift of God to those who accept his revelation by means of which they are able to determine what is right in God's view and not theirs. In this heteronomous view of conscience, there is no fundamental difference between obedience to God when God directly addresses man and listening to the voice of conscience in which also it is the voice of God that is being heard.

If this view of conscience were a tenable one, there would indeed be no conflict between conscience and revelation and Judaism could incorporate such a view of conscience without difficulty. Unfortunately, however, the heteronomous interpretation of conscience is not altogether tenable. To demonstrate this we must however abandon the realm of theories of conscience, with which we have been dealing until now, and direct our attention to the phenomenon of conscience itself. Before we do this, we must make one further observation concerning Barth's treatment of this topic. Because of the deep Reformation roots of his thinking, one could expect conscience to receive considerable emphasis in the thought of Barth. Instead, it plays a rather minor role. While it is true that the *Dogmatics* is incomplete with several of the more ethical volumes missing, it is difficult to believe that conscience could move into a position of centrality when so little groundwork has been laid for it in the more dogmatic volumes. I prefer to believe that the secondary role played by conscience in Barth's thought is an organic development. Where conscience

---

1. Karl Barth, *Church Dogmatics* I/2, trans. T. F. Torrance, G. W. Bromiley (Edinburgh: T&T Clark, 1957), pp. 696-697.

is a more or less independent and internal human power that discriminates right from wrong, we can expect it to play a leading role in theology. But if conscience is a "power which God imparts to those who accept His revelation," then we must not be surprised to find it playing a distinctly secondary role to the study of God's revelation in Scripture. It is the divine word that must then be the focus of interest and while conscience may mirror the word and even perhaps to some extent interiorize it, it can never establish itself as an independent source of authority superior to or even equal to scripture. The reason that Barth cannot pay much attention to conscience is that he cannot ultimately take seriously that which is only human. In the form in which conscience appears in Barth, as an echo of the divine word, it is doomed to leading a shadow existence adjacent to the power and clarity of the divine word.

But let us now return to the phenomenon of conscience. Is the heteronomous interpretation of it persuasive or is it much more plausible to argue that conscience is essentially a phenomenon of autonomy, a turning by man to himself and a trusting of his own powers? There is much to recommend the latter alternative. Very often conscience asserts itself, as we have already seen, as a rejection of another's will, be he a person or an institution. When we hear the voice of conscience we are not, after all, merely hearing the command of another, as Abraham obeyed God at Mount Moriah. No one maintains that in the episode of Abraham's readiness to sacrifice Isaac, we are dealing with conscience. Here we have as clear-cut an instance as we could imagine of obedience, of a heteronomous command that conflicts with everything that Abraham's moral sense tells him is right and which nevertheless is obeyed. We learn here that the command of God pulverizes conscience and that, instead, obedience characterizes Abraham's relationship with God. All this, by contrast, serves to emphasize the prominence of the dimension of autonomy in the experience of conscience. Conscience is not a voice from the outside which speaks to us to censure our actions. Were it that, it could be disregarded with much greater ease than is the case. In conscience it is we who speak to ourselves and the censure is so painful precisely because it is self-inflicted, as we found when Nathan's parable produced David's self-condemnation. Very often conscience begins to make itself felt only after a long series of condemnations emanating from the outside have proven fruitless. Only when the condemnation no longer appears external but is transformed into my voice, my condemnation, do we speak of the appearance of conscience and this is the reason that, prima facie, a heteronomous interpretation of conscience seems to go against the facts.

And yet the heteronomous interpretation of conscience also reflects part of the truth. While it is true that in conscience it is a voice that, in one sense, is part of myself that is speaking, it is also true that this voice is experienced as condemning some past or future enterprise to which I have been committed and which, to that extent, represents the project that I am. The purpose of the call of conscience is to deflect me from the direction my project has taken and, as such, it is a force that is not part of my project but at odds with it. If we are to avoid confusing conscience with the general moral sense, we must distinguish those instances where a person, from the very beginning, has a moral insight by which he organizes his life and in the service of which he labors, from those instances, in which sometimes quite suddenly, an excruciating "no" is pronounced over an act, an undertaking, a life-choice which has been progressing on its path and which now collides with an unforeseen obstacle. The voice that pronounces this "no" cannot simply be the same person's whose enterprise comes under its judgment. At the risk of contradicting what we said earlier, we now argue that in conscience we discover that we are not in fact fully our own masters, that just when we have charted a course we saw fit, something or someone beyond us with a will and project quite his own can pronounce an unexpected condemnation. At times we may try very hard to evade the condemnation, to lose ourselves in a variety of concerns and rationalizations designed either to justify ourselves or at the very least to concentrate our attention on other matters so that our guilt recedes to the periphery of attention, finally, we hope, to disappear. But very often all this is of no avail. We feel a presence that will not disappear, that begins to speak again when the noises of the world abate and when we are with ourselves, constrained once again to listen to a voice that is another's, yet also our own.

It is here, it would seem, that we have reached the heart of the mystery. In conscience heteronomy and autonomy blend into a dialectical unity. The voice of conscience is both the voice of another calling us to our responsibility and it is also the discovery that this voice at the same time seems to be coming from within us, from the deepest levels of our being where we are what we really want to be and in which there is an immediate affinity to the heteronomous dimension of conscience. On this level, he who demands and he of whom the demand is made are no longer in conflict but in harmony. Nevertheless, it is vital to realize that this is never a harmony of identity. It is a harmony in which both moments of the dialectic remain alive. There is the resistance and even rebellion of the human against the demands of the heteronomous authority and there is also the submission in autonomy to an almost self-legislated right through which man becomes a being of freedom instead of a sullen slave.

Whatever the possibilities for reconciling autonomy and heteronomy in conscience may be, the fact of the matter is that for the biblical tradition, especially in Judaism, the autonomous aspect of conscience seemed to have loomed larger and this explains the absence of any serious notion of conscience in a tradition that turned to the divine word for its inspiration.

# III

Our argument until now has led to the conclusion that, within certain limits, an ethics of conscience has the potentiality of drifting into a Godless proclamation of human independence. Equipped with a built-in ethical compass, man can rely on himself to discover the good, not only universally and abstractly, but also in the concreteness of the existential situation in which conscience makes itself heard in judging the right of specific instances. Antithetical as such a view may be to the biblical notion of man's dependence on the word of God as the source of ethical direction, it still does not represent the full flowering of conscience as the basis of human autonomy. The reason for this is that the autonomous direction of conscience we have been discussing until now constitutes an autonomy relative to the divine word; in relation to the moral law, conscience remains a sense that points beyond itself to the good or the right which is not of man's making and which is perceived or sensed by conscience but not created by it. To the extent therefore that conscience retains its essentially moral character, it falls short of total liberation of man from subordination to structures which rule over him, even if these are now rational moral structures and not the sovereignty of God. It was not until our century that an interpretation of conscience makes its appearance in the work of Heidegger which reveals for the first time the consequence that follows a totally secular interpretation of the phenomenon. Heidegger's importance lies in the sophistication of his categories which enable him, in a sense, to do full justice to the phenomenon of conscience without unduly impressing upon it any extraneous categories that obscure the phenomenon before it can introduce itself on its own terms. "The ontological analysis of conscience," he writes, "on which we are thus embarking, is prior to any description and classification of Experiences of conscience, and likewise lies outside of any biological 'explanation' of this phenomenon (which would mean its dissolution). But it is no less distant from a theological exegesis of conscience or any employment of this phenomenon for proofs of God or for establishing an 'immediate' consciousness of God."[2] Lest this be taken to ex-

2. Martin Heidegger, *Being and Time,* trans. John Marquarrie and Edward Robinson (London: SCM Press, 1962), p. 313.

clude the theological but not the moral function of conscience, we soon read the following: "What does the conscience call to him to whom it appeals? Taken strictly, nothing. The call asserts nothing, gives no information about world events, has nothing to tell."[3] And should we finally be perplexed by the question as to who it is that is calling us in conscience, we are told: "In conscience *Dasein* calls itself. "[4]

With conscience deprived of its theological locus, its message emptied of any content whatsoever and its origin located in the very being to whom the call is addressed, it nevertheless remains a phenomenon of the most basic importance to Heidegger. The reason for this is that through conscience man lifts himself out of the mode of existence that is the life of the collectivity or the crowd into which he has been driven inauthentically. The one aspect of conscience that Heidegger seems to respect is its appeal to man in his aloneness, its refusal to attempt making itself heard over the noises of the crowd with its false enthusiasms and superficial interests. Just as guilt emerges in Heidegger shorn of its genesis in wrongdoing and transformed into a fundamental ontological characteristic of human existence, so conscience is no longer connected with any wrong done or contemplated but becomes a means through which man learns to take his destiny into his own hands by coming to terms with his anxiety which all inauthentic existence is desperately escaping. And yet this emptying of conscience of its content does not result in a formalism in the sense in which Kant's categorical imperative is a law whose content is nothing more nor less than the very form of law itself. Since the idea of law seems to be of no interest to Heidegger, the thrust of his interpretation of conscience is in the direction of the uncanny. Law, after all, provides man with a measure of existential security not only by directing his freedom but also by providing some measure of continuity with the rest of creation even if, as Kant insists, the law governing man's moral life is in significant respects different from the law that governs the rest of the universe. Heidegger's purpose is to heighten the sense of the uncanny which for him characterizes man's being-in-the-world as a being who is never fully at home in the world and who is redeemed from total absorption in the world by a voice which speaks in silence, which has no message and which is essentially a soliloquy, an act of calling itself. That conscience understood in these terms has something of the uncanny about it should surprise no one.

We can now see how far we have come since our main problem with conscience was its autonomy which we found to be in conflict with the bibli-

3. Heidegger, *Being and Time*, p. 318.
4. Heidegger, *Being and Time*, p. 320.

cal ethics of obedience. If Heidegger's interpretation of conscience is the end of the road we embarked on when we decided to explore the implications of an autonomous conscience, we now find that this is a road that leads us out of the realm of the ethical altogether. We need not insist that Heidegger's interpretation is in some way the logically necessary outcome of the doctrine of an autonomous conscience. Nevertheless, at the very least it is one of its risks, which goes a long way toward explaining Judaism's reserve toward the notion.

## IV

And yet, is not Judaism the worse for its lack of concern with conscience? We now understand that for biblical theology it is the divine word that is at the center of attention and we also understand the potential implications contained in a doctrine of autonomous conscience for the development of an ethical humanism or even an a-ethical humanism as in the case of Heidegger. And it is therefore not difficult to see why the Jew who looks to the God of his fathers will remain skeptical of all doctrines of human self-reliance, whatever their particular form may be. And yet, can we leave the matter at that, without a sense of uneasiness? Must the believing Jew sacrifice his conscience in obedience to God? Must he give up an ultimate individuality when he embraces the covenant which is more national than individual and must he, together with Buber, reject the Kierkegaardian single one for a relation with God that is always social and in which the ultimate aloneness before God yields to the community of Israel which is ruled by law rather than conscience, by the public more than the private? Perhaps conscience is the Isaac in each one of us which, though we love, we must be prepared to offer on the altar of divine sacrifice. And yet, it is very difficult to teach that the Jew owes nothing to his conscience. Is not the very act of obedience to God ultimately dependent on a dictate of conscience? At the genesis of the God-man relationship there must somewhere be a recognition by man that it is right to obey him whose command he hears and whose word becomes binding by a submission on the part of man that is affirmed in the depth of human existence where the command is heard. Without such an autonomous act of submission, men are the puppets of God and the divine command a facade behind which a divine determinism orders the objects of the world, among which man is merely one.

Today, the community of Israel is more and more a gathering of individuals chosen in faith. It is strange that the bitter assault on Judaism launched by Simone Weil in our century came at a time when her criticisms were least justified. The spirit of the Great Beast of our day hovers over the mass of Jews whose uprootedness from the sacralities of the past reduces them to a degree of contemporaneity that makes their participation and absorption into the mass public of the day natural and inevitable. The minority of Jews that clings to its past, by this very act resists the current and disengages itself from the real Great Beast of our time. To some extent it is much more probable today than ever before that a Jew who remains faithful to the covenant in this day and age is acting out of conscience instead of social conformity.

To resist the profound forces that work to level differences between one faith and another, one community and another, is no easy task and it is for this reason that the faithful Jew, whether he likes it or not, is forced into a degree of individuality much greater than ever before. In this environment, as an individual swimming against the stream, the Judaism of our day can no longer dispense with conscience as part of our theological arsenal. If the effect of this is that we thereby move into the age of conscience, it is a risk that we must be willing to accept because to insist on a Judaism that remains deaf to this voice is even more perilous.

The alternative is to argue that when conscience and the law conflict one must follow the law. In the terminology of the scholastics, this is the problem of whether an erring conscience binds. If an erring conscience does not bind, then one must disregard its dictates when it errs, that is, when the voice of conscience commands a course of action that is in conflict with what is objectively the right or the will of God. But since an erring conscience does not announce itself as erring, it follows that the person whose conscience errs is convinced that the course of action commanded by his erring conscience is in conformity with the right or the will of God. To teach that it is his duty to act against his erring conscience is to maintain that a person whose conscience errs must do that which appears to him wrong or contrary to God's will and that is always wrong. In the words of St. Thomas:

> Erroneous conscience binds even in things intrinsically evil. For conscience binds, as has been said, in this, that if someone acts contrary to his conscience, it follows that he has the will to sin. Thus if someone believes that to omit fornication is a mortal sin, when he chooses not to fornicate, he chooses to sin mortally, and therefore, sins mortally.[5]

It follows, therefore, that as far as St. Thomas is concerned, conscience binds unconditionally, whether or not it is in error, a fact that may surprise those

---

5. In *Epistolam ad Rômanos*, c. 14, 1. 2 (Opera Omnia, ed. Vives, 20, 1876), p. 580, quoted in Xavier G. Colavechio, *Erroneous Conscience and Obligations* (Washington, D.C.: Catholic University of America, 1961), p. 81.

who connect conscience with the Reformation more than with scholasticism. In any case, it is clear that this is a position almost compelled by the logic of the case, if we are to take conscience seriously at all. Otherwise if conscience is to be obeyed only when it is right, there must be some authority other than conscience to distinguish those cases when conscience is right from those in which it is wrong, a state of affairs essentially destructive of the authority of conscience. If conscience is to have any authority, it must have all authority and this is precisely what St. Thomas gives it, alarming as it may sound to maintain that conscience must be obeyed even when it counsels that which on other grounds is patently wrong and contrary to the divine law understood objectively. But since the individual can act only as the divine law appears in his light, as understood in his mind and mediated by his sensibility, in the final analysis he must obey the command as he hears it, in the depth of his conscience.

Must we end on such an anarchic note? Can we do no wrong if we think our action to be right? It is true that we must obey our conscience but it is our responsibility to have a conscience in good working order. This in turn involves two aspects. First, there must be the genuine willingness to listen to conscience, not only to what we want to hear but to what conscience is actually saying, however painful its message may be. And, second, there is the necessity for exposing conscience to those events and documents which constitute the record of Israel's relation with God, immersion in which shapes the conscience of the Jew. Human conscience in general and Jewish conscience in particular are not formed in a vacuum. No man is naturally endowed with an unerring conscience which miraculously leads him to the right irrespective of the knowledge available to him or unavailable to him. Without in any way diminishing the significance of conscience, we maintain that it can be sensitized and developed by the tradition of revelation to which the people of Israel are witness and without which Jewish conscience is impoverished and isolated, cut off from its source of historic sustenance. The study of Torah is therefore a fundamental dictate of Jewish conscience. And because this is so, while no person is guilty for following his conscience, he may be guilty for not giving a hearing to the voices of his tradition which speak to him across the ages and which at least purport to echo the voice of Sinai. Whether they will be perceived by him as such is a matter between him, his conscience, and God. But that he ought to try to listen is a dictate of conscience.

# Judaism and the Land

In this previously unpublished essay, Wyschogrod explores a striking ambiguity in Judaism's relation to the land. On the one hand, the promise of the land is present from the very origins of Israel's election. In this sense, God, Israel, and land are inextricably united in Judaism's self-understanding. On the other hand, Israel becomes a people prior to its entry into the land, and remains a people after it is severed from the land. In this respect, there is a curious dispensability to the tie between Israel and the land. Wyschogrod insists that these clues be interpreted in light of the sovereignty and condescension of the God of Israel. Although not a territorial earth god, but rather the Creator whose jurisdiction extends throughout the earth, God has freely chosen as his people not a spiritual elite but a carnal family, thereby laying claim to the sanctification of human history in all its depths and dimensions.

FROM THE BEGINNING, Israel's right to the land needed to be justified.

It *was* justified. The election of Abraham begins with the first verse of Genesis 12: "the Lord said to Abram, 'Leave your country, your kinsmen, and your father's house, and go to a country that I will show you. I will make you into a great nation, I will bless you and make your name so great that it shall be used in blessings.'" Abraham thus leaves his native land, his right to which requires no justification, and embarks on the divinely commanded journey to a land which, as yet, does not belong to him. "At that time," the Bible (v. 7) tells us, "the Canaanites lived in this land." But their possession of it will not endure. Having told us that "At that time the Canaanites lived in the land," the Bible adds, "There the Lord appeared to Abram and said, 'I give this land to your descendants.'" Thus the picture is clear. The election of Abraham consists of the command to leave a land his right to which could not be contested for a land that was occupied by others and possession of which was promised to Abraham's descendants. Abraham's fate was to be transformed from a native to a foreigner, compelled to exchange a truly native land for one currently owned by others. And that possession was to continue until the days of Joshua. The existence of Abraham and his descendants as aliens in Canaan and Egypt was to be a long one. Only later would they come into possession of the Promised Land. The formative years of the nation would be spent before the possession of the land as strangers in foreign lands. The election and the covenant at Sinai were to occur before the nation obtained possession of the land that first belonged to others. Israel was thus not born in its land but, entering upon it in its adulthood, it was to live in an adopted even if divinely assigned land.

We are therefore able to diagnose a curious ambivalence to the land in Jewish consciousness. On the one hand, it is an integral part of the election. The same act of election which binds Abraham and his descendants to God also binds the people to its land. These three — God, Israel, and the land — are tied one to the other in an indissoluble unity. But, on the other hand, there is also a curious dispensability to the tie between Israel and the land. Israel becomes a full-fledged people prior to its entry into the land. It remains a people, it does not disappear, after it is severed from the land. It is apparently less dependent on the land than any other people. And yet, the longing for possession of the land and for returning to it when separated from it never leaves the consciousness of the people over millennia. In the small villages of the Russian plain, in Jewish homes, the geography of the holy land was far more vivid than that of the surrounding countryside. In our lifetime, Jewish attachment to the land has profoundly affected the international order — and this from the international people *par excellence.* In the case of Judaism, a religious nationalism is abroad at a time when elsewhere the religious consciousness finds itself more and more alienated from the nation which appears to it as a particularly contemporary and dangerous idolatry. The situation cries for clarification.

Nowhere else in the memory of peoples is entry into a land remembered. A people is born out of a soil which is its mother. The people does not pre-date the land. It is the land which pre-dates the people. The land gives birth to a language and a people. And what is more important, out of the land rise the gods. This is so because the gods are the powers of nature which are born and die in the cyclical regularity of nature. The territoriality of the nature-gods is complemented by the territoriality of the political order. Sanctioned by the gods, the king rules over the territory of his sovereignty. His authority ends at the boundary of his land and the authority of the neighboring king and god commences beyond the line that delineates the territory. This is the foundation of polytheism. There are many kings as there are many gods because the authority of each is restricted to a given territory. To leave that territory is to leave the jurisdiction of the god reigning over the territory. The command to Abraham to leave his land to go to a land which God will show him reveals a God whose sovereignty is not limited to one territory but one who is the God of Abraham in Ur of Chaldea and in Canaan and everywhere else that Abraham will visit. Such an international divine jurisdiction is unprecedented. It breaks with the monarchical-territorial model heretofore dominant and makes possible monotheism since one God can now rule over all the earth. If there is any limitation of authority it is God's primary jurisdiction over Abraham and his descendants, i.e., over Israel. But this is not a true limitation but an intensification of interest in the people of election. The basic fact remains that unlike all the other gods of the ancient East, the God of Abraham is the only God who remains Abraham's God wherever he goes.

The God of Israel is therefore not a God of the earth. He is the God of a people that is brought into being in the interval between residence in one land which it is commanded to leave and settlement in another which is still in the future. From the first, the possibility of Jewish existence as international existence is thus established. Because the God of Israel is not a god of the earth, Jewish relationship to the earth is problematical. When Abraham negotiates with the Hittites for a burial place so that he can bury Sarah his wife, he speaks of himself as "an alien and settler" (Gen. 23:3). This condition is repeated in Egypt. What is more, the possession of the land promised to Israel is itself conditional. If Israel is faithful to its covenant, then God will bestow abundant blessing on the people who obey him: "The Lord will make you prosper greatly in the fruit of your body and of your cattle, and in the fruit of the ground in the land which he swore to your forefathers to give you" (Deut. 28:11). But should Israel not prove obedient to the commandments of God, then "The Lord will scatter you among the peoples from one end of the earth to the other, and there you will worship other gods whom neither you have known nor your forefathers, gods of wood and stone" (Deut. 28:64). One almost gets the impression that the gods of the land retain a certain authority from which Israel is freed as long as it is obedient to its God but as soon as — as a result of Israel's unfaithfulness — the protection of Israel's God is withdrawn, the gods of the land reassert their power to the detriment of Israel. The sojourn of the people of Israel is thus a conditional one. The land of Is-

93

rael cannot tolerate an unfaithful people of Israel. And just as the nations whom Israel displaced lost their right to the land because of their wickedness, so Israel is in constant danger of losing its right to the land with its unfaithfulness. But one decisive difference must be noted. For the other nations, to lose their land, to be expelled from it, is to die as a nation. For Israel, to lose its land is indeed a catastrophe but it does not entail national extinction. As Israel was a people before it obtained possession of the land, so it can exist as a people after it has lost its land. And because its existence as a people is never in doubt, its loss of the land cannot be permanent. As long as the people of Israel lives, its return to the land of promise is inevitable.

We must therefore balance Israel's advantages with its disadvantages. Its disadvantage is a certain weakness in its claim to the land. In its deepest consciousness, Israel is aware that it dwells on or lays claim to a previously owned land. It is aware that it is evicting peoples that had an earlier claim to the land. It is commanded by God to evict these peoples but this is a command that Israel does not carry out with the requisite zeal. Again and again, God finds it necessary to chastise Israel for the incompleteness of its conquest of the land. From the first, we might say, Israel is defensive in respect to its claim on the land. It believes that God who created the heavens and the earth is the owner of all the earth and can therefore take it from one people and give it to another. Indeed, the rabbis tell us, the creation account in Genesis was included in the Bible only to make it clear that God, as creator, had the right to effectuate a transfer of ownership from the Canaanites to Israel. But if this is the reason for the creation account, it is not difficult to conclude that we are dealing with a certain lack of ease in respect to the right to the land. The nations who worship the native gods of the land are more firmly rooted. They do not have the need to defend their claim against previous owners because their memory does not extend to the time when others dwelled on the land, because as a nation they did not exist before they dwelled on the land. Israel's claim, from the first, is therefore a contested one and Israel is fully aware of the need to justify its possession of the land.

If this awareness of the contestability of its claim to the land is the disadvantage of Israel's covenant with a God primarily of time rather than space, its advantage as we have already seen, is its ability to survive severed from the land. This is a unique gift which, of course, accounts for the continuing existence of the Jewish people. Separated from its land for almost two thousand years, strewn to the far corners of the earth, it has retained a continuous culture and identity as the people of divine election. While all the other great empires of the ancient world are remembered in history books, the Jewish people maintains a continuous heritage of four thousand years. To assert that this heritage has been continuous is not to deny the reality of history and the changes that history has wrought in the course of time. But a Talmudic rabbi transported to one of the Orthodox sections of New York or Jerusalem would feel very much at home in respect to what people do and believe. Such a degree of continuity in the absence of a common territory is unprecedented and explainable only by emphasis on the religious essence of Jewish identity.

Prior to Israel, all religions were national religions. I am convinced that the reason for this is the rootedness of the gods in the land over which they have jurisdiction. To continue to worship one god in the territory of another god makes as little sense as to obey the laws in effect in Paris while living in New York. The God of Israel, as we have seen, breaks with this pattern. He is God everywhere and his jurisdiction is not evaded by moving from one place to another. Once this is grasped, the bifurcation between religion and nationality becomes possible. Nationality — except for the case of Israel — must remain tied to the soil. But that is not so in the case of religion. As understood by Christianity, a model of dual loyalty develops. The individual belongs both to a nation and to a religion. He is a Frenchman and a Christian or a German and a Christian. As Frenchman or German, he is a member of a national community with territorial and linguistic boundaries. But he is also a member of the supra-national church which has no national boundaries. The fact that the center of western Christendom became Rome which the founder of Christianity had never visited rather than the land which witnessed the events of his life, the fact that Greek and Latin rather than Hebrew and Aramaic became the languages of the church illustrate the distinction the church draws between religion and nationality. The church is a spiritual fellowship into which men bring their national identities because they possess these identities but not because such identities play a role in the church. The church thus understands itself as having universalized the national election of Israel by opening it to all men who, in entering the church, enter a spiritualized, universalized new Israel.

The adherence of the Jewish people to its national-religious election has therefore evoked little sympathy from the church. And this has become particularly true in modern times when secular nationalisms, sometimes of the most criminal variety, have produced major catastrophes. Things were bad enough when the Jewish people clung to its uniquely non-territorial form of nationalism. But, being non-territorial, it was insulated against the worst excesses of common, garden variety nationalism. But with the development of Zionism and the creation of the state of Israel, there suddenly appeared a fully incarnated nationalism which was almost impossible to distinguish from any other nationalism. The Christian mind is therefore deeply perplexed. Is this phenomenon to be interpreted in theological terms or are we here dealing with Jewish secular nationalism having no significance whatsoever for religious history? From a Christian perspective, is the biblically founded Jewish claim to the land of Israel to be taken seriously or is this an illegitimate use of a biblical idea for an essentially secular and political purpose?

These questions cannot be answered *a priori*. From the outset, God could have chosen as his people not the seed of Abraham but men of all nations possessing faith and virtue. But he did not do so. Instead, God elected Abraham and his seed. It could have been foreseen that not all Jews would turn out to be paragons of virtue and faith. While we are told that "Abram put his faith in the Lord, and the Lord counted that faith to him as righteousness" (Gen. 15:6), nowhere are we specifically told that Abraham's election was the result of his extraordinary faith. These feats occur after the election, which is not explained but merely recorded. The need to explain the election of Abraham is rooted in a rationalism that can imagine God only as a sober thinker who does nothing except for good and sufficient reason and whose love for Abraham and his descendants cannot be comparable to the falling in love of a man for a woman or of the love of a parent for a favorite child, instances which are rarely explainable by reasons. But the biblical text does not portray God as an Aristotelian or even Kantian thinker. Instead, it tells us that he chose Abraham, or the man with whom he wished to be associated in history, to whose name he wished to hyphenate his so that, to the end of time, he would be known as the God of Israel. And this association was not to be restricted to Abraham alone but would extend to that numerous — currently, perhaps not numerous enough — nation that was to stem from Abraham. This people was to be the people of God. And not conditionally so. The election would not depend on Israel's obedience. If Israel would prove disobedient, the punishment of God would descend on it. Among those punishments would be the temporary — never permanent — loss of its land. But the basic election was irrevocable (Rom. 11:29). Were the election of Israel contingent upon Israel's behavior, then Israel could walk out on its calling. It could then abrogate the covenant and blend back among the nations of the world instead of living at the white-hot contact point where God meets humankind. But Israel does not have that choice. It remains in the service of God's purpose no matter how unfaithful it is to itself and to God. The election of Israel is seared into its flesh and not only its consciousness.

That God should have anything whatsoever to do with the flesh of humankind and not only its soul is a thought quite foreign to the ruling neo-Platonic Aristotelianism of the Roman world. Matter was the irrational; all knowledge was of forms or ideas. At death, the soul shakes off its destructive association with the body and rises to a state of purely spiritual existence which is, of course, far superior to its earthly condition. Gentile Christianity absorbs much of the attitude, which is easily converted into a flaunting of the spirituality of the new Israel over the carnality of the old. And yet, the Jewish dimension of the church never disappears. Modified by the gentile Greek consciousness, severed from its roots in the Hebrew and Aramaic of Jesus and the apostles, estranged from the land of Jesus, headquartered at the old central office of the Roman Empire, the church clings to the Hebrew Bible, even as it proclaims it superseded and fulfilled in the New Testament. And above all, the church clings to the crucifixion and the resurrection and later comes to define the incarnation, all carnal conceptions rooted in the Judaism of its origins.

Take the notion of resurrection. To the Greeks, this is utter madness. The goal of the rational soul is to shed the body. Having done so, what possible purpose could be served by the promise of reattachment to the body? Maimonides, the twelfth-century Jewish philosopher deeply influenced by Greek thoughts, probably found the belief in resurrection something of an embarrassment. For much of his life he ignored the doctrine, so much so that rumors began to circulate that he did not believe in the resurrection of the dead. Late in his life he wrote an "Essay on the Resurrection of the Dead" in which he affirms that at the end of days resurrection will take place. He merely adds that after it has taken place, those risen will die again but this time for good, never to be burdened with a body again. Augustine, when faced with the same dilemma, also reaffirms the resurrection of the dead, merely adding that the risen body will be an incorruptible one, leaving his readers to wonder whether incorruptible corporeality is not a contradiction in terms. Nevertheless, in spite of all these problems, the church held fast to the resurrection both of Jesus and of all others on the day of judgment. And it did so because of its Jewish roots which it was not prepared to annul. The human being is body and soul. A disembodied soul is a partial and not a fulfilled human being. Death is therefore not an occasion for joy, as it was for Socrates, but for grief as it was for Jesus on the cross. And, strangely enough, even the doctrine of the incarnation, that Jesus was all God and all human, which has been perhaps the single most serious issue dividing Judaism from Christianity, has a Jewish element in it. If Christianity is a movement away from carnal to spiritual election, then ought not Docetism to have triumphed in the church? Is not the assertion that God became flesh the extension of perhaps the foundation of Israel's carnal election? Judaism does not accept the contention that God became flesh. But it does teach that God elected a people of the flesh as the people of God. In some sense, this irrevocable election constitutes a unique dwelling of God among or in this people. And it is an indwelling not only in the spiritual and ideological sense but in the physical one. The enemies of God hate the commandments of God, his moral demands which they find contrary to their plans. But they do not find only God's commandments unacceptable. They also find the physical existence of the Jewish people unacceptable first and foremost because the Jewish people preaches God's commandments but not only for this reason because even when Israel ceases to preach God's commandments, his enemies still insist on the physical liquidation of the Jews because the Jews, however silent and however ideologically estranged from the commandments of God, proclaim God's sovereignty and the truth of his commandments by their very physical being because they are the people of election of the flesh.

God is thus not only the God of spirit. He is the God that speaks not only to a portion of the human being, namely his spirit, but to all of him, his spirit and body. An election by faith alone would have been a purely spiritual election. It would have left unhallowed the human body and the extensions of the body, such as his nationality and the historical order. Instead, God elected a historical people. Having been elected, it ceases to be a normal historical people. It is able to survive millennia without a homeland. Its national essence is its relationship to God. But its election does not destroy it as a people. It makes it a unique people, but a people nevertheless. The same is true of its relationship to history. In one sense, Israel is beyond the "laws" of history. It is not subject to the rise and fall of all other peoples and empires, a fact which causes angry philosophers of history whose schemes Israel undermines to refer to it as a fossil not subject to historic destruction. But at the same time, Israel does not abandon the domain of history. It refuses to exchange its historical and national messianism for a doctrine of individual salvation. Israel refuses to invent the idea of a church which forces men to live in two jurisdictions and to assume two identities: a member of a nation and a member of a church. When such a bifurcated existence is decreed for human life, European wars in which Christian fights Christian, not as Christian but as German, Frenchman, or Pole, become possible. That such a church-sanctioned conflict was the rule rather than the exception in the history of Europe was not simply the result of a failure of Christianity. Once religion and nationality are separated, the historical order in which national destinies are realized is almost inevitably de-Christianized. And to the extent that Christianity desires to remain a factor in the historical order, it chooses for itself a central-Italian state whose temporal ruler is made to coincide with the spiritual leader of the church. For Judaism the retention of messianism as a national-historical expectation thus hallows the historical order by foreseeing redemption as coming in history, amidst the realities of international relations, interpreted in the concrete terms of the daily newspaper. And this is the reason that the first question addressed by the Jerusalem community to the risen Jesus (Acts 1:6) is "Lord, is this the time when you are to be established once again over the sovereignty of Israel?" This Zionist question is addressed to the risen Jesus because to establish once again the sovereignty of Israel is the essential task of the Messiah as understood by Judaism. In the second century many Jews, including the famous Rabbi Akiba, believed that Bar Kochba, who came near to freeing Israel from its Roman rule, was the Messiah. They discovered their error when Bar Kochba failed. There is reason to believe that the disciples of Jesus were also deeply shaken in their faith in him during the interval between the crucifixion and the resurrection. It is therefore easy to understand how the resurrection made it possible once again to hope that the messianic task, the national liberation of Israel, would be accomplished and this explains the questions the community poses the risen Jesus.

We are trying to explicate the carnal election of Israel — that God did not choose a community of faith but a people of the flesh, the descendants of Abraham, Isaac, and Jacob. I have maintained that in so doing God confirms the carnality of the human person, that he is soul and body and that God can love the body as well as the soul. Because the human being is not only soul but also body, he belongs to a historic nation. Were he only soul, his primary identity would be self-chosen as mathematician or biologist, philosopher or musician. As it is, while we do belong to such intellectual or spiritual groupings, our historical identity is a national one that, in most instances, is not of our choosing. And once we understand the seriousness of national identity, we have entered the historical order which is hallowed through the national election of Israel. It is hallowed because, God tells us, "a kingdom of priests and a holy nation" is a possibility. Not only an individual, or a collection of individuals can be holy, but a nation can. The institutions of the nation can be, as can its laws and traditions, its collective awareness as a community bound together in a common destiny. All this can be hallowed. And if we are suspicious of such claims, if we can remember the idolatry that the state and the collectivity have in the past and continue in the present to generate, we must be forgiven our suspicion because it is based on much bloody evidence. Yet, precisely because of the numerous idolatrous imitations of the concept of a holy nation, the possibility of a truly holy nation must be of special interest. Idolatry, the worship of a false god as the true God, is possible only because there is a true God who ought to be worshiped. That history is replete with instances of nations that have claimed a special relationship to God and have used that claim to justify their human ambitions does not rule out the possibility of genuine national election and a calling for being a holy nation. And even the fact that Israel also has not always been faithful to its calling as a holy nation does not annul its election nor in the slightest diminish the urgency of the demand laid upon it to become a holy nation through whom all the nations of the world will be blessed. Instead, it compels us to take national and historic existence seriously. It makes it impossible for us to withdraw to islands of redemption composed of select individuals who have banded together in a spiritual Noah's ark to sit out the calamity that is about to descend on the rest of humanity. We need only think of the people of the Qumran community who withdrew from the cities of Israel in the expectation of just such an apocalyptic holocaust. While there are elements in the teaching of Jesus which suggest an ambivalence toward the political activism of the tradition, in the final analysis Jesus did not leave the city for Qumran-like isolation but took his stand in Jerusalem where history was being made, where the spiritual power of Israel was in conflict with the temporal power of Rome.

We must now return to the question of the land. But we do so in the context of an understanding of the nature of the election of Israel. Were this election purely spiritual, were Israel a church instead of a people, it would not need a land. And because it is a unique people chosen by God to serve as the instrument of his redemption for all humankind, its relation to its land is unique. It was not born in the land but entered it as a fully mature people. It was expelled from its land and has continued to be a people after it was separated from its land. It is therefore not as bound to its land as other peoples are. It is, in a sense, an international people, not only because the exigencies of history have made it so but because its election takes place so that other peoples will be blessed through it (Gen. 12:3). Israel can therefore not be oblivious to the history of any people. But while all of this true, it is also true that Israel is not destined forever to remain without a land. The land is promised to it from the beginning when God appears to Abraham (Gen. 12:7) and says, "I give this land to your descendants." This promise, like so many of the other promises of God, is not immediately fulfilled. All the difficulties that faced the patriarchs, the suffering of Joseph, the slavery of Egypt, the wandering in the desert and the pain of the conquest of the land — all this intervenes between the promise and its fulfillment. Perhaps most importantly, the bad conscience of having to take the land away from those currently in possession of it intervenes between Israel and the land. Israel does not have its heart in the conquest. Time and again it performs an incomplete act of conquest, leaving intact this or that settlement, permitting itself to be fooled into a treaty of peace (Josh. 9) with those not to be appeased. But while all this intervenes between the promise and its fulfillment, the promise of God is not in vain. After a time, the wandering of Israel comes to an end. It gains possession of the land and settles into it. The land is inherited from the patriarchs and on it the descendants of the patriarchs now reside. It is the land on which the people of Israel practices the commandments pertaining to the land such as leaving it fallow every seventh year during which the orphan and widow have unlimited access to the produce of the earth. And above all, it is the land in which God takes his residence, in the Temple, in the Holy of Holies.

Fundamentally, God's residence is in the midst of the Jewish people. This is the community whose king God is, over which he exercises sovereignty. God, as we know, opposes the institution of monarchy in Israel because he is the ruler of this people. But because the people insist on a king, he acquiesces reluctantly. Nevertheless, God's kingship over Israel remains the preeminent institution of the Jewish polity, exercised by the prophets who never hesitate to call the king to task when so commanded by the real king of Israel, God. God's dwelling with the people he rules is typical of the God of Israel who enters the world and the affairs of human beings. While this people is forced to wander for forty years in the wilderness, God dwells in a portable tent which is carried from location to location, disassembled when the time comes to move and assembled again when the temporary resting place is reached. Once the people are permanently settled in the land, the place where Abraham was prepared to sacrifice his son becomes the temple mount, the place where Solomon builds his permanent temple as the spatial center of Judaism. Here Solomon dedicates the Temple and says:

> "O Lord who has set the sun in heaven
> but hast chosen to dwell in thick darkness,
> here have I built thee a lofty house,
> a habitation for thee to occupy for ever."
>
> (1 Kings 8:12)

Solomon is not unaware of the God of the philosophers: "But can God indeed dwell on earth? Heaven itself, the highest heaven, cannot contain thee; how much less this house that I have built!" (1 Kings 8:27). But he has built the house as "a habitation for thee to occupy forever," therefore, the answer to the question "can God indeed dwell on earth?" must be at least partly answerable with a "yes." God dwells in heaven. When the people of Israel sin and are exiled from their land, and "pray to thee, turning towards their land which thou gavest to their forefathers and towards this city which thou didst choose and this house which I have built in honor of thy name; then in heaven thy dwelling do thou hear their prayer and supplication, and grant their justice"

(1 Kings 8:48-49). While heaven is God's dwelling place — though this itself is problematic since "heaven itself, the highest heaven cannot contain thee" — in addition to heaven he also has an earthly dwelling place which is the city of Jerusalem, the Temple, the Holy of Holies. God therefore dwells in a particular place on earth which is the Temple in Jerusalem. This is God's address, in the midst of the people whose king he is and in whose holy city he dwells. It is of course necessary to mumble a formula of philosophic correction. No space can contain God, he is above space, etc., etc. But this mumbled formula, while required, must not be overdone. It must not transform the God of Israel into a spatial and meta-temporal Absolute, in short, into the god of the philosophers. With all the philosophic difficulties duly noted, the God of Israel is a God who enters space and time, who dwells in Jerusalem on the temple mount and therefore, by his presence, sanctifies the land of Israel beyond any other land on earth. There are, in fact, two spatial locations of God in the world. One of them — and the preeminent one — is the people of Israel. This indwelling is also to be understood, at least partially, in spatial terms. God dwells not only in the spirit of Israel, in their study and prayer and faith. He also dwells in their bodies, which are not excluded from the domain of the holy. The second spatial location of God in the world is the Temple in Jerusalem and therefore the land of Israel. Because of this dual indwelling of God in the people and the land, when the people of Israel is missing from its land, the land is incomplete. There is thus a triadic relationship: the indwelling of God, Israel, and the land.

We have thus reached the theological root of Israel's relationship to the land. The land of Israel is the land chosen for God's indwelling and for the indwelling of the people of God. When Israel sins, the divine indwelling in the people and in the land is diminished. God's presence, to some degree, is withdrawn from the people and the land. But never completely and never permanently. The divine presence remains with Israel and in the land, though it is now less visible, more obscured. The people is evicted from the land but here again, not completely and permanently. From 70 C.E. to the present, there always was a Jewish presence in the land, particularly in Jerusalem where Jews often constituted a majority of the population. Nevertheless, there is a withdrawal of the divine presence and of the presence of the Jewish people from the land, to last until the reconciliation of God, Israel, and the land, a reconciliation that God promises through the prophets of Israel.

In our time, the people of Israel has returned to its land. Was it justified in doing so? Does this return signal the beginning of the redemption promised by God or is it a human act of will resulting from impatience and the secularization of Jewish consciousness? These are difficult questions to answer and will ultimately be answered by history. But whatever the answer to these questions may be, they concern only the issue of whether we should have waited longer. But that sometime Israel will return to the land which it has been promised by God cannot be in question because God has so promised.

And if all this is true, then no claim to the land of Israel other than the Jewish claim is divinely validated. And this is so even if this was the wrong time to reestablish Jewish sovereignty and if, therefore, God is temporarily interposing another people between Israel and its land. The people who have come to dwell in the land during the estrangement of Israel from its land have been drawn into the vortex of a theological drama not of their making. Their pain must be felt by Israel and the compassion that is the deepest dimension of Jewish consciousness must be brought to bear on the problem. But none of this can obscure the eternal link between Israel and the land, a link that must, sooner or later, be reestablished.

I need only add that everything I have said has proceeded from the point of view of faith. Seen from the point of view of secular history, little of what I have said would retain much cogency. Whether a case for the Jewish right to Israel can be made apart from faith is another question. But Jews, Christians, and Muslims are people of faith and it is because of this crucial fact that the discussion can proceed.

# Reflections on the Six Day War
## after a Quarter Century

Jews around the world were euphoric after the Israeli victory in the Six Day War (June 1967), and even secular Jews found themselves speaking of the event in religious and even messianic terms. That summer, the journal *Tradition* invited several prominent Jewish thinkers from Israel and America to participate in a public symposium on the topic "The Religious Meaning of the Six Day War." Twenty-five years later, the journal invited the original participants to publish short reflections on the topic of their earlier conversation. Wyschogrod's reflections appear below.

Of the participants in the original symposium, Wyschogrod was the least willing to ascribe religious significance to the Six Day War. At the time, he warned, "It is necessary to proceed with caution, listening obediently to the Divine Word, rather than human emotion, and to the judgment of God on the affairs of men." He continued: "All events, as events, are equivocal. . . . Jewish faith is therefore not based on events as such, be they events that appear redemptive or those, such as the Holocaust, that seem to point to God's powerful anger with the people He loves above all other. Jewish faith is based on events as they are transformed by the Word of God from the realm of ambiguity to that of clarity. . . . Because we in our day do not have such a Word concerning the Six Day War we remain in the realm of ambiguity. . . . To tie the fate of Judaism to the fortunes of the State of Israel, for whose preservation and prosperity we all fervently pray, is simply unauthorized and therefore irresponsible. Along this path could lurk, God forbid, a catastrophe similar to those that was the fate of other messianic claims."

Twenty-five years later, Wyschogrod reaffirmed his earlier caution and went on to call for "a largely non-violent Zionism, a messianic Judaism that keeps alive the living expectation of the Messiah but also the messianic repudiation of violence." The original symposium appeared in *Tradition* 10:1 (Summer 1968): 5-20; the retrospective essays were published in *Tradition* 26:4 (Summer 1992): 24-25.

ALMOST A quarter century has passed since the 1968 symposium on the "The Religious Meaning of the Six Day War" in which I argued that events, as such, are always ambiguous and that it is only the prophetic word that provides an authoritative interpretation of events. It seemed to me that messianic claims with respect to the Six Day War were premature and to be treated with great caution. If anything, my wariness about messianic claims has grown.

It is not that messianism plays a minor role in my Judaism. The opposite is the case. Most of Orthodox Judaism is rooted in sacred history, in the revelation at Sinai and the authority of the past. Messianism is the open future, that which lies ahead and cannot be fully envisaged in the present. Messianism points to God's future intervention in history in the form of possibilities we cannot even imagine. It prevents us from sinking into the psychological rut of thinking that that there is nothing new under the sun, that the future will be like the past, that repetition is human destiny and that God has done and said everything important that he will ever do and say. Messianism tells us that we haven't seen anything yet because the God we worship is a living God who has a few tricks up his sleeve that will surprise us. Messianism is thus an essential complement to halakhic Judaism with its emphasis on the predictable and the established.

In recent years it has become clear to me that I stand for messianism without violence. I have deep sympathy for Gush Emunim but I have deep reservations about Gush Emunim's lack of discomfort with violence. Now I am not a pacifist. There are tragic situations in which violence cannot be avoided. But the shedding of human blood is a frightful enterprise and extreme measures have to be taken to prevent violence and injustice. I agree with Gush Emunim that the bond between the Jewish people and the land of Israel is eternal because it is rooted in God's promise of the land to the seed of Abraham. Jews therefore have a God-given right to live everywhere in the land, on either side of the Green Line.

But not every right must be exercised, especially if the cost is the shedding of human blood. On biblical grounds, the Arabs are wrong in objecting to Jewish settlement in Judea and Samaria. They should recognize the validity and cogency of the biblical word and welcome Jews as the rightful owners of the land. But they do not because their religion teaches them that the Hebrew Bible is a corruption of the true word of God which is to be found only in the Koran. And Arabs are not averse to violence.

So we have a choice. We can enforce our rights to the hilt and get sucked into more and more violence and killing or we can leave the enforcement of our rights to God while we deal with our misguided Ishmaelite cousins with love. Wrong and unjustified as they are, they are created in the image of God and if the only way we can obtain residence rights in Hebron is to become accustomed to shedding Arab blood, then we ought to opt for a less obvious form of messianism: non-violence. Nonviolence rather than residence in Hebron is the deepest layer of messianism. Apocalyptic stories about the wars of the end of days to the contrary notwithstanding, I cannot believe that the peaceable kingdom of the Messiah will be brought about by lethal strikes of the Israeli Air Force or the small arms fire of settlers in fear of their lives.

To repeat, I do not preach absolute non-violence under all circumstances. But I preach a high degree of non-violence, a hatred of violence, a love of the land combined with a high degree of non-violence, a largely non-violent Zionism, a messianic Judaism that keeps alive the living expectation of the Messiah but also the messianic repudiation of violence, a love of all human beings whether Jewish or non-Jewish, a willingness to wait and even temporarily yield territory if this will save us from bloodshed.

We may be on the verge of the messianic era but whether we are or not may depend on us. I simply cannot believe that the messianic era will be preceded by the reality of Jews becoming accustomed to killing. I find it much easier to believe that the messianic era will be preceded by the reality of Jews recognizing the image of God in all human beings, even those foolishly convinced that God did not promise the land to his people.

# The Revenge of the Animals

In this brief but memorable essay, Wyschogrod draws on rabbinic sources to cast unexpected light on the familiar opening chapters of Genesis, and proposes an intriguing answer to one of the Bible's enduring puzzles. Originally published in *Hören und Lernen in der Schule des Namens: Mit der Tradition zum Aufbruch*, Festschrift für Berthold Klappert zum 60. Geburtstag, ed. Jochen Denker et al. (Neukirchen-Vluyn: Neukirchener, 1999), pp. 23-25.

IN GENESIS 3:1 the serpent, who is characterized as "the shrewdest of all the wild beasts," poses the following question to Eve: "Did God really say: You shall not eat of any tree of the garden?" Eve replies that God had given her and Adam permission to eat of any tree except "the one in the middle of the garden" (v. 3) which may not be eaten or touched. Eve does not refer to the forbidden tree as "the tree of knowledge of good and bad," the term God had applied to it (2:17), and she broadens the divine prohibition to include touching in addition to eating. The serpent assures Eve that she will not die but "that as soon as you eat of it your eyes will be opened and you will be like divine beings who know good and bad" (v. 5). Immediately, Eve eats the fruit of the forbidden tree and gives her husband to eat.

It is clear that the serpent played a key role in causing Eve and Adam to sin.

It is not far-fetched to speculate that had the serpent not intervened, Eve and Adam would not have sinned. But who is the serpent and what motivated his intervention? The most common interpretation is that he is Satan.

But when the Bible speaks of Satan it does not hesitate to refer to him by that name (e.g., Job 1:6). The snake in Genesis seems to be a snake and even if he is Satan, why does he appear in the guise of a snake? I know of no other place in the Bible where an animal causes human beings to sin. Why does an animal play a decisive role in this, the most decisive of all sins?

The answer, it seems to me, is found in the verses just prior to those we have been discussing. In 2:18 we read: "The Lord God said, 'It is not good for man to be alone; I will make a fitting helper for him.'" This verse should have been followed by verse 21 where we are told of the deep sleep God cast over Adam during which he removes one of his ribs and shapes it into woman. The natural progression would have been verses 18, 21, 22, 23, and 24.

Verses 19 and 20 interrupt the smooth flow of the story. These two verses report that God formed the wild beasts and the birds of the sky out of the earth and presented them to Adam to be named. He did so but then we are told (v. 20): "But for Adam no fitting helper was found." It seems more was at stake here than just naming the animals. Verses 19 and 20 follow verse 18 where God determined that "it is not good for man to be alone; I will make a fitting helper for him." Having made this determination, God introduces the animals to Adam and requires of Adam that he name them, and "whatever the man called each living creature, that would be its name" (v. 19). Whatever the significance of this naming ceremony was, it concludes with the observation that "for Adam no fitting helper was found" (v. 20). It seems that God had expected that as Adam got to know (name) the animals, one of them would appeal to him and become his fitting helper. A rabbinic text (B. Talmud Yevamoth 63a) comments that Adam had sexual intercourse with all the animals but found no satisfactory mate among them. It is at this point that God decided to create another kind of mate for Adam.

About this new mate, Adam exclaims (v. 23):

"This one at last
Is bone of my bones
And flesh of my flesh.
This one shall be called Woman,
For from man was she taken."

The other animals were not proper helpers for Adam because they were not bone of his bone, flesh of his flesh. Because Eve is precisely what the animals are not, he can unite with her and "become one flesh" (v. 24). It seems that only that can become one flesh that originally was one flesh. While a certain level of friendship with animals is possible, this friendship cannot rise to the level of the union possible between two human beings. It is most curious, of course, that God did not know this all along. He apparently thought that one of the animals would prove a proper helper for Adam. Only when this proved not to be the case did he decide to create a human helper for Adam. Because this is so, our evaluation of the bond between humans and animals must rise. We can now understand better the companionship animals can provide human beings, a recognition strengthened by recent research on the beneficial effects of pets on old people living alone or in nursing homes.

Much of what I have said until now can be found, more or less, in ancient rabbinic sources. But I now want to connect the events at the end of Chapter 2 of Genesis with those at the beginning of Chapter 3. Why does the snake suddenly appear in Chapter 3 in the role of instigating Eve to sin? The answer is obvious. The feelings of the animals have been hurt. They wanted someone from their ranks to become Adam's helper but he did not accept any of them. Instead of an animal, Eve was chosen by Adam and the animals were furious. They chose the shrewdest among them to extract revenge by causing Eve and Adam to sin. The animals, the rejected lovers, punish the successful one, Eve. This also explains, to a degree, why the snake approaches Eve instead of Adam with his malevolent plan. While the animals are also angry at Adam, their primary enemy is Eve who has replaced them in Adam's affection. She must be made to pay for alienating Adam's affection.

For me, the most important lesson that emerges from all of this is a recognition of the proximity, from God's perspective, of human beings and animals. However great the gulf may seem from the human perspective, from the perspective of God who is infinitely above both humans and animals, the gulf is not as absolute as it seems to humans. It is, of course, true that only the human being was created in the image of God (1:26-27) which at the very least means that humans are closer to God than animals. But it does not mean that the gulf between humans and animals is as absolute as that between humans and God. Humans and animals are both finite creatures and while, in the final analysis, only woman is the proper companion of man, animals are also companions though less than fully satisfactory ones.

This comes to the fore most sharply in the question of whether human beings may eat animals. At first, God permitted human beings to eat plants only (1:29; 2:9). After the flood, God recognizes (8:21) that there is something ineradicably evil in man and it is then, apparently as a concession to his innately evil drive, that he permits the eating of animals (9:2-3). But this is circumscribed by a number of restrictions: some animals may be eaten and others not, some parts of animals may be eaten and others not, blood may not be eaten, and so on. It is as if, even in permitting human beings to eat animals,

God circumscribes this permission with so many restrictions that it is not easy to forget that animals were almost the proper companions for human beings and that they are much closer to us than those who eat meat without second thought might think.

Finally, I cannot help noticing that when God permits Noah to eat animals (9:2-3), he quickly speaks of the prohibition (9:5-6) to shed human blood. The danger in permitting humans to kill animals and eat them is, it seems, that they will slide into shedding human blood. If animals were absolutely different from humans, this danger would be minimal. But because they are not absolutely different, the danger is real and this prompts God to reiterate the prohibition against shedding human blood even as he permits the shedding of animal blood for dietary purposes. It is difficult to escape the conclusion that God would prefer a vegetarian humanity.

# Faith and the Holocaust

"Faith and the Holocaust" is a review of Emil Fackenheim's *God's Presence in History: Jewish Affirmations and Philosophical Reflections* (New York: New York University Press, 1970), a major early contribution to theological reflection on the Holocaust. There Fackenheim argued that the commanding word of Auschwitz is that "Jews are forbidden to hand Hitler posthumous victories!" That is, the Holocaust imposes on Jews a sacred obligation to survive. In his frequently cited reply, Wyschogrod takes issue with the idea that the Holocaust can provide a rationale for contemporary Jewish existence, characterizing the notion as "a kind of negative natural theology with the survival of the people, rather than the existence of God, as the conclusion." After the Holocaust as before, the sole viable basis for Jewish existence is revelation, which alone has the power to speak louder than the wholly destructive voice of Auschwitz. Originally published in *Judaism* 20:3 (Summer 1971): 286-294.

—————

SPEAKING OF the Holocaust, Emil Fackenheim writes in *God's Presence in History: Jewish Affirmations and Philosophical Reflections*: "Silence would, perhaps, be best even now, were it not for the fact that among the people the flood-gates are broken, and that for this reason alone the time of theological silence is irretrievably past."

The flood-gates are, indeed, broken and silence no longer surrounds the Holocaust. Whether it was the people who broke the flood-gates or whether it was a small number of Jewish writers who, in recent years, have not permitted the people to forget what many have very much wanted to forget, remains an open question. From their side, the Holocaust thinkers (Fackenheim, Eli Wiesel, and one or two others) have been driven above all by the terror that the people will forget, that the Holocaust will cease to be the central event of contemporary Jewish existence and become, instead, one memory among the many others that make up Jewish history. The people, for their part, have been ambivalent. On the one hand, they have certainly wanted to forget: Jewish life, after all, has not been transformed by the Holocaust, business continues as usual and time has shown once again that it heals all wounds — a fact for which men cannot help thanking God while recognizing the horror of the process when such wounds as the Holocaust are involved. On the other hand, the Jewish public has also wanted to remember: the reception accorded the writings of Eli Wiesel demonstrates the point. Whoever addresses Jewish audiences with any frequency can testify to the kind of charge generated when the Holocaust is mentioned. This is the one common experience of the Jewish people today, believing and unbelieving, learned and simple, young and old. Not to be addressed by the Holocaust is the one sure sign of exclusion from the Jewish people, it is the great divide that separates those in from those out. It is this ambivalence of forgetting and remembering that characterizes, it seems to me, the attitude of the people.

It was the philosopher Ludwig Wittgenstein who announced that concerning those matters of which we cannot speak we ought to remain silent. While, of course, he had nothing like the Holocaust in mind, it is difficult, as Fackenheim well understands, not to apply the rule of silence to it. The peril is blasphemy. In fact, it seems to me that nothing but blasphemy can be the result if we view the Holocaust from the human point of view. If we find ourselves continuing to believe in the biblical God after the Holocaust, we can neither forgive him nor love him. Or, following Richard Rubenstein, we blaspheme by denying the existence of the God of history and are driven into some form or other of atheism.

Fackenheim, for his part, has little sympathy for Rubenstein. He speaks (p. 71) of "the view of a 'radical' Jewish theologian who asserts that . . . the Midrashic framework is shattered by Auschwitz; the God of history is dead." Without mentioning Rubenstein's name in the body of the text (though he is identified in a footnote), Fackenheim calls him to task for having the temerity to speak: "What assures him (Rubenstein) of his capacities to deal with the trauma — or stills his fear that some other mechanism may cause him to utter words which should have never been spoken?" Fackenheim's lack of sympathy for Rubenstein's total rejection of the "for our sins are we punished" theology would make good sense if Fackenheim could see his way to embracing this standpoint, a standpoint which is, after all, not unhallowed by Jewish history. The fact of the matter, however, is that Fackenheim, too, finds it impossible to embrace the theology of "for our sins are we punished." As a response to Auschwitz, this doctrine, according to Fackenheim, "becomes a religious absurdity and even a sacrilege" (p. 73). Fackenheim buttresses this contention by reference to the work of N. N. Glatzer who had claimed, in his *Untersuchungen zur Geschichtslehre der Tannaiten,* that the "for our sins are we punished" view was rejected by the ancient rabbis, "perhaps not in response to the destruction of the Temple by Titus, but in response to the paganization of Jerusalem by Hadrian" (Fackenheim, p. 73). This being so, what is so dreadfully wrong with Rubenstein's rejection of the biblical God once he found himself rejecting the view that, in Hitler, Israel was once more feeling the scourge of God?

In the section of the book entitled "The Midrashic Framework and the Holocaust" (pp. 69-79), Fackenheim examines the various standpoints that attempt to deal with the Holocaust from within the circle of faith and finds them all lacking. He then examines "Jewish Secularism and the Holocaust" (pp. 79-84) and finds that Jewish secularism, in stubbornly persisting in its Jewish identity after the Holocaust, is also involved in a profound contradiction, because the logic of its position would dictate assimilation, a solution that would seem to be indicated by the cost of Jewish survival, especially in the twentieth century, but which the Jewish secularist nevertheless refuses to embrace. The two frameworks, the theological and the secular, from which the Holocaust can be approached are, therefore, rejected by Fackenheim, and this explains his dissatisfaction with Rubenstein to the extent that he reads Rubenstein as simply representative of the secular option. It should, however, be kept in mind that Fackenheim rejects with equal firmness the standpoint of simple faith, be this in the "for our sins are we punished" form or perhaps an even more simple faith which refers to the inscrutability of God's will. All these are inadequate. What then, is adequate?

Only obedience to the voice of Auschwitz. This voice, as heard by Fackenheim, commands the survival of Jews and Judaism. Because Hitler was bent upon the destruction of both, it is the duty of those Jews who survived Hitler to make sure that they do not do his work, that they do not, by assimilation, bring about the disappearance of what Hitler attempted but ultimately failed to destroy. For the religious Jew, this means that he must go on being religious, however inadequate Auschwitz has shown his frame of reference to be. And for the secular Jew, the voice of Auschwitz commands not faith, which even the voice of Auschwitz cannot command, but preservation of

Jews and Judaism. Speaking of the significance of the voice of Auschwitz for the secular Jew, Fackenheim writes: "No less inescapable is this Power for the secularist Jew who has all along been outside the Midrashic framework and this despite the fact that the Voice of Auschwitz does not enable him to return into this framework. He cannot return; but neither may he turn the Voice of Auschwitz against that of Sinai. For he may not cut off his secular present from the religious past: The Voice of Auschwitz commands Jewish unity" (pp. 88-89). The sin of Rubenstein is, therefore, that he permits Auschwitz further to divide the Jewish people at a time when survival is paramount if Hitler is not to be handed a posthumous victory, and survival demands unity. Because this is so, Rubenstein should presumably soft-pedal his doubts so as not to threaten the Jewish people at a time when everything must be secondary to the issue of survival.

What can be said about all this?

Since all criticism proceeds from a point of view, it would be best for me to state mine. I do not think that a voice can be extracted from the Holocaust which will speak to believer and non-believer alike. I do not think that the question of faith can be circumvented by means of Auschwitz. Finally, I do not think that Judaism can be given a new hold on life by means of Auschwitz. For me, the Holocaust was a totally destructive event which makes my remaining a Jew infinitely more difficult than it has ever been. I can only marvel at Fackenheim's effort to extract a positive result from the Holocaust, a kind of negative, natural theology with the survival of the people, rather than the existence of God, as the conclusion.

Let us first examine the contention that the voice of Auschwitz speaks to the secular Jew and commands him to adhere to his Jewishness so as not to hand Hitler a posthumous victory. At the risk of drawing simplistic analogies, it is necessary to examine the logic of the argument. Let us imagine that there arises a wicked tyrant who sets as his goal, for his own depraved and psychotic reasons, the extermination of all stamp collectors in the world. It is clear that it would be the duty of every decent person to do everything in his power to frustrate the scheme of that tyrant. Let us further imagine, however, that before the tyrant is made harmless, he succeeds, in fact, in murdering a large proportion of the world's stamp collectors. Does it now follow that subsequent to the tyrant's demise it becomes the duty of the remaining stamp collectors not to lose interest in their stamp collecting so as not to hand the tyrant a posthumous victory? Isn't there all the difference in the world between exterminating persons who wish to be stamp collectors just because they wish to be stamp collectors and the right of individuals or groups to lose interest in something they no longer wish to remain interested in? Would it be a posthumous victory for the tyrant were stamp collecting to disappear from the world as long as this disappearance is due, not to force, but to free choice? I cannot see why, if I am a secular, non-believing Jew, it is incumbent upon me to preserve Judaism because Hitler wished to destroy it. What was incumbent upon me was to destroy Hitler, but once this is accomplished, the free choice of every individual is restored and no further Hitler-derived burdens rest on the non-believing Jew.

It is, of course, true that there are secularist Jews who insist on remaining Jews even after the Holocaust. Fackenheim seems to be convinced that, if not for the voice of Auschwitz, these secularist Jews would have every reason to embrace assimilation in light of the price that Jewish existence extracts. The desire of some secularist Jews to remain Jews may be due, however, to the fact that they find positive value in remaining Jews independently of the Holocaust. Jewish secularism, with its national and ethnic identification, existed long before the Holocaust, when surely no voice from Auschwitz could be heard. In such circles, assimilation was resisted, partly because of a genuine and deep pride in the historic contribution of the Jewish people to civilization and, partly, I would think, because assimilation was never quite as possible as Fackenheim seems to think it was and is. And finally, there is the possibility that there is something slightly irrational about the desire to perpetuate Jewish existence when this desire is combined with secularist premises. To the believer, this can be taken to demonstrate that Jews remain in the service of God even in their state of disbelief and that forces deeper than those known to the individuals concerned shape Jewish existence. But all this is a far cry from turning this state of affairs into an ideology, which is precisely what Fackenheim attempts to do.

I have already termed Fackenheim's enterprise "negative natural theology," a phrase which deserves brief explanation. Traditionally, natural theology has been the enterprise whereby the existence of God is demonstrated on the basis of some rational evidence, without recourse to faith or revelation. Most commonly, the point of departure for such an attempt was some "positive" feature of the world as it appears to man: its order, its beauty, or its harmony. It was then argued that such characteristics could not be the result of pure chance and that it was, therefore, necessary to posit some all-powerful and rational being as the author or creator of a universe possessing the respective positive characteristics. Such an argument was presumably persuasive to the nonbeliever and could force him to concede the existence of an intelligent creator, all without having to leave the framework of reason with which we started.

Fackenheim's point of departure is, of course, the opposite of the "positive." Instead of being the order, beauty, harmony, or justice of the universe, it is a totally unique crime, unparalleled in human history. But once we get over this initial difference, similarities appear. In the positive version, a positive characteristic of the universe is noted and it is argued that no natural explanation for it is adequate. In negative natural theology, an evil is pointed out for which also, it is alleged, no natural explanation is possible. Of course, the conclusion in negative natural theology cannot be identical with that of positive natural theology, inasmuch as the problem of theodicy cannot here easily be ignored. Nevertheless, the conclusion which Fackenheim draws, the sacred duty to preserve the Jewish people, is the functional equivalent of the existence of God in positive natural theology, inasmuch as it becomes a total foundation for the continued existence of Judaism, a foundation as fully serviceable to the secularist as to the believer. One is almost driven to the conclusion that in the absence of the Holocaust, given Fackenheim's profound understanding of the irreversibility of the secular stance, no justification for the further survival of Judaism could have been found. With the Holocaust, amazing as this may appear, Judaism has gotten a new lease on life.

Because the Holocaust becomes, for Fackenheim, the fulcrum of his negative natural theology, he apparently finds it necessary to claim that it was, and remains, a unique event in human history. Strictly speaking, this is not necessary, since any sufficiently terrible negative event can become the foundation of a negative natural theology so long as it can be argued that it is not amenable to natural explanation. Nevertheless, it is understandable that an overwhelmingly terrible event such as the Holocaust would be even more useful if it could be demonstrated that in addition to everything else it was totally unique. Now this is precisely what Fackenheim maintains. According to him, the uniqueness of the Holocaust consists of the fact that there was no "rational" purpose in the crime. "Whole peoples," writes Fackenheim, "have been killed for 'rational' (however horrifying) ends such as power, territory, wealth, and in any case supposed or actual self-interest. No such end was served by the Nazi murder of the Jewish people" (p. 70). In a footnote, he adds: "I feel constrained to stress once again that I assert only that the Nazi genocide of the European Jews is unique, not that it is a greater or more tragic crime than all others. Thus, for example, the fate of the gypsies at the hand of the Nazis (itself an 'ideological' project) is at least in one sense more tragic — that no one seems to bother to commemorate them. Even this example of genocide, however, though itself a product of Nazi ideology, still differs from the Nazi genocide of European Jewry: no comparable hate propaganda was directed by the Nazis against the gypsies. Whence this groundless, infinite hate, indiscriminately directed against adults and children, saints and sinners, and so relentlessly expressed in action" (p. 100). What are we to make of this claim?

It would be rather beside the point, though not without logical force, to argue that, in one sense, all events are unique, since there can be no event which does not have at least one characteristic not shared by any other event — if only its exact place and time of occurrence. In another sense of the word "unique," no event is unique for there is no event which does not share at least one characteristic with at least one other event — if only the fact that both are events. This being so, it might not be altogether unreasonable to expect some discussion of the sense of the word "unique" in such a vehement claim by a philosopher of the uniqueness of an event. Even so, the issue far transcends such relatively technical considerations. The crux of the matter is a moral one.

Although, as we have seen, Fackenheim restricts himself to the claim that the Holocaust was a unique crime and not that it was a greater or more tragic crime than all the others, the claim of uniqueness reflects an existential fact: that for Fackenheim the focus of his life is the destruction of European Jewry and not the extermination of the gypsies or of the residents of Hiroshima in World War II, the Armenians in World War I or the illiterate peasants of Vietnam in the recent past. In some way, the fate of European Jewry is for Fackenheim in a class by itself, having an existential significance for him that these other horrors do not have. We will soon have to ask why this is so or, perhaps, more to the point, what justification Fackenheim can offer for this being so. It is not to be expected that the obvious reply, namely, that since Fackenheim is a Jew he is more reached by the fate of Jews than by that of others, will satisfy either Fackenheim or his critics. Fackenheim's insistence on the uniqueness of the Holocaust indicates that he feels constrained to justify his preoccupation on grounds other than simple ethnic or national partiality. And he feels constrained to justify his preoccupation because he senses an accusation in the air, an accusation emanating from those who present themselves as equally reached by the death of any child, be he in Warsaw or Biafra, in 1943 or 1970. To this sensibility, such dwelling on a catastrophe of the past is an evasion of the crime — as they see it — being committed today about which something can still be done but about which Fackenheim does not write books and articles. For such people, the ultimate object of reverence is man wherever he appears, rather than just "one's own," which is the light in which they see Fackenheim's enterprise.

It is at this point that Holocaust theology as practiced by Fackenheim finds itself on the defensive. At this point, it is essential to be scrupulously honest. It is necessary to admit that we are fixated on the Holocaust to an extent quite unacceptable in a universalistic framework. The moral force of those who cannot share this fixation must be recognized. It is, I believe, necessary to abandon the attempt to find "objective" criteria in accordance with which such a fixation on the Holocaust will be made plausible, simply because any and all such criteria bestow uniqueness on the Holocaust at the expense of diminishing the other occasions of human suffering. To argue that one is asserting only the uniqueness of the Holocaust and not that it is a greater or more tragic crime than all others, simply won't do because the uniqueness which is asserted ("groundless, infinite hate indiscriminately directed against adults and children, saints and sinners, and so relentlessly expressed in action") turns out to be morally decisive and not just an attribution of abstract uniqueness. It is necessary to recognize that, from any universally humanistic framework, the destruction of European Jewry is one notable chapter in the long record of man's inhumanity against man, a record which compels the Holocaust to resign itself to being, at most, a first among equals.

If we therefore remain fixated on the Holocaust it must be for another reason. It is true that the Holocaust is our catastrophe and one is entitled to mourn more intensely for the death of a relative than for that of another. But this consideration cannot have ultimate significance. On the psychological plane such partiality is understandable: on the final, moral plane, all men enjoy the same dignity as my relatives and it therefore follows that crimes against them cannot be qualitatively different from those against others.

To justify Emil Fackenheim's and my fixation with the Holocaust, I must resort to theology. To make clear my meaning, I must recount an episode that I witnessed quite recently.

A devout Catholic philosopher of my acquaintance returned from Mass one Sunday morning in a state of agitation. Some progressive members of the parish had removed the crucifix from its usual position and substituted for it a contemporary crucifix on which, instead of the suffering Jesus, there was affixed a collage depicting suffering Vietnamese men, women, and children. My friend was outraged. "How can they," he asked, "equate human suffering with the suffering of the Incarnate Son, a person of the Godhead?" I had no doubt of his deep and genuine compassion for the suffering of man, wherever and whenever it occurs. But it was only the suffering of the Son of God at Golgotha that, he argued, redeemed the sins of the world and healed the suffering of man. To substitute the suffering of man for this saving event was to confuse man with God, something that benefits neither.

Must we not say something at least somewhat similar if we are to remain really honest? The fate of Israel is of central concern because Israel is the elect people of God through whom God's redemptive work is done in the world. However tragic human suffering is on the human plane, what happens to Israel is directly tied to its role as that nation to which God attaches his name and through which he will redeem man. He who strikes Israel, therefore, engages himself in battle with God and it is for this reason that the history of Israel is the fulcrum of human history. The suffering of others must, therefore, be seen in the light of Israel's suffering. The travail of man is not abandoned, precisely because Israel suffers and, thereby, God's presence is drawn into human history and redemption enters the horizon of human existence.

Can we deny that all this must be a scandal in the eyes of non-belief? Can we expect the non-believer to concede that somehow the fate of Israel is more central, more decisive, more important than the fate of any other people? We cannot and must not expect this; we must learn to live with the knowledge that there is an abyss between belief and non-belief, that for non-belief Auschwitz is a member of a large and tragic class of human evil whose voice, if it commands anything, commands men to struggle against evil and injustice wherever perpetrated. When we observe the Holocaust fading from the consciousness of men, as it inevitably will, when we observe it fading to some extent even from the consciousness of our young, we must be neither surprised nor outraged. To remember is not, after all, the really natural inclination of man. Were this not so, the Torah would not find it necessary to command the remembering of the Amalekite assault on Israel. The Torah commands it precisely because it is natural for man to forget, for memories to fade, for emotions to be calmed and for wounds to heal. The Torah commands remembering because only a believing community can transcend time, can fixate on events of very limited "historic" significance (how "significant" was the exodus to the ancient world whose records never mention it?) and find in them the significance of a redemption history apparent only to the eyes of faith. For believing Israel, the Holocaust is not just another mass murder but, perhaps, the final circumcision of the people of God. But how else, except by the power of God, can anyone believe that?

One final word about the theology of Emil Fackenheim. Israel's faith has always centered about the saving acts of God: the election, the exodus, the Temple, and the Messiah. However more prevalent destruction was in the history of Israel, the acts of destruction were enshrined in minor fast days while those of redemption became the joyous proclamations of the Passover and Tabernacles, of Hannukah and Purim. The God of Israel is a redeeming God; this is the only message we are authorized to proclaim, however much it may not seem so to the eyes of non-belief. Should the Holocaust cease to be peripheral to the faith of Israel, should it enter the Holy of Holies and become the dominant voice that Israel hears, it could not but be a demonic voice that it would be hearing. There is no salvation to be extracted from the Holocaust, no faltering Judaism can be revived by it, no new reason for the continuation of the Jewish people can be found in it. If there is hope after the Holocaust, it is because to those who believe, the voices of the Prophets speak more loudly than did Hitler, and because the divine promise sweeps over the crematoria and silences the voice of Auschwitz.

# Franz Rosenzweig's
# The Star of Redemption

A significant form of Wyschogrod's literary activity over the years has been the book review. Of the several dozen he has written, none sheds more light on Wyschogrod's own thought than that devoted to Franz Rosenzweig's *The Star of Redemption* on the occasion of the *Star*'s first appearance in English translation. Touching on philosophy, theology, and the relation of Judaism and Christianity, the review is an invaluable resource for understanding Wyschogrod's relation — both appreciative and critical — toward perhaps the greatest Jewish religious thinker of the twentieth century. The review originally appeared in *Man and World* 6, no. 1 (February 1973): 100-107.

The review originally appeared in *Man and World* 6, no. 1 (February 1973): 100-107.

—◈◈◈—

WRITTEN PARTLY on army postal cards from the Balkan front in 1918 where Franz Rosenzweig was serving with a German anti-aircraft unit, completed, after his return from the front, in his native Cassel, *The Star of Redemption* has been for many years a legend in the English-speaking world. Relatively short excerpts from it appeared in Nahum N. Glatzer's *Franz Rosenzweig: His Life and Thought* in 1953 but that book served more as an introduction to Rosenzweig's life than his thought. The result was that religiously inclined Jewish intellectuals in this country knew Rosenzweig as a life more than as a thinker. Coming at a time, after World War II, when many Jews found themselves reexamining their Jewish origins and the possible meaning of Judaism for their lives, Rosenzweig appeared as the paradigmatic example of the Jew who, deeply rooted in Western enlightenment thought, rediscovers the faith

121

of his fathers, acquaintance with which had been denied him by his assimilated home.

The story of Rosenzweig's life is a particularly concentrated version of this scenario. He was born in 1886 in Cassel, Germany, as the only son of a well-to-do, assimilated Jewish family. In 1912 he received his doctorate for a dissertation on Hegel's political thought which appeared in 1920 as *Hegel und der Staat*. This book was extremely well received in German academic circles and a university career in philosophy seemed to beckon the young scholar. But this was not destined for realization. Starting in 1911, Rosenzweig made the acquaintance of Eugen Rosenstock-Huessy, a man deeply learned in jurisprudence, sociology, and history, who was also a deeply believing Protestant Christian. For Rosenzweig, this friendship came at a time when the religious dimension had become more and more his primary concern. Indications are that Rosenzweig was on the verge of conversion to Christianity except that some deep instinct persuaded him that he "could turn Christian only qua Jew," i.e., by remaining loyal to Judaism during the period of preparation and up to the moment of baptism. Faithful to this condition, Rosenzweig attended a Day of Atonement service at a traditional synagogue in Berlin in October 1913. It apparently changed his life. Later, he was to write: "Anyone who has ever celebrated the Day of Atonement knows that it is something more than a mere personal exaltation (although this may enter into it) or the symbolic recognition of a reality such as the Jewish people (although this also may be an element), it is a testimony to the reality of God which cannot be controverted." From this point on, conversion to Christianity became an impossibility. In a letter written on October 31 of that year, while acknowledging that to the Christian no one can reach the Father save through the "Lord," he claims "the situation is quite different for one who does not have to reach the Father because he is already with him." At the same time, his interest in an academic career in philosophy disappeared. In a letter to his philosophy teacher, Friedrich Meinecke, Rosenzweig wrote: "In 1913, something happened to me for which collapse is the only fitting name. Suddenly I found myself on a heap of wreckage, or rather I realized that the road I was then pursuing was flanked by unrealities." He added: "My life has fallen under the rule of a 'dark drive' [a term Meinecke had used in his letter to Rosenzweig] which I am aware that I merely name by calling it 'my Judaism. . . .'"

Rosenzweig devoted the rest of his life to his Judaism. With Martin Buber, he worked on a remarkable translation of the Hebrew Bible into German. He headed the "Lehrhaus" in Frankfurt which he conceived as an adult education center where Jews could rediscover their origins. He became one of the great personalities of German Jewry, heroically fighting his neurological paralysis, which he first noticed in 1922 and which, until his death at the end of 1929, progressively reduced his control over his body. During the last several years of his life, when he could no longer turn the pages of a book, write, or speak, he continued to work by dictating to his wife and by the use of various devices specifically designed for him. During these years, daily services were held in his room. Those who were present speak of the joy that shone from his eyes when, from his bed and in words almost indistinguishable, he recited the blessing over the Torah. He died a faithful Jew, spared the ultimate agony of German and European Jewry that lay ahead.

Because of the dimension assumed by the Rosenzweig life story, it is difficult to read the *Star of Redemption* in its own light, divorced from its setting in Rosenzweig's life. Now that the work is available in an excellent English translation, the effort must be made to evaluate the work on its own terms, uninfluenced by whatever admiration we may have for its author as a human being and a Jew. It may turn out that the man is much greater than his writings. In that case, it will help in balancing the scale against all those instances in which the man behind the writings has turned out to be far inferior as a human being.

The *Star of Redemption* is a highly written book, i.e., a book that seems to have taken shape in the process of writing. To some extent, of course, this is true of all writing. However well thought out a writer's ideas may be, they receive concrete existence in the act of writing and in this process of incarnation they may assume a form often quite surprising to the writer. Nevertheless, in the majority of instances the brush strokes, as it were, are largely imperceptible in the final product. Not so in the case of Rosenzweig. The style is rhetorical, almost asking to be read aloud. In the *Church Dogmatics* of Karl Barth this effect is attributed both to the fact that Barth was a superb preacher as well as to the central role occupied by preaching the Word of God, by proclamation, in his theology. In the case of Rosenzweig the rhetorical effect of the work is also not simply accidental. It is connected, it seems to me, with the stance Rosenzweig adopts toward philosophy. The case of death can serve as an example. Philosophy, he argues, is out of touch with the realities of human life. While man trembles before the reality of death, philosophy, with strained equanimity, proclaims the eternity of the All, a fact which it offers as consolation to the death-threatened individual. Exposing the hollowness of such a sham consolation pushes the writer into a rhetorical stance because the weapons that present themselves naturally in such an enterprise are rhetorical weapons: irony, sarcasm, indignation, etc. In the case of Kierkegaard, whom Rosenzweig had read, the prevalence of such techniques as irony and sarcasm is well known. They are not absent in Rosenzweig either but they are less prominent than a generally declamatory style combined with the full arsenal of German philosophical terminology wielded with great enthusiasm. In addition, Rosenzweig is a highly allusive writer. Frequently, the reader feels that he somehow misses the exact meaning of a sentence or paragraph because the writer is alluding to some text or concept which he does not explicitly mention but which was in his mind as he wrote and knowledge of which would clarify matters instantly. The translation under discussion appends an index of nine pages which is very helpful in fathoming the Jewish allusions. There is no such index for the large number of other allusions.

The argument of the *Star of Redemption* is an exercise in Jewish philosophy. For Rosenzweig there are two trilogies which sum up the Jewish stance: God, Man, and the World is one of these, and Creation, Revelation, and Redemption the other. Divided into three parts, the first two parts, or approximately two-thirds, of the book, are devoted to a detailed examination of these two trilogies. Here there is relatively little explicit mention of Judaism though, of course, the very trilogies under discussion reveal the underlying Judaism. The third part of the book, entitled "The Configuration, or the Eternal Hyper-Cosmos," is a full-blown exposition of Judaism centered around Jewish liturgy and the Jewish festivals. Reading the book is like listening to some complex tone poem in which a theme struggles to emerge. At first it is lost among the many other themes and variations, itself appearing only in vestigial or embryonic form. Gradually, as it is better defined, it gains ascendancy until it bursts forth in full Wagnerian splendor. It is thus that the Judaism of the *Star* fares. The most striking and significant fact about this whole process is that whereas the first two sections of the work, suggestive and learned as they are, are also deeply murky, the third or explicitly Jewish section of the book is incomparably clearer. There is almost an experience of emergence into the light, an exodus into a promised land where the sun shines and speech need not be by allusion, where the names of things have been discovered. In the pre-Jewish (comparatively speaking, of course) sections of the book there is almost a will against clarity, as if the forces being struggled against cannot be properly taken hold of, slipping out of one's hands just when something definite is identified. I could not help thinking of Jacob (Gen. 32:24-30) wrestling with the unknown man in the dark, who, with the appearance of the dawn, begged to be released, apparently because he could not exist in the light. Jacob extracts a blessing from his opponent but neither has prevailed as the morning dawns. It must be added that it is as a result of this struggle that Jacob becomes Israel.

If there is a will against clarity in the pre-Jewish portions of the book, by no means must this be interpreted as a rejection of philosophy. Were

Rosenzweig's attitude more Barthian, were there a clear division in his mind between the truths of philosophy and those of theology, it is quite possible — though, of course, one can only speculate — that the result would have been far less clouded. Barth, after all, is quite able to give philosophy its due precisely because its results need not be continuous with theology. The philosophical terrain does not therefore have to be landscaped to conform with the edifice with which it is destined to coexist. In the case of Rosenzweig, on the other hand, the thrust of a corrected philosophy is seen as embedding the Judaism into friendly terrain from which it can take some sustenance, even if it never becomes totally dependent on its philosophic soil. In the case of Rosenzweig there is nothing secret about this since the Judaism of the work as a whole cannot possibly be missed by anyone. For Emmanuel Levinas, the French Jewish phenomenologist greatly influenced by Rosenzweig, things are not quite that open. His major work, *Totalité et infini* (*Totality and Infinity,* Pittsburgh, 1969), is a sustained ethical metaphysics deeply Jewish in intention, but conducted as an exercise in phenomenological philosophy, it presumably being a happy coincidence that the net result is a sort of Judaism in philosophic idiom. While the reader of Levinas's work is never told of the Jewish energies of the project, Rosenzweig hides nothing. Nevertheless, the first two-thirds of the work have an atmosphere of a generalized philosophic religious sensibility rooted much more in universal religious experience than in biblical or even rabbinic documents. In these portions of the work, the term "soul" occurs frequently, finding its way in one case even into a section heading as in "Revelation, or the Ever Renewed Birth of the Soul." It is, of course, the atmosphere of German romantic philosophy that we are meeting here, not the robust anthropological monism of the Bible which does not separate man into body and soul, with the seat of the religious being the latter.

The fundamental question raised by the pre-Jewish portion of the *Star* is therefore whether such an approach is good philosophy or good Judaism or possibly neither. As Rosenzweig sees it, the central idea that holds philosophy together, the idea that has now been shattered, is the idea of the All. First and foremost, the All is philosophy's answer to death. While man is terrified of death "philosophy deceived him . . . by weaving the blue mist of its idea of the All about the earthly. For indeed, an All would not die and nothing would die in the All. Only the singular can die and everything mortal is solitary" (p. 4). This cure works only so long as the individual is willing to give up his point of view and substitute for it that of the All. But if he is not willing to do this, if he insists on the right to his individuality and resists absorption into the All, then "man became a power over philosophy — not man in general over philosophy in general, but one man, one very specific man over his own philosophy. The philosophy ceased to be a negligible quantity for his philosophy" (pp. 9-10). Man had become master of philosophy instead of philosophy being master over him. Rosenzweig applies this consistently for being, logic, and ethics. For each of these, he develops the corresponding meta-: metaphysics, metalogic, and metaethics. The metaversion of each of these is that version which does not absorb its domain into a unified whole but, instead, leaves a discrepancy between object and subject. "The metaethical in man makes man the free master of his ethos so that he might possess it and not vice versa. The metalogical in the world makes the logos a 'component' of the world entirely emptied into the world, so that it might possess the logos and not vice versa. Just so the metaphysical in God makes physics a 'component' of God. God has a nature of his own, quite apart from the relationship into which he enters, say, with the physical 'world' outside himself" (p. 17). Elsewhere he adds: "Metaethical, too, was of course not intended to mean a-ethical. It was not meant to express absence of ethos but solely its unaccustomed placement, that is to say that passive position instead of the imperative one to which it was otherwise accustomed. The law is given to man, not man to the law. This proposition is demanded by the new concept of man. It runs counter to the concept of law as it appears in the realm of the world as ethical reasoning and ethical order. Accordingly, this concept of man has to be characterized as metaethical" (p. 14). Rosenzweig's purpose is to drive a wedge into the tight philosophy originating with Parmenides and retained in varying degrees by philosophers like Plato, Plotinus, Spinoza, Leibniz, Hegel, and others. The concepts around which such philosophy clusters are: the one, the necessary, identity, eternity, the universal, the identity of logos and being, etc. Rosenzweig's aim is to open this solidity to the contingent, the temporal, the individual, the historical. In his philosophy, God, man, and the world are not absorbed into each other but retain their individuality instead of being derived one from another by some emanation-like process. In so doing, he lays the philosophical groundwork for his Judaism.

The question that must then be posed is whether this explosion of the tight Parmenidian universe is something that happens immanently or whether it is fractured from the outside. Is there something in the logic of Parmenides' case that is flawed, or is it revelation that breaks into this tight circle and pries it apart? Is Rosenzweig asserting that the tight universe is poor philosophy which can be refuted on its own ground or is there something from the outside, the word of God, which shatters its unity? These questions deserve an answer because we do not understand Rosenzweig fully if we cannot answer them.

It is quite clear that Rosenzweig cannot be read in a Barthian light. For

Rosenzweig, the security of philosophy is not shattered by something foreign to it, something for which it is not prepared and which it did not expect. The pre-Jewish portion of the *Star*, quantitatively the largest part of the book, is a bridge to his Judaism, the process by which someone rooted in the totalism of German idealism, the philosophy of All, is made ready for Judaism by a recognition of the shortcomings of the totalistic position. While it is true that Judaism is a presence in the pre-Jewish portion of the book, it is also true that it is a somewhat veiled presence, its categories appearing, as it were, in translation, expressed in a universalistic vocabulary. There is a polemic against the philosophy of All such as could not be conducted by Barth. In fact, Barth takes pains to emphasize the internal coherence and human adequacy of those philosophies which revelations supplant because, in the absence of the event that is the word of God, man is so deeply sunk in his error that he does not even suspect that he lacks the truth. It is quite otherwise with Rosenzweig. The inadequacy of the philosophy of All is demonstrated in considerable detail, page after page, section after section. And yet it is not internally refuted. It is refuted as being inadequate to the human condition so that it is really man who shatters the philosophy of All and not pure reason. It is man who asserts dominance over philosophy and makes himself master of the law. Man rejects philosophy's solution to his fear of death as unsatisfactory, a sham solution. It is in some sense the human condition that philosophy does not adequately understand. But which man is Rosenzweig talking about? The human condition as interpreted by what tradition discovers the inadequacy of philosophical totalism?

At first sight, it might be thought that Rosenzweig has a notion of man as such, independent of historical particularity. To some extent this is undoubtedly the case, especially in the pre-Jewish portion of the work. His constant reference to the soul leaves the reader with the impression that the author is mapping the morphology of religious man. Heidegger after all builds, or attempts to build, an ontology on his notion of abstract man, named by him *Dasein*, who has nothing historically specific, not even a sex, for that matter. While Heidegger's man is afflicted with anxiety, projected into temporality and capable of authenticity, Rosenzweig's man, it might be argued, has a more religious bent and it is about him that we read in the *Star*. But, in the final analysis, this is hardly a tenable possibility. This is so for two reasons. The first, and for our purposes the less important, is the difficulty that haunts Heidegger's *Dasein* and must therefore also apply to Rosenzweig's abstract man, if that in fact is the man he is talking about. I am referring to the inconsistency that is involved when a philosopher whose basic purpose is to liberate man from the universalizing and objectifying categories of traditional philosophy finds himself positing some universal human nature which, he alleges, resists such universalization but which is being universalized in that very process. In the case of Heidegger it emerges when, for example, he distinguishes between the death of others and my death, and then transforms "my death" into the commonly held heritage of the race which the philosopher can analyze and weave into his notion of man. It emerges equally when a philosopher, for whom the historical is as vital a dimension of man as it is for Heidegger, seems to ignore the possibility that the portrait he draws of man may not be of man in general but the man of Freiburg of 1922 or whatever other place and time it may be. To put the same point in a slightly different way, how can Rosenzweig be so certain that the consolation for death offered by philosophy, a consolation which he finds so eminently unsatisfactory, is inherently unsatisfactory to man? It seems to have worked for Socrates whose equanimity in the face of death is a sharp contrast to the more Jewish death of Jesus of Nazareth, with its immense agony and grief. The choices that civilizations make are diverse as are those of individuals. To build a philosophy on some stable entity called man is a risky undertaking.

But for Rosenzweig there is a second and more important reason for not positing such a man. It has to do with his Judaism and particularly with his understanding of it. What is the relation between Jew and man? Is Judaism a set of ideas which is offered to man and which man can accept or reject as he does all other ideas? What is the relation between Judaism and Jews? What is the mystery of Israel? These are the questions which are at the heart of the final third of the *Star*, the Jewish portion. Speaking of the Jew, Rosenzweig writes: "His belief is not in something: he is himself the belief. He is believing with an immediacy which no Christian dogmatist can ever attain for himself" (p. 342). Across the centuries, the charge of tribalism has never been silenced. The Christian faith is open to all men who can believe that God gave his son for the sins of mankind, that Jesus was born, crucified, and that he rose on the third day. The church is thus catholic because the New Israel is an Israel of the spirit instead of the flesh. Israel, whatever else it may also be, and it is many other things, is first and foremost a commmunity of family, of kinship, of descent from Abraham, of blood communion. "There is only one community," writes Rosenzweig, "in which such a linked sequence of everlasting life goes from grandfather to grandson, only one which cannot utter the 'we' of its unity without hearing deep within a voice that adds: 'are eternal.' It must be a blood community, because only blood gives present warrant to the hope for a future." There is therefore no idea that encompasses Israel because Israel is, as it were, an idea incarnated in the flesh of a people. The contrast between baptism and circumcision defines the difference. The one is water, symbol of the spirit, leaving no external change but an internal transformation. The other is a cutting into the flesh, the organ of generation, leaving a permanent mark in the flesh of a people that thereby embraces the covenant with its flesh.

If God's covenant is with a biological people, the seed of Abraham according to the flesh, then history is fully brought within the circumference of redemption because history deals not with individuals or ideological groupings but nations constituted by descent or common territory. It is true that while other nations grow out of soil, loss of which equals loss of nationhood, Israel is made into a nation prior to its entry into its land and, unlike all other nations, it can live after it is banished from its soil until it returns to the land which it was given. Nevertheless, the relation of the Jewish people to its land and language is altogether different from that of Christianity. Though Christianity's central focus has consistently been on the life, death, and resurrection of Jesus of Nazareth, no major Christian group has ever made the soil which Jesus walked the geographic center of the Church. Similarly, though it is universally agreed that Jesus' language was Aramaic, the Church did not preserve the words of its savior in the language in which he spoke them but in Greek translation. From this, the Roman Church moved to Latin and in recent years we have seen the almost total disappearance of Latin from the liturgy of the Roman Church. All this would be inconceivable for Israel.

The attachment of the Jewish people to the land of Israel and to the language of the Bible is such that, to take but one example, the revival of Hebrew as a spoken language, which occurred during the first several decades of the twentieth century, is unprecedented in the annals of dead languages, none of which has ever been raised from the dead (the efforts in the case of Gaelic are well known, as is their failure). It is not possible within the confines of a review to develop fully Rosenzweig's view of the Jewish people, the topic that occupies the third part of the *Star*. It will however be amply clear already that Rosenzweig is very much aware of the extent to which Judaism is incarnated in the Jewish people which preserves its history in its faith. It is for this reason that no generalized philosophy of religious "man" can adequately serve as propaedeutic to the faith of Israel. With the election of Abraham, a series of events is set in motion which, in a sense, shatters the unity of the human race and with it, as Rosenzweig seems to grasp quite clearly, the authority of any universal ethics before which all men, as rational beings, are equal. The election of Israel cannot be digested by any philosophy nor, for that matter, can any philosophy lay the ground for such an event. The absence of an emphasis on ethics in the *Star* must be seen as a sign of Rosenzweig's understanding that the ethicization and universalization of Judaism which had become the specialty of Western-oriented, German liberal Judaism had outlived its usefuless and that a time had come for a new beginning. The *Star of Redemption* is a beginning which has really never been continued. Since its publication, much has happened, both to the world and the Jews. It is good that this book is finally available to the English reader.

# A Jewish Death in Heidelberg

Love, death, and the mystery of election are central themes in this true and previously unpublished story in which only the names of participants have been changed. The story recounts the drama that ensued upon the death of "Franz Redner," a Jewish Holocaust survivor who taught Hebrew and Yiddish for many years on the Theological Faculty at the University of Heidelberg. When Redner's Christian friends sought to bury him according to his wishes alongside the ashes of a gentile woman in a Christian cemetery, Redner's Jewish acquaintances objected. Unexpectedly, Michael Wyschogrod came to play a central role in how the matter was resolved.

ALL DURING the month of June it was cold and rainy in Heidelberg. But on the first day of July the sun came out and after that it never rained again. After a week of sunshine, nobody remembered the cold and rain of June. It had turned into a lovely European summer, the kind without the unbearable heat of New York. Week after week, it was warm and invigorating, conducive both to suntanning and to getting work done.

A new College of Jewish Studies had opened in Heidelberg the year before. It was the first Jewish institution of higher learning in Germany since the Nazi years and it had begun to operate the previous fall. Since there were very few Jewish scholars left in Germany, the decision was made to start with a faculty of visiting lecturers. I had agreed to come immediately after the conclusion of my semester in New York. The German summer semester ended in the middle of July so I was able to pick up half a semester by arriving toward the end of June. The semester in Heidelberg had now ended but I stayed on for several weeks to tie up loose ends. Edith and I had also wanted to spend several days in Strasbourg. We were going to take a 10:30 train that Friday morning so I stopped off early at the College to pick up mail. We had our weekend luggage with us and were going to the station from the College.

It was then that I first heard the name of Franz Redner. Someone said that Redner had died the day before and somehow I learned (I do not now remember from whom) that he had taught Yiddish and Hebrew at the Theological Faculty of Heidelberg University. While the College of Jewish Studies was not part of the University, it had close relations with it. Our courses could be taken for credit by the students of the University and our students had to take a minor at the University. I had met many faculty members of the University but not Redner. That Friday morning, the news of his death did not make much of an impression on me.

We left Strasbourg early Sunday morning for Frankfurt. Edith was returning to New York and I accompanied her to the airport. The check-in went smoothly and Edith was boarded by early afternoon. I spent several hours walking around a Sunday-empty Frankfurt and then I took the train to an equally Sunday-stricken Heidelberg. I ate, went for a walk along the Neckar River, and read for several hours. By eleven, I was asleep.

Because I had only nine more days left in Heidelberg, I made sure to get to the College early next morning. There was a paper I had to finish, any number of letters to write and phone calls to return, so I had no time to waste. I had an early breakfast and was at the College by 9:15. But as soon as I had climbed the two flights of stairs to the office of the College, I knew something was up.

I noticed that there were no students around. The office was located in an apartment on the third floor of a three-hundred-year-old building. The nerve center of the College was a medium-sized room in which there were two desks facing each other, belonging respectively to the Rektor and Pro-Rektor of the College. The room also had an old sofa, several chairs, and some bookcases with books in them. The door to this room was generally open and students and faculty drifted in and out. The Rektor and Pro-Rektor conducted business in a charmingly chaotic way, giving the institution a warmly Jewish family feeling. But this morning the door to the room was closed.

I asked Miss Steuermacher, the secretary, whether Prof. Guttenberg was in. She said that he was conducting a meeting with some faculty and students. She explained that since my last visit to the College on Friday morning, something of a crisis had arisen. It had to do with Redner, about whose death I had heard on Friday. It seemed that some Christian friends of his were determined to have him buried in the Christian cemetery of a small town near Heidelberg. The Heidelberg rabbi was away on vacation and therefore Prof. Guttenberg had tried to intervene. But so far, he had failed. The funeral was scheduled for four o'clock that afternoon. First, a memorial service would be held in the chapel of the cemetery, conducted by the members of the Heidelberg Theological Faculty, and he would be buried immediately thereafter. The few Jews left in Heidelberg during this vacation period were frantically trying to reverse the arrangements. That is, Miss Steuermacher told me, what the meeting was about.

I knocked on the door and entered the room. There were fewer than ten persons in the room and they were agitated. Idiomatic German was flying back and forth in great volume and at high speed. It took me a little time to discover that the facts as reported by Miss Steuermacher were essentially correct. Gradually, the picture became clearer. Redner was a Polish Jew who had come to Germany in the early thirties to study medicine. When Jews were expelled from the universities, his studies came to an end and in 1938 he was arrested and sent to Dachau. From there he made the round of camps, including Auschwitz, until his liberation in 1945. As soon as he had his strength, he proceeded to Heidelberg to continue his medical studies which he completed in a few years. But for some unexplained reason, he never practiced medicine. Instead, he started teaching, at first Hebrew and then Yiddish, at the Heidelberg Theological Faculty. For many years, he did not hold a regular academic appointment — after all, his degree was in medicine, not Hebrew or Yiddish. But as the years passed, he worked his way into the academic ranks. But even at his death at the age of seventy-three, he was not a full professor but held some lower rank. During the early years of his stay in Heidelberg, he had been an active member of the Jewish community. While the community had never been large, after the war it was particularly small, made up mostly of Eastern European Jews from the nearby DP camps who had been attracted to Heidelberg because it was one of the few cities in Germany that had escaped damage. Under such circumstances no Jew stayed away from the only institutional Jewish presence in the area: the Jewish community. But after a while, various frictions arose (most of the survivors were not in the best psychological health) and Redner left the community, never to be seen in the synagogue again. Even on the Day of Atonement, Redner did not attend services. He maintained relations with a few individual Jews but not with the community.

Redner never married. But for the last ten years of his life, he had lived with a German gentile woman and it was this relationship that was the source of all the current difficulties.

It seems that these years had been the happiest of his life. The woman was a widow. Her husband had died in the war and after it she dedicated herself to working with the Jewish victims of Nazism. For many years she lived alone but as soon as she met Redner she was drawn to him and he to her. At first, he came for dinners at her little house about twenty minutes outside of Heidelberg. Gradually, he came to spend a night now and then and soon he was essentially living there. He never gave up his small apartment in the old section of Heidelberg near the university. But it gradually turned into a kind of office that he used only during the day. He never married the German woman, referring to her to the end as "my hostess," "*Meine Wirtin.*" But his deep affection for her could not be doubted.

She had died two years before he did. She left everything she owned, including her house, to him and he continued to live in it, spending the days with his books in the city apartment. In her will, she asked to be cremated and the ashes to be buried in the country cemetery near her house. Redner had taken care of all this, and from time to time, it seems, he expressed the wish that when he died, he was to be buried next to her. That was all he said. He did not say either that he was to be buried in a Christian cemetery or that he was not to be buried in a Christian cemetery. He said only that he was to be buried next to her, the woman who had given him the only happiness he had ever known. Nor did he put this in writing, in a will, or in any other form. He merely mentioned it to some Christian friends who were now determined to carry out his wishes. And that is why he was going to be buried that afternoon in a Christian cemetery.

Things were moving toward a climax. For the last two days, negotiations had been conducted with Redner's friends. A Dr. Wolfgang Plotze who was described as a philosopher and an American young woman whose name I did not at first catch were mentioned. These two had been Redner's closest friends during the last two or three years of his life and it is to them that he had expressed the wish to be buried near the ashes of Frau Gebel. They had arranged the funeral for 4:00 that afternoon and a notice to this effect had appeared in the Heidelberg morning newspaper. Since Sunday morning, Guttenberg had been in telephone contact with Plotze, trying to convince him that a Jew, particularly a Holocaust survivor, ought not be buried in a German Christian cemetery. Guttenberg thought that most of the Theological Faculty was on his side, made uneasy by this "kidnapping" of a Jew. But it was all to no avail. Plotze and his friends were carrying out the wishes of the dead man and they were not going to fail in the fulfillment of their obligation to him, as they saw it.

Most of the conversation in the room concerned the legalities of the matter. Did Plotze have the right to do what he was about to do? In the absence of a written will, who had the authority to determine where Redner should be buried? Was there still time to go to court and obtain some sort of injunction?

As soon as I heard that Plotze was a philosopher, I knew that I had to talk with him. Perhaps I could accomplish what the others could not. I offered to call Plotze to see whether anything could still be done. Guttenberg and the others said they were sure he could not be moved. But they agreed that there was nothing to lose. So I left the Rektor's room and walked across the hall to Miss Steuermacher's office to make the call.

Plotze answered the phone. I gave him my name and told him that I had been teaching philosophy and Jewish theology at the new College for Jewish Studies.

"I am calling," I said, "about the funeral this afternoon of Franz Redner. There is a great deal of concern here about burying a Jew in a Christian cemetery. I think it is urgent that we talk. But you must postpone the burial because there is no use talking if he has already been buried."

"The memorial meeting will take place at 4:00," he replied. "Why don't you come to that? We can then talk afterward, before the burial. There should be about an hour from the end of the memorial meeting to the beginning of the funeral. In any case, I cannot call off the memorial meeting. It has been advertised and people will show up. But we can talk afterward."

I told him I would be there. He then gave me directions to the cemetery and the hall where the memorial meeting was going to be held. It was just after noon when I hung up with him.

I was rather confused. I would be attending a memorial meeting and then conducting a dialogue while the funeral was waiting. This was an extraordinary situation. But what choice did I have? Plotze did not turn me down completely. He was ready to talk. But under what circumstances! But I had to go. There was no choice.

One of the Jewish students at the College offered to drive me to the cemetery and stay with me during the service and the negotiations. But nobody else from the College was to go. Earlier, Plotze had asked Guttenberg to speak at the memorial service but had refused because that would sanction the whole procedure. So the funeral was going to be boycotted by the College. Only I and the student, Jacob Fenster, were to go.

We arrived about a quarter to four. It was a sunny and warm afternoon. The chapel at the cemetery in which the memorial meeting was to be held was a modernistic church-like structure with a high ceiling made of wood. There were pews for perhaps 200 persons and the chapel was about a quarter full. Up front, the covered coffin was resting on a low, wheeled bier. And on the front wall, there was a huge wooden cross which dominated the room. It dwarfed everything in the chapel, especially Franz Redner's beautifully polished coffin with brass handles attached. There was a buzz of conversation in the room. People were waiting for the meeting to begin.

I asked some people who Dr. Plotze was. They directed me to the first row where four or five persons were conversing. One of them was Dr. Plotze. I introduced myself and asked whether I could have a word with him. He agreed and we left the chapel for an adjoining corridor.

Plotze was a tall man, in his fifties, wearing thick glasses. He seemed to me a bit formal but not unfriendly. There was something strange about the way he moved but at first I could not define it. I soon learned that he had a severe vision problem. Though he wore glasses, he was really almost blind. He had to be guided wherever he went and when he was not, he bumped into things. But from the first, he seemed to me a person of sensitivity, even profundity. He was a spiritual presence.

I told him that I realized we would be talking after the memorial meeting (which was now about five minutes away) but that I had to tell him immediately that placing the coffin of Redner under the huge cross in the chapel was improper. Redner, I pointed out, was a Jew and not a Christian and in the light of everything that had happened, I could not see conducting a service for a Holocaust survivor under the cross. Couldn't the coffin be wheeled out of the chapel and the memorial meeting be held without the coffin present in the chapel?

Plotze agreed. He gave orders to the attendants to wheel the coffin out of the chapel and the service began.

It consisted of several speeches and the playing of some Jewish tunes on a lute. The speech I remember best was given by a member of the Heidelberg Theological Faculty who stressed Redner's contribution to the school. Without him, Christian students preparing for the ministry would never have come to understand what Judaism was all about. Redner, he said, was a living embodiment of Jewish culture and it was a privilege for the University of Heidelberg to have had such a faculty member. The speeches were quite moving, the lute playing was rather amateurish, and one could sense the affection some of the people in the chapel had for the deceased.

But the most memorable incident of the memorial meeting did not emanate from up front. It happened in the back of the chapel where the door was located through which one entered the chapel.

When the service first began, I had the feeling that Fenster and I were the only Jews at the service. Twenty minutes into the service, I heard footsteps on the path leading to the chapel and very soon the footsteps could be heard on the wooden porch of the chapel. This all took place while the theologian I referred to earlier was speaking and total silence was reigning in the chapel. Finally, the door opened, many necks turned to see who was entering and I discovered at a glance that a number of Heidelberg Jews were putting in their appearances. Among them was Ludwig.

I had made Ludwig's acquaintance about two months before this incident. He attended the Heidelberg synagogue regularly, made something of a nuisance of himself, and was known all over town by Jews and gentiles alike as "Crazy Ludwig." It was said that Ludwig and his family had lived in Heidelberg before the war, his mind gone even then. He could be found anywhere attempting to sell outdated newspapers, matches, or anything else he happened to see lying around. He dressed in rags except on the Sabbath and Jewish holidays — of which he clearly kept track since he appeared regularly in the synagogue on those days. His clothing on such occasions was far from elegant but incomparably better than on weekdays. And Ludwig appeared in the doorway, together with six or seven other Jews, in his Sabbath best.

It took Ludwig about ten seconds to size up the situation and to make the decision not to keep his point of view secret.

"What is going on here?" he hollered. "What is this cross doing here? Redner was a Jew. Why is he being buried from a Church? I knew Redner. He was a Jew. What is going on here?"

These questions were not whispered, but asked in a loud voice, audible to everybody in the chapel. The Heidelberg professor who was speaking stopped and looked bewildered. Ludwig's Jewish companions shushed him, he quieted down and sat down with the other Jews. But I felt Elijah had come in the guise of a madman and said what needed to be said. Ludwig had earned his place in the world to come in those twenty seconds.

The service was over and the audience drifted outside to wait for the funeral to begin. Fenster and I drifted toward Plotze to begin the dialogue. It was a tense moment.

Plotze shook many hands. It seemed that people respected him for having organized the funeral and they wanted to thank him for it and to express their condolences, as if he were a mourning relative. After a few minutes he sensed my presence (I never learned just what he was and was not able to see) and said that we would go to a room near the front of the chapel. By this time, a woman in her thirties was with him. She was somewhat heavy with an intense but not German appearance. Introduced to me as Nancy Whitford, an American, who was teaching English in Heidelberg, she was the other close friend of Redner's who was jointly responsible with Plotze for the funeral arrangements.

About five or six of us left the chapel and walked along a rather dark corridor in which Redner's coffin had been placed before the memorial service. The room in which we found ourselves was some sort of cemetery office. There were several chairs and one or two desks.

Plotze and Nancy Whitford were clearly in charge. Others drifted in and out, but they were basically listeners. My dialogue partners were the German philosopher and the American from Kansas.

I knew that there was no chance of changing their minds right then and there, in the small cemetery office, while a hundred persons were milling around outside awaiting the beginning of the funeral. So I argued for a postponement of the funeral. Once the man is buried, I said, no further dialogue would be of any use. According to Jewish law, a body may not be dug up once it is interred. So burying Redner would be an irrevocable act, while postponing the funeral would leave all options open. I refused to go into the question of where Redner ultimately should be buried. I hammered away at the postponement issue and of the irrevocability of burial compared with the compatibility of postponement with all future solutions. I succeeded in convincing them.

Plotze gave orders that the funeral was to be postponed. The body was to be loaded into the hearse and returned to the Pathology Department of the University of Heidelberg which had the proper facilities for the refrigeration of bodies. Plotze sent Nancy Whitford to tell the waiting mourners that due to unforeseen circumstances, the funeral had to be postponed. Nancy went out to deliver the message and, upon returning, reported that the crowd accepted the news with some puzzlement but without very much of a reaction. After a number of other details were taken care of, we proceeded to Wolfgang's home (by this time we were all on a first-name basis) to continue — or better, to commence — the dialogue.

Wolfgang lived a ten-minute drive away from the old part of Heidelberg, in an area of newer apartment buildings, somewhat in the style of American garden apartments. He lived on the ground floor in a comfortable, book-lined apartment. He explained that his wife and child were away on a trip and that he was being looked after by a Jewish neighbor who had been a childhood friend. She had married a Lithuanian before the war and settled in Lithuania where she survived the war, enduring many difficulties. A year ago, they had been permitted to emigrate to Germany from the Soviet Union together with their son who was well on the way to becoming a violinist of international reputation. This lady was with us for the next three days. She made coffee, served cookies, and acted as hostess. She did not say much, though I had the distinct feeling that she was not very sympathetic to me and my enterprise. I cannot be sure of her reasons. Possibly she just found the endless discussions boring. While Jewish, she did not seem to have much sympathy for Jewish religious considerations. But she did not have much of a role in the negotiations.

As I have already said, most of the talking was done by Wolfgang, Nancy, and me. With each of my dialogue partners, I had a specific advantage. To Nancy I was an American, and countrymen become somewhat sentimental about each other in foreign lands. And for Wolfgang, I was a Heideggerian philosopher. He had studied with Heidegger both during and after the war and had written his dissertation under Heidegger. As soon as I told him that I considered Heidegger one of the greatest philosophers of the century, a certain bond was forged. I made very clear my unequivocal condemnation of Heidegger's unrepentant Nazism but this could not, in my view, change the fact that Heidegger was nevertheless a great philosopher. Wolfgang's manner from the first was open and respectful.

From this point on a dialogue lasting three full days ensued. There is no point reciting it minute by minute. Suffice it to say that the first session did not adjourn until midnight. During the following days, we would begin at about 8:30 in the morning and continue until midnight, interrupted only by short meals and various trips around town as will be described. But it was a three-day marathon during which this matter occupied my total energy. I was ready to dialogue forever if that was what it took to prevent Redner's burial in a non-Jewish cemetery. I think my friends sensed my determination and this had something to do with the outcome.

Their story was more or less as I had heard it. They had known Redner for the last three or four years of his life. Nancy had taken courses in Yiddish at the University with him. I asked her what accounted for her interest in Yiddish. She said she was not sure but living as an American in Germany for ten years had made her think about many things, including the Holocaust. This, in turn, aroused her interest in Jews and Judaism and Franz Redner turned out to be the embodiment of the Jewish spirit — its humor, compassion, gentleness, and love of learning. Wolfgang had met him and was instantly attracted to him. These three had spent many evenings together, always in Redner's small Heidelberg apartment. Redner spoke endlessly about Eastern European Jewry, sang Yiddish songs, and held Talmudic discourses. When it turned late, he would lock up the apartment and take a taxi to Frau Gebel's house to spend the night. Even after she died, he spent the nights in her house and the days in his apartment.

Redner had had a serious heart attack several months after Frau Gebel's death and from that time on he indicated, on two or three separate occasions, that he wanted to be buried next to her ashes. Redner had inherited Frau Gebel's house and money and he also said that after his death, he wanted the house sold and the whole fortune (close to one million German marks) used for the benefit of orphans in Israel. Wolfgang and Nancy had tried several times to persuade Redner to draw up a will but he never did. He left nothing in writing. They did not know why he would not prepare a will. They speculated that it had something to do with his attitude to death — having seen so many human beings die without any preparation, he could not write a will as if death were still surrounded by all the protections of civilized society. In any case, there was nothing in writing, either about the funeral arrangements or the disposition of the money. But they were sure that he wanted to be buried next to the ashes of Frau Gebel and because they loved him, they intended to carry out his wishes.

I said that I understood and sympathized with everything they said. In fact, I had no doubt that they had the best of motives. From the first — and to this day — I believed that they loved Redner and desired only to carry out his wishes. To carry out the wishes of a dead person, I continued, was a holy task from the point of view of Judaism. But a wish expressed by a Jew before his death had no binding force if that wish was contrary to Torah law. Thus, a Jew's will in which he requested cremation was null and void. Because cremation was contrary to the Torah, a desire to be cremated after death must not be carried out. A Jew has no power to order a violation of the Torah. And burying a Jew in a non-Jewish cemetery was contrary to the Torah.

Plotze was very interested in this argument. He pointed out that Redner had not attended the Heidelberg synagogue for over twenty years. Was he still a Jew? Had he not, in fact, left Judaism?

I replied that a Jew cannot leave Judaism. Someone born to a Jewish mother was a Jew whether he liked it or not. Being a Jew does not depend on adhering to certain beliefs or even practices. Being a good Jew did. But whether or not a Jew was a good Jew — and no Jew is perfect — a Jew born a Jew or validly converted to Judaism remained a Jew and subject to all obligations of Judaism.

Why did it matter, Plotze asked, where a person is buried? Isn't the immortal soul the real person and didn't the soul leave the body at death? Judaism, I replied, was not all that spiritualized. It was Plato and the Gnostics who put all the emphasis on the soul while speaking of the material world as illusion. For Judaism, the material world was created by God who found it good. The body and matter in general was neither illusion nor evil. The election by God of the Jewish people was an election of the seed of Abraham, Isaac, and Jacob. The Jewish people was a holy people, both spiritually and materially.

Therefore, the Jewish body was holy too. Hitler, in his evil malevolence, understood this very well. He knew that as an enemy of the God of Israel whom he could not reach, he had to murder the body of Israel that was a holy vessel in which the God of Abraham dwelled in the world. A Jew such as Redner who had seen the mountains of Jewish corpses created by Hitler during the Holocaust should not be separated from these mountains in his death. He should not be buried in a cemetery where many Nazis were buried.

I have no intention of recording the details of our conversations. At times they became profound, at times foolishly technical. Heidegger figured prominently, as Plotze and I, as I have already said, were both deeply influenced by him. We discussed Heidegger's critique of the mind-body dualism and his writings about death. We discussed Heidegger's Nazism, the German Jewish symbiosis, Christian theology, Karl Barth, and many other topics. All this time, Franz Redner was lying dead in the cooling facility of the University of Heidelberg Pathological Institute and I was desperate to get him buried as quickly as possible because Jewish law demands quick burial. But it forbids burial in a gentile cemetery and I was therefore willing to dialogue until hell froze over.

Gradually, I began to detect a shift in Wolfgang's and Nancy's attitude. They began to understand what a Jew was and who a Holocaust survivor was. After all, they had been attracted to Redner in the first place because of their interest in Jews and Judaism. Nevertheless, they remained troubled by the prospect of not carrying out Redner's last wish.

By this time, I also was looking for a solution that would enable Redner to be buried in a Jewish cemetery and at the same fulfill his wish that he be buried next to Frau Gebel's ashes. And I invented a solution. I proposed that Redner be buried in the Jewish cemetery and that the ashes of Frau Gebel be disinterred and inserted in Redner's grave. This solution seemed possible to me because the ashes of Frau Gebel, from the Jewish point of view, were not a body. A gentile could not be buried in a Jewish cemetery. But Frau Gebel's ashes were not a body and could, according to Jewish law, be inserted in Redner's grave. In this way, all sides, living and dead, Jewish and gentile, could be satisfied. We agreed that this was the perfect solution. But could it be carried out?

In the final analysis we discovered that it could not. Because Redner had died without a will, the Heidelberg court had assigned a lawyer to protect his interests. This lawyer was an elderly gentleman of aristocratic bearing who had been mayor of Heidelberg for some years, left office, and returned to his law practice. I met him on the second day of the dialogue when Nancy and I drove out to the little town near Heidelberg where Frau Gebel's house was located. Dr. Heide, the lawyer, listened very carefully to the story we told him and to the solution we proposed. He agreed that it was an excellent solution. But we had to touch two bases. The first was the office of the municipality of Heidelberg that dealt with burials. And the second was the cemetery in which Frau Gebel's ashes were buried. The cemetery authorities had to agree to the disinterring of the ashes. Heide phoned the city burial office and set up an appointment for Wolfgang and me for the next day.

We were received by an official with a working-class air about him. He listened to the story carefully and agreed to the procedure. As far as he was concerned, nothing was happening. Redner was being buried in the Jewish cemetery and that was all. If anyone inserted ashes into the grave, as far as he was concerned, it was just so much more earth. And he also agreed to take no notice of the disinterring of Frau Gebel's ashes. If we returned the urn emptied of the ashes to the grave, who would be the wiser for it?

But the cemetery authorities demurred. What if some remote relative of Frau Gebel got wind of these activities and demanded to see the ashes? If the urn was found to be empty, the cemetery could be sued for permitting the removal of the ashes. For this reason, they refused to permit the removal of the ashes without a court order and thus our plan came to naught.

I have spoken earlier of the visit to Frau Gebel's house. The purpose of the visit was to conduct a ritual search for any possible written last will that Redner may have left.

Nancy and I drove to the village where we went to see the mayor, who had sealed the house immediately after Redner's death. He told us how Redner had died. He was standing at the bus stop in the village shortly after 9:00 A.M. with two shopping bags of books in his hands, on his way to his apartment in Heidelberg where he spent his days. He collapsed at the bus stop, scattering the books in all directions. The single doctor in the town was summoned and declared him dead. The body was transported to the Pathological Institute, the contents of the shopping bags were taken to the city hall, and the house was sealed. From the city hall, the mayor, Nancy, and I drove to the house where we met Dr. Heide.

It was a comfortable, solidly built, small house. As are most houses in Germany, it was surrounded by a wall. The gate in the wall was sealed and the mayor unsealed it in our presence. We walked through a small garden in which flowers grew. These had been Frau Gebel's interest but, after her death, Redner had taken over their cultivation. The house itself was not large. On the ground floor there was a kitchen and several rooms. The living room and two bedrooms were upstairs. The house was not in disarray but neither was it in excellent shape. During the two years that Redner had lived there alone his care of things had been good but probably not quite up to Frau Gebel's standards.

One room downstairs was apparently an extension of Redner's Heidelberg apartment. It was full of books and articles, many of them in Hebrew and Yiddish. In the kitchen, the breakfast dishes were in the sink, unwashed. We spent an hour or so looking in drawers and other likely places for a will. Of course, we did not find one. But it was the closest I had come to meeting Redner. A place where a man lives becomes part of the person. Redner's presence could be felt in the house.

After the plan to insert Frau Gebel's ashes in Redner's grave collapsed because of the cemetery's refusal to permit the ashes' disinterment, Wolfgang and Nancy gradually came to agree that Redner should be buried in the Jewish cemetery. The ashes, we agreed, could be added later. Perhaps some way would be found in the future to disinter the ashes, but meanwhile, Redner had to be buried. Jewish law, I explained, demanded burial as soon as possible, preferably on the same day as death. Many days had already passed and Franz Redner had not yet been buried. No more time could be lost.

In the final analysis, I convinced Wolfgang and Nancy that Redner should be buried in the Jewish cemetery because they were good people. Their love for Redner was love for Redner the Jew. And they came to believe that Redner belonged to the Jewish people in death. His love for Frau Gebel was not being ignored. The happiness she had given him was the only happiness he had known. But his being in the world as the seed of Abraham transcended such happiness. We convinced ourselves that Frau Gebel would understand and even approve. The funeral was set for Monday morning at 11:00 A.M. A notice was inserted in the newspaper.

Before a Jew is buried, a rite of purification is required. Essentially, this consists of a very thorough washing of the body, the cutting of the fingernails and the dressing of the body in a white shroud and in a *tallith* (prayer shawl). Jewish law requires burial in a simple wooden coffin so that all Jews, rich and poor, are equal in death. Franz Redner's purification was set for 8:00 A.M. on Monday morning in the Pathological Institute.

Abraham was the person who usually conducted the purification. He was an Estonian Jew who had lost his family in the Holocaust and remained in Heidelberg. He was one of the persons who led services in the synagogue and prepared the modest communal meals usually served after services. He was a simple, gregarious person who had performed many purifications.

For the purification, three or four men are required. I volunteered, as did Jacob Fenster, who had been with me through most of the events described. And another Heidelberg Jew also participated.

For me, this was something new. I had never been present at a purification and — to be truthful — I was rather apprehensive. For one thing, I wanted it done right. And while I had been present at one or two deaths, I had never had so much contact with a corpse. In view of the length of time elapsed since death, what would be the condition of the body? And how would I take it? But I knew I had to be there, after everything that had happened. Franz Redner had seen many corpses in his seven years in Nazi camps. If — by the grace of God — I had not, this last act of respect I owed Redner. But I was apprehensive.

We met a little before eight at the drive-in entrance of the Pathological Institute, the entrance through which the hearses entered the building. Abraham knew the men who worked there. While his German was not perfect, it was good enough to exchange working-class banter about their jobs and his. As we were waiting, a phone call came in for me. It was from Wolfgang and Nancy. They wanted to be sure that I was there. Because of Redner's break with the Jewish community, they were not altogether comfortable in turning him over to them. But with me present, they felt better about it.

The men directed us to the walk-in refrigerator which held the body. It was dark inside and very cold, with a powerful chemical odor that assailed us as soon as we entered. There were several bodies covered with sheets on wheeled stretchers. To the hand of each body a name tag was attached. As soon as Redner was located we wheeled him out of the refrigerator into an adjoining room. The employees of the Institute left and we were alone with Franz Redner.

The purification was conducted as required. Finally I met Franz Redner at his purification. He was a short, heavy-set Jew with a Ben-Gurion-like face. The right side of his face was injured from the fall at the bus station. Otherwise, the body was in surprisingly good condition. On his right hand, the number 0007 was tattooed. It was an Auschwitz number, one of the lowest I had ever seen. Redner had been among the first prisoners in Auschwitz. Very few of those survived. Abraham, who was participating in the purification, also had a number on his arm.

It is customary to address the deceased as the purification proceeds. As he is lifted up, water is poured on him and the other procedures are performed, he is asked for pardon if anything is done improperly, or if his dignity is in any way being impaired. We so addressed Franz Redner. When we finished, he was a Jew lying in a coffin like many others before him. He was ready for burial.

I returned to my hotel to rest. The pungent odor of the chemical that pervaded the Pathological Institute clung to my hands. I could not get rid of it, even after washing my hands several times. The washing of the body had not been easy for me. But I felt good that I was able to participate. The ancient rabbis refer to burying the dead as the only true work of mercy. Whenever we do something for living persons, the possibility that they might somehow reward us lurks in the back of our minds: make us rich if we are poor; make us powerful if we are powerless. But a dead person will never repay us. Therefore, say the rabbis, burial of the dead is mercy without expectation of reward. And I was privileged to help with the burial of one of the first prisoners of Auschwitz.

The next day was a beautiful, warm, and sunny day. I arrived at the Jewish cemetery more than an hour before the service was scheduled to begin. The service was going to be the standard Orthodox Jewish burial service but I knew that German translations of the Hebrew parts of the service were necessary. I could find no one book that had a complete translation so I pieced it together from a number of books in the library of the Jewish College. I had no idea of how many would attend but I knew that during the last few days word of the goings-on in connection with the burial of Franz Redner had gotten around. So I did not expect a very small funeral.

It was not a very large one either, though the Jewish chapel in the cemetery was filled to capacity. There were probably close to 200 people. Among them were many Jews and a large part of the Heidelberg Theological Faculty. One of the Jewish families of Heidelberg brought along a German gentile who was visiting them. He was the son of a German soldier who had saved them from death. The father had died and the son kept up relations by spending a few days with them every year. So they brought him to the funeral.

The Jewish cemetery in Heidelberg is really just a part of the municipal cemetery, though clearly marked off as a Jewish cemetery. The old Jewish cemetery is elsewhere, the part we were in went back to the 1920s. And the post-war years were also represented. Only the 1938-45 period was missing. During that time, Heidelberg was *Judenfrei.*

Abraham, who had participated in the purification, was accustomed to chanting the El Mole Rachamim and he did so. I read some psalms, first in Hebrew and then in German. And then I eulogized Redner. I spoke of his seven years, from 1938 to 1945, in the murder camps, of his being one of the first prisoners in Auschwitz and of his life in Heidelberg after the war. I pointed out that for many of the students of the Theological Faculty he had been the representative Jew through whom they acquired some knowledge and in some cases even love of Judaism. As I said this I looked at Wolfgang Plotze and Nancy Whitford who sat in the first row of the chapel. And then I switched to Yiddish.

The idea of delivering part of the eulogy in Yiddish had been growing on me in the last few days. Redner had been a Polish Jew who loved Yiddish. Wolfgang and Nancy had pointed out several times that he seemed to be himself most when he sang Yiddish songs. In fact, he had published two collections of Yiddish songs with music and German translation. They told me that they had a tape of Redner singing and explaining the songs. He had done this one evening in Plotze's home and they had taped it, somewhat over his protest. But there was no time for me to listen to the tape. Nevertheless, the significance of Yiddish in Redner's life had become clear to me. So I knew that some Yiddish words were right.

In recent years, Yiddish had become an exotic and interesting language for Germans. A mixture of German (maybe eighty percent), Hebrew (ten percent), and Polish, Russian, and other languages, Yiddish had been an embarrassment to German Jews eager to be accepted as full-fledged Germans. Eastern European Jews who emigrated to Germany spoke it, but their children were eager to get rid of it as quickly as possible. But however low the esteem was in which it was held by German Jews — not to speak of German gentiles — Yiddish mirrored Jewish feelings and attitudes as nothing else did. In Yiddish, I spoke of Redner's love of the language. I said that it was the language of the vast majority of the victims of the Holocaust. In it, the Jews of Eastern Europe expressed their world and its religious framework. Yiddish was a language of great tenderness in which God was an elementary reality and compassion the essence of his teaching. In this ocean of Yiddish life, Franz Redner had become who he was and it was good for us to remember.

After the service in the chapel was over, the coffin, followed by the mourners, was wheeled to the graveside. There an Israeli student of Redner's recited Kaddish. The coffin was lowered into the grave and we began shoveling earth so as not to leave it uncovered, as is the Jewish custom. And then we left.

That evening, a dozen of us were reunited in Wolfgang Plotze's apartment. The atmosphere was warm. There was a consensus that we had done the right thing.

About six months later, on a snowy February day, a tape arrived at my New York City apartment. It was snowing heavily all day and by the time I was able to play the tape in the evening, the city was snowed in. But out of my hi-fi speakers, the thick Warsaw Yiddish of Franz Redner sang about Jewish children in cradles, Jewish maidens in love and about burning villages. He sounded just as I thought he would.

I have often asked myself, did I do the right thing? Did I have the right to separate him from the ashes of Frau Gebel? Could Franz Redner be angry at me?

I think I did the right thing, but who can be sure?

# JEWISH-CHRISTIAN RELATIONS

# A Jewish View of Christianity

This essay provides a general introduction to Wyschogrod's understanding of the historical context, goals, and major themes of Jewish-Christian dialogue. In it, he explains why his own approach to Jewish-Christian relations differs from that of his teacher, the philosopher and Talmudist Joseph Soloveitchik, who advocated restricting dialogue between Christians and Jews to secular matters. Originally published in *Toward a Theological Encounter: Jewish Understandings of Christianity*, ed. Leon Klenicki (New York: Paulist Press, 1991), pp. 104-119.

IN THE LAST forty or so years, several dozen Christian bodies have adopted statements about Jewish-Christian relations. It is widely conceded that this concentration of attention on the Jewish issue by Christian bodies is largely the result of the Holocaust. It is possible that even without the Holocaust, Christian interest in Judaism would have escalated in the closing decades of the twentieth century. The maturation of the historical method made it more and more difficult to overlook the deeply Jewish character of early Christianity. So even without the Holocaust, it is not unlikely that Christian scholarship would have been forced to deal more seriously with the Jewish roots of Christianity.

But this was not to be. The Holocaust occurred, and instead of an organic development prompted by scholarly and theological considerations, a world historical evil event of unprecedented proportions intervened and cast Jewish-Christian relations, and many other things, in an entirely new light.

The Christian side in the dialogue found itself burdened with a heavy guilt. While Nazism was hardly a Christian phenomenon, there was widespread agreement that two thousand years of the Christian teaching of contempt prepared the ground for the "final solution." Christianity was forced to face up to the implications of its teaching which were taken to insane extremes by the Nazis but which also built on Christian foundations.

On its side, Judaism entered the dialogue in the post–World War II period in a seriously weakened position. The Holocaust was, of course, the deepest reason for the weakening. No people could suffer the fate European Jewry did without showing signs of deep trauma. But the trauma the Holocaust inflicted on world Jewry must be understood in the context of Jewish history since the Enlightenment. This history, in turn, must be viewed in the context of Jewish self-understanding rooted in the doctrine of election and the Jewish self-image that this doctrine generates. The product resulting from the interaction of these influences yielded a deeply injured Judaism that embarked on Jewish-Christian dialogue after World War II.

## Defeat and Secularism

When we consider the three monotheistic religions — Judaism, Christianity, and Islam — we can conclude that of the three, Judaism and Islam have been wounded religions and Christianity much less so. Islam, from its inception, has seen itself validated by its early success. Starting out as the faith of a small group of believers on the Arabian Peninsula, the message of Islam quickly conquered vast territories that were brought under Muslim hegemony by means of both the book and the sword. Islam's success validated the faith as nothing else could, an attitude not unknown to either Judaism or Christianity. Religions often interpret worldly success as a sign of divine favor but this is perhaps more deeply rooted in Islam than in the other two monotheistic religions. The existence of a political realm in which Islam is supreme is thus essential to the spiritual health of Islam, largely because of Islam's refusal to separate the religious from the political. The existence of territories where Islam has not yet succeeded in establishing its authority can only be interpreted as a temporary state of affairs to be remedied at the earliest possible moment.

It is for this reason that European imperialism of the nineteenth century was so profoundly painful to Islam. By the end of the century, the Muslim world was largely subordinate to the power of Christian Europe. Largely due to the superiority of Western science — but not only for that reason — the Muslim world found itself deprived of its sovereignty or reduced to the status of vassal states of European Christian powers that had set out to establish empires in Africa and Asia.

How could this happen to Islam, the true faith that was destined to rule the world and to unite all of humanity under the banner of the teaching of the prophet? Failure of such magnitude after so much success was also unbearable because Islam never embraced suffering as a desirable part of the religious life. Where suffering could not be avoided, a highly detailed doctrine of otherworldly rewards rushed in to take the sting out of the suffering and to assure the faithful that the suffering was as nothing compared to the assured reward.

Since the advent of the age of imperialism until the defeats suffered in the Arab-Israeli conflict, Islam has been a wounded faith that has had great difficulty in coming to terms with its relatively weak position in a world that should have yielded long ago to the message of the one true religion. The wounds imposed on Islam manifest themselves in various ways among which fanaticism and the development of denial mechanisms are the most prominent. Such manifestations can also be observed in contemporary Judaism.

The injuries suffered by Islam are of interest because they enable us to understand better the injuries suffered by Judaism. Muslims see themselves as followers of the last and the greatest of the prophets whose revelation is God's final message to humanity. Jews see themselves as members of a people chosen by God for special proximity and service to him. While God loves all of his children, he has a special love for the people of Israel, particularly when that people is faithful to him and obeys his commandments. But even when it does not — and it frequently has not — God's undeserved love for the people of his election is not erased but only temporarily suspended. After God's anger passes, the original love returns, perhaps in increased measure. Like the love of a parent for an erring child, God's affection for Israel is indestructible. It is the expression of God's eternal faithfulness.

If this is so, then why does Israel suffer so much? Why does Israel live in exile, despised and persecuted everywhere? Is this the fate appropriate to the chosen people? These are questions Jews have asked over the centuries and with particular vehemence since the Holocaust. Since there are no satisfactory answers to these questions, a certain spiritual injury has taken up abode in the Jewish soul. And it is an injury which, we will see, injects itself into the Jewish-Christian dialogue.

It is, of course, not the case that there are no answers at all to these questions. Traditionally, Jewish suffering has been explained as the result of sin. When Israel is faithful to the covenant, all goes well, and when it is not, all sorts of calamities befall the people (for the biblical source of this idea see

Deut. 11:13-17). On the frequent occasions that calamities did occur, the standard explanation was the sin of the people. This left the traditional system intact and held out the promise of improvement if the people improved their ways.

The messianic idea was an integral part of this system. Given Israel's sense of election, its particular closeness to God and God's profound faithfulness to Israel, no defeat of Israel could be final. However final the defeat seemed, it could only be a temporary reversal. God would redeem his people from exile. God would reestablish the destroyed kingdom and Israel would dwell safely in its homeland once again. Messianic redemption was the expectation that would not die because the current situation of exile could not last forever. God will fulfill his promises to his chosen people.

When truly accepted, this system of beliefs did much to shield Israel from deep psychic and spiritual injury. Persecution was a sign of election, of the jealousy and hatred of the nations who could not accept Israel's special status and rebelled against God's sovereign election of Israel. While Jews rarely turned suffering into something inherently desirable, they learned to accept it because they were convinced of its nonpermanence and that, by changing their ways, their situation would change for the better.

Gradually, however, this system of beliefs began to be eroded. A number of factors contributed to this. First, there was the length and severity of the exile. For how long can a situation be termed temporary? How much suffering is compatible with the conviction that it is an expression of God's passing anger, soon to be replaced by the returning love of a temporarily angered parent-God? Could it be that God's love for Israel was much less intense than had been believed or perhaps even nonexistent? Such questions were, until recent times, rarely permitted to enter Jewish consciousness. But even below the conscious level, they could do much damage.

And then there was, of course, the crisis of modernization. The secularization that swept over Europe during the enlightenment had an immense impact on European Jewry. It undermined in large measure the theological worldview that has been outlined. But that is only the beginning because secularization was not the exclusive enterprise of Jews. With the French Revolution, much of Europe began a process of secularization. For Jews, the enlightenment was experienced as the beginning of the end of exclusion.

For Jews as for no others, secularization was not a cultural-historical phenomenon connected with the end of the middle ages and the rise of science but a development that promised to end the exclusion of the Jews from the cultural and economic life of Europe. The fact that medieval civilization had been deeply Christian accounted for this exclusion. Suddenly the prospect of a de-Christianized Europe opened up, and it is not difficult to understand that many Jews seized this prospect as the beginning of Jewish liberation. Citizens would no longer be Jews or Christians but members of the human race. The faculty of reason would unite all of humanity.

There was a price to be paid for this liberation, however. It consisted of a weakening if not an abandonment of Jewish identity. Here is the source of the deep attraction to secularism that is inherent in modern Judaism. This tendency was, of course, much more pronounced among Western Jews. The Jews of Eastern Europe continued to live in a largely pre-modern society. But even there, the *haskalah*, the Jewish version of the enlightenment, began to assert itself and had not the Holocaust intervened, it would undoubtedly have changed the orientation of Eastern Jewry in a secular direction.

In summary, then, Judaism, like Islam, found itself injured even before the period of the Holocaust. While the enlightenment seemed to promise an abatement of Jewish suffering, this did not materialize and the Holocaust proved once and for all that the dangers for Jews in the modern period were not smaller but greater than before. It became more and more difficult, especially after the Holocaust, to sustain the doctrine of the chosenness of Israel. When we add to this the fact that many Jews experienced secularization as the price of admission into European society, we cannot evade the conclusion that the Judaism that entered into dialogue with Christianity after World War II was a seriously weakened version of the faith.

What was the condition of Christianity? It, too, was weakened but not as much as Judaism or Islam. Like Islam, Christianity had originally also been an incredible success story. Unlike Judaism and Islam, Christianity had never been defeated by a civilization expressive of another faith. It was, of course, weakened by secularization and various schisms, particularly the Reformation, but Christianity never had to ask itself why Christians are living under the oppression of Jews or Muslims. It was the West that was ruling the world, and even if the West was not doing this altogether in the name of Christianity, the fact that Western civilization and its technology became the dominant influence in the modern world did nothing to undermine Christianity's self-confidence.

Other than the growth of secularism, Christianity in the twentieth century was seriously threatened by left- and right-wing totalitarianism. For the first time since Constantine, there were countries in Europe ruled by explicitly anti-Christian regimes. This was perfectly clear in the Soviet Union and its post–World War II satellites, but it was also partly true in Nazi Germany where an ideology ruled that was anti-Christian even if not as explicitly so as Marxist totalitarianism.

The Holocaust was a trauma for Christianity because it made visible the possibility of a non-Christian or even anti-Christian transmutation of Christian anti-Semitism, more virulent even than the original form. Nevertheless, these post-Christian forms of anti-Semitism were seen by many to owe much to Christian anti-Semitism, and that is the reality Christianity now had to face.

## Orthodox Judaism and Dialogue

With this background in mind, I now move to our actual topic: a contemporary Jewish view of Christianity. My focus will not be on the historical aspect, though history cannot be eschewed altogether. But history must not be permitted to reign unchallenged. The temptation to do so is very great. History is a convenient way of escaping the necessity for taking a position. Ever since the middle of the nineteenth century and the advent of *"Wissenschaft des Judentums,"* the "scientific" study of Judaism, an atmosphere was generated as if Judaism had only a past but no present or future. Yet the "scientific" study of the past was possible only because in the past there were people who were making Judaism happen. If all we do now is study the past of Judaism, those who come after us will have nothing to study but detailing the way in which we looked at the past — in other words, writing a history of the way we wrote history.

The issue, then, is how today's Jews view today's Christians. But the Judaism of today is a fragmented entity. The fact is that a significant portion of Judaism, namely the Orthodox branch, refuses to engage in any dialogue with Christianity. For many Orthodox Jews, Christianity is a foreign religion with which Jews should have as little to do as possible. From the point of view of right-wing Orthodoxy, dialogue with Christianity can only lead to a blurring of the division between the two faiths, and to Jewish conversion. The first priority of Orthodox Judaism is the preservation of the Jewish people as the people who observe the Torah. In the modern world this requires building very prominent fences around Jews, who are characterized in the Bible as "a people that dwells apart" (Num. 23:9). Since this even requires separation from non-Orthodox Jews, how much more so from non-Jews. The result of this is that the Israeli chief rabbinate, the leadership of the Israeli and American Yeshiva world, and the other organizations that speak for right-wing Orthodoxy exclude themselves completely from the Jewish-Christian dialogue. While this does not, technically speaking, constitute a theological evaluation of Christianity, it is, in fact, even worse than a negative theological evaluation.

There is nothing as bad, in my mind, as the refusal to speak with the other. Where there is communication there is hope, but where there is no communication, the very basis of hope is absent.

Left-wing Orthodoxy, the Orthodoxy that does not reject modernity but tries to combine faithful Torah observance with secular education and participation in the professions, takes a more complex stand with regard to dialogue with Christianity. In an article that appeared in the Spring/Summer 1964 issue of *Tradition* published by the Rabbinical Council of America, Rabbi Joseph B. Soloveitchik laid down the guidelines on Jewish-Christian dialogue that are widely accepted by modern Orthodox Jews.

Soloveitchik says: "We have always considered ourselves an inseparable part of humanity . . . committed to the general welfare and progress of mankind," and "We are interested in combating disease, in alleviating human suffering, in protecting man's rights, in helping the needy, et cetera. . . ." Because this is so, we are prepared to deal with Christianity with respect to the secular problems that we both face. "In the secular sphere," he writes, "we may discuss positions to be taken, ideas to be evolved, and plans to be formulated. In these matters, religious communities may together recommend action to be developed and may seize the initiative to be implemented later by general society."

But, continues Soloveitchik, "it is important that the religious or theological logos should not be employed as the medium of communication between two faith communities whose modes of expression are as unique as their apocalyptic experiences." "The word of faith," Soloveitchik insists, "reflects the intimate, the private, the paradoxically inexpressible cravings of the individual for and his linking up with the Maker. It reflects the luminous character and the strangeness of the act of faith of a particular community which is totally incomprehensible to the man of a different faith community." He adds: "As a matter of fact, our common interests lie not in the realm of faith, but in that of the secular orders."

Having said this, Soloveitchik reveals his understanding of the weakness of his case by remarking in a footnote: "The term 'secular orders' is used here in accordance with its popular semantics. For the man of faith, this term is a misnomer. God claims the whole, not a part of man, and whatever He establishes as an order within the scheme of creation is sacred."

This, of course, is the crux of the matter. Soloveitchik requires that when Orthodox Jews enter into dialogue with Christians, they do so as human beings and not as Jews. There exists a neutral realm in which Jews and Christians can interact without their religious commitments having to play any role. In this neutral realm, questions of social policy, such as war and peace, poverty and medical-ethical issues can be discussed. But it is essential that no religious or theological topics be raised because the religious "reflects the intimate, the private, the paradoxically inexpressible cravings of the individual for and his linking up with the Maker." These matters are so private that they cannot be shared or, at the very least, should not be shared, almost as if sharing them constituted a form of voyeurism that Soloveitchik finds unacceptable.

But how would such a Jewish-Christian dialogue function in which the participants were determined to exclude their religious commitments? Suppose the discussion turned to abortion, to take one example. Could the Jewish side discuss this without taking into account the halachic stand on this issue? Should the Jewish side pretend that it is approaching this question and other similar questions purely from a secular, rational point of view, uninfluenced by the written and oral Torahs which are documents of revelation accepted in faith? And the very same will be true of Christians. Many Christian attitudes to social and ethical issues are deeply rooted in the standpoint of Christian faith. Were this not the case, both Jewish and Christian faiths would be irrelevant to the issues that agitate a troubled humanity. Both of these faiths fuse the religious with the secular. In any case, Judaism does in a marked way.

Soloveitchik is, of course, aware of this, and it is for this reason that he inserts the footnote, previously noted, in which he writes that the term "secular orders," as used in his statement that "our common interests lie not in the realm of faith, but in that of the secular orders," is a misnomer. "God claims," he writes, "the whole, not a part of man, and whatever He established as an order within the scheme of creation is sacred." So the world does not come divided into a "secular" and a "religious" realm, and the participants in Jewish-Christian dialogue must react not only as secular but also as religious persons.

Because it is clear that Soloveitchik understood all of this, a slightly Machiavellian interpretation of his position suggests itself. Right-wing Orthodoxy, as we have seen, opposes all dialogue, indeed almost all contact, with Christians and other non-Jews. Soloveitchik does not share this isolationism. As a Western-educated person, he believes that contact with Western culture is permissible and even desirable, and this includes contact with the churches. But he had to cover his right flank, and in order to do so, he invented this theory of bifurcated dialogue. Religious topics may not be discussed because they are too private but social and ethical topics may be. It seems possible that he understood quite clearly that the distinction is not defensible, that once dialogue begins with ethical and social issues, the religious and theological plane will quickly be reached. If I am correct, this was his prudent way of approving something for which he could have been criticized severely by the Right had he not veiled his position to some degree. In other words, this would be another instance of "persecution and the art of writing," to quote the title of Leo Strauss's essay about writers who are forced to disguise their true meaning but leave hints so that an elite will be able to discover their real teaching.

Nevertheless, American modern Orthodoxy has adhered to the surface meaning of Soloveitchik's guidelines. Wherever they have been able to exert their influence (as in the Synagogue Council of America) they have seen to it that the dialogue avoided theological issues. This has inhibited the development of a theological dialogue and has particularly inhibited the formation of a Jewish theology of Christianity.

## Trinity and Incarnation

As in ages past, the most difficult problem the Jew faces when viewing Christianity is the topic of Christology. In Judaism and Islam, the highest level a human being can reach is that of prophet. Unlike the philosopher, the prophet does not teach a truth he has discovered by means of reason, but he teaches a truth or message committed to him by God for transmission to humanity. The question whether a particular person was or was not a true prophet is, of course, one of great importance. It is the question that separates Judaism from Islam. Judaism does not accept Mohammed as a prophet, particularly not as the greatest of the prophets, while Islam does. Significant as this disagreement is, it pales to insignificance when compared to the disagreement between Judaism and Christianity about the divinity of Jesus. A prophet is a human being chosen by God to transmit God's message to humanity. The contention that Jesus was both fully human and fully divine blurs, from the Jewish point of view, the difference between God and man and therefore raises the possibility of idolatry.

Because our orientation here is not primarily historical, we will make no pretense of surveying Jewish comments about the Trinity and the incarnation. We need only note that all Jewish writers have expressed varying degrees of disagreement with these doctrines. The only question left open was whether these doctrines turn Christianity into an idolatrous religion, a category with serious implications for Jewish law. The majority opinion seems to have been that Christianity is not idolatry, particularly for non-Jews. This is based on the perhaps curious idea that the precise definition of what constitutes idolatry is not the same for Jews as for gentiles. It becomes more understandable when we remember that, from the rabbinic point of view, different legal requirements apply to Jews and non-Jews.

While recognizing the intractability of this problem in the past, what about the present and the future? Can we hope for any progress, for a narrowing of the gap, for a reduction of the intensity of the disagreement? Is such a hope desirable? Is it not best to accept the reality of the disagreement and to leave it at that?

I would argue with conviction that such a non-interventionist policy is religiously unacceptable in this situation. The necessity for dialogue even about such issues as the Trinity and the incarnation is rooted in religious reality. If I, as a Jew, believe that the Trinity and the incarnation are false doctrines that either border on or constitute idolatry, then it is my duty as a Jew to persuade my Christian friends to abandon these teachings. Non-Jews are required to adhere to the so-called Noachide commandments based on Genesis 9:1-7, one of which prohibits idolatry. The only remaining question then is whether Jews have a responsibility to teach the Noachide commandments to gentiles. Since it is difficult to see where else but from Jews gentiles could obtain information about the Noachide commandments, it seems reasonable to conclude that Jews have a responsibility to teach to gentiles the Noachide commandments, including the prohibition against idolatry.

But there is more. The natural tendency has been for Jews to view Christianity as a foreign faith whose otherness is nowhere displayed more clearly than in the teachings of the Trinity and the incarnation. Focusing exclusively on the discontinuity between the two faiths, Judaism and Christianity have become more and more estranged, with little effort on either side to supplement the element of discontinuity with the significant dimensions of continuity that must not be ignored. Some Jewish authors in the past have recognized the positive role Christianity has played in God's redemptive plan, but even they have not found any positive elements in the Trinity and the incarnation, the teachings which Judaism finds most difficult to understand.

The effect has been a kind of polarization. The more Christianity has moved in an incarnational direction, the more Judaism moved in a transcendental direction. The divine and human natures, Judaism insists, are very different. God is above any human categories of understanding. Biblical anthropomorphism does not mean what it says. God is an absolute who is above time and space, and no attributes can be attached to him. In short, there has been a tendency to transform the God of the Bible into the God of the philosophers.

I am firmly convinced that this does not constitute a service to Judaism. I am not arguing that this tendency in Judaism is solely the result of a recoil from Christian ideas. But it is at least partly that, and we have here a situation in which both faiths have damaged one another. It seems to me that just as Judaism recoiled from the Trinity and the incarnation toward a non-biblical absolute rather than to the personal God of the Bible, so Christianity responded to the Jewish rejection of Jesus as the Messiah by raising him to the status of a divine being co-equal in his divinity to that of the Father who sent him.

All this was possible because the God of the Hebrew Bible was depicted as harboring within himself two divergent characteristics. On the one hand is the absolute dimension. He is not merely one God among many, but the only God. Even if there are other beings with superhuman powers, the God of Israel is more powerful than any of them. There is no limit to his power; in effect, he can do anything. While there is relatively little in the Hebrew Bible that makes God out to be omniscient (at times, he seems surprised by developments he did not anticipate), his knowledge is clearly greater than that of humans, and the lack of omniscience might even be interpreted as a self-imposed limitation. In short, the God of the Hebrew Bible is so overwhelmingly powerful that absolutist claims about him seem to have considerable biblical support.

At the same time, the biblical God is also very human. The Bible has no difficulty depicting God as a personality interacting with human beings. He has emotions, needs, desires, disappointments. He can be influenced, positively and negatively. He seems to profit from experience. He has his likes and dislikes and sometimes he develops a particular affection for an individual or a group. But he also gets angry at those he loves when they do not obey him, and when he does, he can be very punitive. However his anger generally passes and then the love returns. Very often he is best understood as a parent whose love for his child waxes and wanes as the conduct of the child varies.

These two dimensions of God are not easy to hold in balance. It is easiest to choose one of the two dimensions as primary, with the other not to be taken too seriously. Maimonides, within Judaism, focuses on the absolutist dimension and expends a great amount of energy to explain away the anthropomorphic passages in the Bible. That is, however, rather an exception. Most Jews, ancient or medieval (Rashi would be an example of the latter), had no great difficulty with the problem of anthropomorphism, but they certainly did have difficulty with the doctrine of incarnation.

The doctrine that one of the three persons constituting God became incarnate in the body of the Jew from Nazareth is thus a particular sharpening of divine personalism. The humanity of God is transposed from an anthropomorphic way of speaking about God which, it is understood, is not to be taken fully literally, to an ontological assertion that God actually *became* man, that the divine and human natures were blended in at least one case into one personality with two natures. Needless to say, this is deeply troubling to Jewish ears even if we keep in mind that the transcendental aspect of God is preserved, in a fashion, by maintaining that God the Father does not participate in the incarnation. Were this not the case, were Christianity to have taught that there is a non-triune God who became incarnated in the body of a human being, the break with Jewish sensibilities would have been even more profound.

So the teaching of the triune and incarnated God remains a source of deep difficulty between Judaism and Christianity. It is incumbent upon Jews to deal with this teaching. It is a teaching not difficult to caricature, and Jews have not missed the opportunity to do so. But many teachings can be caricatured, and it behooves Jews to ask themselves whether interpretations of these doctrines can be developed that would make them less objectionable to Jews. Chances are that such less objectionable interpretations might be more faithful to the Christian message than interpretations which make the gulf with Judaism as great as possible.

By the time of Nicea, the church had very little interest in how Jews would react to any particular doctrine. If anything, a negative Jewish reaction recommended a teaching because it strengthened Christian as against Jewish identity. This may have changed now. For Christians the views of Jews cannot and should not be decisive in determining the soundness of any particular teaching. But perhaps the time has come when a negative Jewish reaction is no longer a recommendation. All things being equal, many Christians today believe that a version of Christianity which reduces the gulf toward Judaism may be preferable and more authentic. In that spirit, dialogue about the Trinity and the incarnation — the most difficult issues between the two faiths — may be of advantage to all concerned.


## Torah

The Trinity and the incarnation are the very first topics contemporary Jews see in regard to Christianity. Second is Christianity's view of the Torah. It has been said that Christianity teaches salvation through Jesus Christ, all man and all God, while Judaism teaches salvation through obedience to the Torah of Moses. There is an element of truth in this, though it is probably not accurate to speak of Judaism as teaching salvation by any means, including the Torah of Moses. A religion does not teach salvation unless it sees man posed between salvation and perdition, with the latter likely in the absence of some extraordinary intervention. While punishments of various sorts, including some very severe ones, are not unknown in Judaism, the stark options of salvation or perdition in the otherworldly sense are not at the center of thinking. In that sense, Judaism is not a salvational religion.

Nevertheless, the Torah plays a central role in the Judaism that evolved after the destruction of the Temple in 70 c.e. It played a central role before the destruction of the Temple as well. The service in the Temple, the roles of the priests and the Levites, and many other details were all regulated by the commandments of the Torah. But with the destruction of the Temple the Torah came to occupy an even more central role. It was God's guidance to Israel, cleaving to which meant eternal life for the people and abandoning of which meant disaster. The Torah became the portable temple which Jews could carry into exile and by means of which they remained attached to the God who had chosen them. It was the lifeline of the Jewish people to God.

Over the ages, most Jews have experienced Christianity as a deadly assault on the Torah. The truth of the matter is, of course, much more complex and the complexity of the Christian position is the source of hope for the future. But we must start with the uncomplex truth that Christianity is an assault on the Torah, at least as Jews have understood and lived the Torah.

For Jews, the Torah is the expression of God's will for the conduct of the Jewish people. It is not only that. It is the telling of the stories that collectively constitute the history and self-understanding of the Jewish people. Also, an essential part of the Torah comprises the commandments which Israel takes very seriously. They deal with all imaginable areas of life, from the spiritual to the most mundane, and Israel tries, to the best of its abilities, to obey them.

Juxtaposed against this view is the Christian view — or what many consider the Christian view — of the Torah as a law of death. The Torah bestows death because it bestows guilt. Nobody can live up to the demands of the Torah, and when man violates its commandments — which he inevitably does — then the result is catastrophe. Instead of being a gift of love, then, the Torah is a trap, a Trojan horse which appears at first sight as a divine gift but which really turns out to be a potent poison that causes the painful death of those who place their trust in it. Those who place their trust in the Torah are, of course, the Jews who have paid dearly for their foolish confidence in the works of the law. Christians place their trust in Jesus and are saved because they know that faith saves and law condemns. As long as they lack faith, Jews will be condemned by the very Torah whose commandments they adhere to without any profit.

If this is an accurate summary of the Christian view of Torah, then the Jewish view of Christianity cannot be a very positive one. This is true even though many Jews since the enlightenment no longer obey the commandments of the Torah in the comprehensive way of Jews in the past. Liberal Judaism, deeply committed to an historical and evolutionary view of Judaism, has discarded some of the Pentateuchal commandments as time-bound and no longer significant for the contemporary Jew. From a certain perspective, liberal Judaism's freedom with the law could be interpreted as drawing closer to the Christian view. If Christianity early on proclaimed that all foods are permitted, then liberal Judaism came to that conclusion in the nineteenth century. So at least non-Orthodox Jews finally came to agree with at least part of Christian teaching, even if not the most central part.

But there is less here than meets the eye. Christianity's critical attitude to the law is based on the conviction that the law results in guilt rather than salvation. Liberal Judaism's, on the other hand, is based on the view that the law is largely a human creation that shows the marks of the age in which it originated. Many portions of the law, it is thought, are not divine in origin and can therefore be modified or even cancelled. The essence of God's will, according to liberal Judaism, is expressed in the moral rather than cultic law. So while it is true that liberal Judaism shares with Christianity flexibility with respect to the law, the reasons for the flexibility are quite different, and not too much should be made of the common flexibility.

If the Christian view of the law as a law of death remains in force, then the estrangement between Christianity and Judaism will prevail. Fortunately, there is reason to believe that the Christian view as I have expounded it is at least incomplete. Starting with the New Testament (e.g. Matt. 5:17-20), there are passages which speak very positively about the law. The key to the matter is Christianity's acceptance of the Old Testament as the word of God. However much significance is attached to the new covenant as transforming and fulfilling the old, the fact remains that God speaks not only in the New but also in the Old Testament and that his commandments there were a valid expression of God's will at least for a time.

Over the centuries, Christian debate about the law has revolved around the before-Jesus and after-Jesus axis. The idea was that the law was in full effect before the coming of Jesus, but that with his coming, large parts of it were suspended. The problem then was which parts were declared inoperative and which not. This question was never answered with the requisite clarity, though not a few Christian authors have tried. There is yet another way of looking at the problem which may be more productive for Jewish-Christian relations. Jews have long believed that the full Mosaic law was binding only on Jews. Non-Jews were duty-bound to obey the Noachide commandments, and if they did so, God was fully pleased. The tendency was to discourage gentiles from abandoning their Noachide obligations and entering the covenant of Israel. Life under the yoke of the commandments was not easy. Israel had often proven inadequate to the task and had to pay dearly for its failure. Why then subject gentiles to this burden? Only if the gentile insisted, contrary to all advice, to enter the covenant of Abraham was he accepted as a full Jew.

It seems that this problem played a crucial role in early Christianity. The Jerusalem church consisted of Jewish believers in Jesus of Nazareth, but soon gentiles were attracted to the Jesus-believing community. Did these gentiles require circumcision and full Torah-obedience, or could they be accepted as followers of Jesus while living in accordance with the Noachide commandments? It seems, judging from Acts 15, that the Jerusalem church was divided on this issue. One faction believed that gentiles who wished to follow Jesus had to be circumcised and obey the Torah of the Jews, while the other faction required only faith in Jesus and obedience to the Noachide commandments. The latter group carried the day at the first Jerusalem council described in Acts 15.

It is quite clear, however, that both factions in Jerusalem agreed that Jews, even after Jesus, remained under the prescriptions of the Torah. If the Jesus event had changed Jewish Torah obligation, then it would hardly make any sense to argue whether non-Jews required circumcision and Torah obligation. The debate concerned gentiles; both sides agreed about the Torah obligation of Jesus-believing Jews.

If all this is true, then it puts Paul's criticism of the law in a totally new light. Paul's letters in which he criticizes the law were written to gentiles who were being influenced by Jewish Jesus-believers to accept circumcision and Torah observance. Paul wishes to persuade them that this is neither necessary nor desirable. In so doing, he emphasizes and even exaggerates all the disadvantages and dangers of living under the law. He carefully omits all the advantages of Israel's covenant under the Torah because he has a specific purpose in mind: to dissuade gentile Jesus-believers from placing themselves under the obligations of the Torah. Were he writing to Jews, his evaluation of Torah observance would have been very different.

At present, this alternative reading of the early Christian attitude to the law is not widely accepted. Some Christian scholars seem to have sympathy for it, but they are in a minority. Still, much is at stake here. Jews cannot view with much sympathy a Christianity that adheres to the teaching of contempt for the Torah of Moses.

We have dealt with two of the crucial issues in the Jewish-Christian relationship: Christology and the Torah. They are, of course, not the only outstanding problems between the two faiths, though they are probably the most difficult ones. On the Torah issue, I have proposed a direction which might make it possible for Christians to accept the obligatory nature of Torah commandments for Jews even after Jesus. Jews will continue to follow with deep interest the attitudes of Christians to these issues.

As Christians deepen their understanding of Christianity's Jewish roots, Jews must try to understand Christianity's role in God's redemptive work. In respectful dialogue, the estrangement of the past will be overcome.

# Incarnation and God's Indwelling in Israel

Centered at the intersection of theology and philosophy, the topic of the incarnation is rarely examined in the context of post–World War II Jewish-Christian dialogue. The reason for this, presumably, is the widespread assumption that there is little to be gained from examining a topic that so fundamentally divides Christians and Jews. Yet while Wyschogrod concurs that the Christian doctrine of the incarnation poses a fundamental obstacle to Jews, he is perhaps unique among contemporary Jewish thinkers in drawing attention to an important line of convergence between the Christian doctrine and Judaism's own understanding of God's presence in the midst of the Jewish people. In this essay, Wyschogrod explores the dimensions and limits of this convergence. Originally published in *Incarnation*, ed. M. M. Olivetti (Cedam, Biblioteca dell 'Archivo di Filosofia,' 1999), pp. 147-157. See also "Incarnation," *Pro Ecclesia* 2:2 (Spring 1993): 208-215, and "A Jewish Perspective on Incarnation," *Modern Theology* 12:2 (April 1996): 195-209.

IN RECENT YEARS, my thinking has become more theological, even scriptural. I like to think that my theology and my reading of scripture are enriched by philosophical concerns and techniques. But the basic data with which I work are scriptural. The foundation of Jewish or Christian identity cannot derive from the enterprise of thought but must derive from the encounter with the alterity of God who speaks to believing Jews and Christians in scripture. Once we have gathered some of the data — and we never have more than some of it

— philosophical investigation can begin. But philosophical investigation cannot be the point of departure if our intention is to remain within the Jewish or Christian frame of reference. This is particularly true of a topic such as incarnation as Christians, and perhaps Jews, use the term or the idea to which the term refers. There are, of course, purely philosophical analogues to the idea of incarnation, such as the mind/body problem as discussed in the analytic tradition, but the mind/body problem is not the Christian contention that God became man in Jesus of Nazareth. It is this claim — and any possible Jewish analogue to it — that is the focus of my remarks.

Earlier I wrote:

> The most difficult outstanding issues between Judaism and Christianity are the divinity of Jesus, the Incarnation, the Trinity, three terms which are not quite synonymous but all of which assert that Jesus was not only a human being but also God. Compared to this claim, all other Christian claims, such as Jesus as the Messiah, become secondary at most. The divinity of Jesus has been unanimously rejected by all Jewish (and Muslim) authors as incompatible with true monotheism and possibly idolatrous. For Jews, once this issue is raised, it is no longer necessary to examine seriously any teachings of Jesus. A human being who is also God loses all Jewish legitimacy from the outset. No sharper break with Jewish theological sensibility can be imagined.[1]

I cannot dilute the severity of these words. To point to a human being and to say of him that he is God can only arouse terror in the Jewish soul. When we are told (Exod. 20:4-6):

> "You shall not make for yourself a graven image, or any likeness of anything that is in heaven above or that is in the earth beneath, or that is in the water under the earth; you shall not bow down to them or serve them; for I the Lord your God am a jealous God, visiting the iniquity of the fathers upon the children to the third and fourth generations of those who hate me, but showing steadfast love to thousands of those who love me and keep my commandments,"

we hear a very decisive rejection of the worship of anything that can be represented. True, the emphasis in this passage and others like it is to images created by man and not the worship of a human being who is not created by other human beings as a representation of God. Nevertheless, the teaching

1. "A Jewish Perspective on Incarnation," *Modern Theology* 12:2 (April 1996): 195-209, pp. 197-198.

that there can be no image of God, that an image cannot be God, is very clear. I am made particularly uncomfortable by Christian paintings that depict not only God the Son but also God the Father. Depiction of the Father, it seems to me, follows from depiction of the Son. If they are equally divine and the Son can be depicted, then so can the Father.

If the teaching of the incarnation of a person of the triune God in Jesus of Nazareth creates such a gulf between Judaism (and Islam) and Christianity, then what, if anything, prevents this gulf from turning into a total and radical separation between the two faiths? I do not doubt that there are Jews and Christians who believe in just such a total separation. While we cannot underestimate the depth of the gulf between the two faiths, it is also necessary to remember what unites us. And that brings us back to scripture. What unites us is not so much a philosophical or even theological orientation — though these, of course, are important — but the fact that we share the Hebrew Bible. When the church accepted the Hebrew Bible as part of its scripture, it made a momentous decision. Christians could insist on reading the Hebrew Bible through the lenses of the New Testament and Jews could challenge the validity of such a reading. But as long as we agree on a common text, the arguments about the proper interpretation of that text cannot assume the magnitude of the disagreement that would obtain were there no common text. With all deference to the masters of interpretation in some strains of contemporary hermeneutics for whom the text seems less important than its interpretation, I cannot resist the conclusion that the deepest bond between Judaism and Christianity is a common text, the Hebrew Bible. However vehemently we argue about its correct interpretation, sooner or later the text will reassert itself and, as it were, judge among interpretations. It must be remembered that, while the church has insisted on reading the Hebrew Bible through the lenses of the New Testament, it has not taught that the New Testament annuls or renders inoperative the Hebrew Bible. For classical Christianity, the New Testament interprets but does not cancel the Old. That is why a form of Judaism lives in the church and the church cannot understand itself without coming to terms with the Judaism within it.

How does all this apply to the question of the incarnation? Is there anything in the Hebrew Bible that is not totally anti-incarnational? Is there an element of continuity even with respect to this most non-Jewish article of Christian faith?

The extreme opposite of incarnational thinking is the God of Maimonides. For Maimonides, the greatest interpretive error a Jew can commit is to understand literally the anthropomorphic passages of the Hebrew Bible. Among the anthropomorphic passages, the most damaging are those that attribute corporeal characteristics to God. Maimonides insists that God has no body and that all expressions which seem to state or imply that he has a corporeal dimension cannot mean what they seem to assert. God and corporeality are totally incompatible and this, for Maimonides, is the essential message of Judaism. The unity of God, as he understands it, is but a corollary of his incorporeality because the material is infinitely divisible while the idea is one. The concept of the atom was invented to bridge the gap between divisible matter and the indivisible non-material. We need not judge the success of this bridging maneuver. The indivisibility of God for Maimonides is the result of God being on the extreme opposite of the continuum on which matter is the other opposite. The result is a God without material or any other attributes. Maimonides, of course, thought he was protecting God from what he saw as primitive idolatry, which is the only term he could apply to a theology of a corporeal God. He apparently did not consider the danger of an overly rarefied God who is so beyond all conception that he cannot be distinguished from no god at all.

The Hebrew Bible speaks about God in anthropomorphic terms. I will focus on one aspect of this anthropomorphism — the indwelling of God in the Tabernacle, in the Temple of Jerusalem, and in the Jewish people — because I detect a certain diluted incarnation in these ideas that will narrow, though not eliminate, the gap between the two faiths on the issue of incarnation. My aim is not a comprehensive survey of the relevant passages (Bernd Janowski in *Gottes Gegenwart in Israel,* Neukirchener, 1993, comes close to such a survey) but the consideration of a small number of passages that are representative of many others.

Let us start with passages that describe God's dwelling in or among the people Israel:

"There [the tent of meeting] I will meet with the people of Israel, and it shall be sanctified by my glory; I will consecrate the tent of meeting and the altar; Aaron also and his sons I will consecrate, to serve me as priests. And I will dwell among the people of Israel, and will be their God. And they shall know that I am the Lord their God, who brought them forth out of the land of Egypt that I might dwell among them; I am the Lord their God." (Exod. 29:43-46)

When Solomon began building the Temple in Jerusalem, God said (1 Kings 6:12-13):

"Concerning this house you are building, if you will walk in my statutes and obey my ordinances and keep all my commandments and walk in them, then I will establish my word with you, which I spoke to David your father. And I will dwell among the children of Israel and will not forsake my people Israel."

When the Ark of the Covenant was brought to the newly built Temple,

a cloud filled the house of the Lord, so that the priests could not stand to minister because of the cloud; for the glory of the Lord filled the house of the Lord. (1 Kings 8:10-11)

Solomon was not oblivious of the difficulties raised by the conviction that God can dwell in an earthly house. "But will God indeed dwell on the earth?" he asks (1 Kings 8:27). "Behold, heaven and the highest heaven cannot contain thee; how much less this house which I have built!"

But the question does not invite the response that God indeed does not dwell on this earth, in this house, in Jerusalem. Quite the contrary. The glory of the Lord filled the house. The priests cannot minister because of the cloud of glory. God dwells in the Temple even if he is also greater than anything a building can encompass. But the transcendence of God is not newsworthy. What is newsworthy is that God dwelled in the Tabernacle, in the Tent of Meeting, and now dwells in the Temple built by Solomon. God has taken residence among the people Israel. That is what makes the space and its environs — Jerusalem and Israel — in which he dwells holy and it makes the people among whom he dwells holy.

God has thus two dwelling places or addresses: the Temple and the people Israel. He dwells in the Temple and among the people. After the destruction of the Temple, the psalmist laments: "Oh God, why dost thou cast us off for ever? Why does thy anger smoke against the sheep of thy pasture? Remember thy congregation, which thou hast gotten of old, which thou hast redeemed to be the tribe of thy heritage! Remember Mount Zion where thou hast dwelt" (Ps. 74:1-2).

But does he dwell in the people as well? Before God took up residence in the Jerusalem Temple, he resided in the mobile Tent of Meeting. The Tent moved with the people so his loyalty was to the people that carried the Tent. Later, his residence is the Temple in Jerusalem because Jerusalem is in the midst of the people Israel. God's affinity to the people is thus deeper than his affinity to the land. The people had its relationship to God before it entered the land and is able to maintain its relationship after it has been severed from the land. When the people is exiled from its land, the divine presence moved into exile along with the people. David Stern ("*Imitatio Hominis*: Anthropomorphism and the Character(s) of God in Rabbinic Literature," *Prooftexts* 12

[1992]: 158), summarizing a passage in *Eikhah Rabbah*, a classical Amoraic midrash on the book of Lamentations, writes:

... when God initially sought to destroy the Temple, he realized that so long as He was inside the building, his presence protected it. In order to allow the gentiles to destroy the Temple, God had to remove himself. He therefore swore not to live in the Temple until the final redemption. Immediately, the Gentiles invaded the building and destroyed it.

But apparently God's self-removal was not total. The divine presence did not leave the Temple Mount, at least not completely. But wherever a community of (ten) Jews gather, the divine presence is with them. Anywhere.

Does this amount to an indwelling of God in the people Israel? In some sense, I suppose it does. The Hebrew *betochom* can be translated as "among" them or "in" them. But I do not think this is a philological issue. It is not even so much a philosophical as a spiritual issue. It is an issue of the image of God in man and of God's love for Israel. It is drawing together of a God who creates a human family in his image and then chooses a segment of that family for a special measure of love. As this love intensifies, as lover and beloved draw closer together, a certain indwelling of God in his people results. This indwelling does not result in the erasure of the difference between the two but rather in an indwelling of the one in the other.

God's drawing to man occurs in two stages. First, there is the creation of man in the image of God (Gen. 1:26-27). The significance of this statement can easily be underestimated. That the ancient rabbis did not underestimate it emerges from a midrash[2] which recounts,

Said R. Hoshaiah, "When the Holy One, blessed be he, came to create the first man, the ministering angels mistook him [for God, since man was in God's image] and wanted to say before him, "Holy [holy, holy is the Lord of hosts]." To what may the matter be compared? To the case of a king and a governor who were set in a chariot, and the provincials wanted to greet the king, "Sovereign!" But they did not know which one of them was which. What did the king do? He turned the governor out and put him away from the chariot, so that people would know who was king. So too when the Holy One, blessed be he, created the first man, the angels mistook him [for God]. What did the Holy One, blessed be he, do? He put him to sleep, so everyone knew that he was a mere man.

2. Gen. R. VIII:X, quoted in Jacob Neusner, *The Incarnation of God: The Character of Divinity in Formative Judaism* (Philadelphia: Fortress Press, 1988), p. 3.

Being created in the image of God produced a resemblance between man and God that was great enough to confuse the angels. Man's body, it seems to me, cannot be excluded from this resemblance. It is, of course, tempting to restrict man's resemblance to God to his rationality or some other non-corporeal aspects of the human person. But that would be neither biblical nor rabbinic. Man is created by God as a physical being and if there is a human resemblance to God then his body also resembles God. That is why the human corpse does not fully lose the divine image and must therefore be treated with great respect. And if the human body can resemble God, then there must also be a physical aspect to God's being. But we must be careful not to go too far. God is not prepared to acquiesce in the error of the angels. However much resemblance there is, there is also the ultimate difference: man and God are not one, though they resemble each other.

The image of God that is impressed on all human beings, Jew and gentile, is the first and possibly most fundamental (can I say ontological?) sign of God's love of man. True, the first eleven chapters of Genesis do not overflow with God's love of his creatures. We read about a number of unfortunate events — the eating of the forbidden fruit and the expulsion from Eden, Cain's killing of Abel, the flood, and the tower of Babel — most of which arouse God's anger and his judgment. The love of God is in the background but it is not absent. Punishment must not be interpreted as a lack of love. Pre-Abrahamic humanity is loved and disciplined when disobedience warrants it. The creature who resembles his creator must learn to obey him.

And then suddenly Abraham appears and God's love flows over him and Israel without limit. Perhaps it is because God has observed the consequences of his anger and has been chastened. Whatever the reason, we now witness an outpouring of love for an individual and his descendants that becomes the central motif of the rest of the Hebrew Bible.

Here are some representative texts, biblical and rabbinic:

"For you are a people holy to the Lord your God; the lord your God has chosen you to be a people for his own possession, out of all the peoples that are on the face of the earth. It was not because you were more in number than any other people that the Lord set his love upon you and chose you, for you were the fewest of all peoples; but it is because the Lord loves you, and is keeping the oath which he swore to your fathers, that the Lord has brought you out with a mighty hand, and redeemed you from the house of bondage, from the hand of Pharaoh king of Egypt." (Deut. 7:6-8)

Further:

"Is Ephraim my dear son? Is he my darling child? For as often as I speak against him, I do remember him still. Therefore my heart yearns for him; I will surely have mercy on him, says the Lord." (Jer. 31:20)

Further:

"Who is a God like thee, pardoning iniquity and passing over transgression for the remnant of his inheritance? He does not retain his anger forever because he delights in steadfast love. He will again have compassion upon us, he will tread our iniquity under foot. Thou wilt cast all our sins into the depth of the sea. Thou wilt show faithfulness to Jacob and steadfast love to Abraham, as thou hast sworn to our fathers from the days of old." (Mic. 7:18-20)

Nowhere is God's love for Israel demonstrated more clearly and in more vivid imagery than when Israel is addressed as the son of God.

"And you shall say to Pharaoh, Thus says the Lord, Israel is my first-born son, and I say to you, Let my son go that he may serve me." (Exod. 9:22-23)

Further:

"You are the sons of the Lord your God; you shall not cut yourselves or make any baldness on your foreheads for the dead." (Deut. 14:1)

Further:

"With weeping they shall come, and with consolations I will lead them back, I will make them walk by brooks of water, in a straight path in which they shall not stumble; for I am a father to Israel, and Ephraim is my first-born." (Jer. 31:9)

Further:

"When Israel was a child, I loved him [or "fell in love with him"], and out of Egypt I called my son. The more I called them, the more they went from me, they kept sacrificing to the Baals, and burning incense to idols. Yet it was I who taught Ephraim to walk, I took them up in my arms; but they did not know that I healed them. I led them with cords of compassion, with the bands of love, and I became to them as one who eases the yoke on their jaws, and I bent down to them and fed them. . . . How can I give you up, Oh Ephraim! How can I hand you over, Oh Israel! How can I make you like Admah! How can I treat you like Zeboiim! My heart recoils within me, my compassion grows warm and tender." (Hos. 11:1-6, 8)

The application of the term "son" or "first-born" to Israel is not a rarity. While at times the term is also applied to the king of Israel (e.g., 2 Sam. 7:14; Ps. 2:7), it is most frequently applied to the people Israel and to the king as the representative of the people before God.

I now turn to some rabbinic texts that deal with God's love and intimacy with Israel. We read:

> Said R. Nahman bar Isaac to R. Hiyya bar Abin, As to the phylacteries of the Lord of the world, what is written in them? He said to him, 'And who is like your people Israel, a singular nation on earth' (1 Chron. 17:21). And does the Holy One, blessed be he, sing praises for Israel? Yes, for it is written, 'You have avouched the Lord this day . . . and the Lord has avouched you this day' (Deut. 26:17-18). Said the Holy One, blessed be he, to Israel, You have made me a singular entity in the world, as it is said, 'Hear Oh Israel, the Lord our God, the Lord is one' (Deut. 6:4). And I shall make you a singular entity in the world, as it is said, 'And who is like your people Israel, a singular nation on the earth' (1 Chron. 17:21). (b. Ber. 6a-b)

There are two aspects of this passage that attract our attention. There is first the flagrant anthropomorphism of depicting God as wearing phylacteries. It is not easy to understand how the ancient rabbis intended such texts to be understood. One wonders whether they distinguished between a "literal" and a "figurative" sense of their texts. At times, they invoked the formula *kivyachol* which seems to mean something like "as it were," thereby indicating that their words were not to be taken quite literally. But that word is missing in the text just cited, though it may be implied. But even if some version of *kivyachol* is hovering over the text, the boldness of the anthropomorphism is remarkable. They were certainly not as disturbed by anthropomorphism as Maimonides was later.

Equally important for our purpose is the level of dignity God bestows on Israel in this text. The key word is *echad* which is best translated in this context as "unique." Israel attributes *echad* of God and God attributes *echad* of Israel. The Jewish philosophical tradition interprets the *echad* of Deuteronomy 6:4 to mean "one" in the metaphysical sense. According to Maimonides, the reason God cannot possess attributes is that he is absolutely one and if there were any attributes that could be connected to God, his absolute oneness would be compromised. However, this is probably a misunderstanding

173

of Deuteronomy 6:4. The Jewish Publication Society translation of the Hebrew Bible gives Deuteronomy 6:4 as "Hear, O Israel! The Lord is our God, the Lord alone." This translation — which I think is correct — reads the verse not as making a metaphysical statement about God, namely, that he is one and indivisible, but rather that God alone is to be worshiped to the exclusion of all other gods. Nevertheless, it is of the highest importance that our text has God attach the quality of *echad*, which Deuteronomy 6:4 attaches to God, to the people Israel. If *echad* attributed to God means that only he is to be worshiped, then *echad* attributed to Israel must mean something comparable. Among the nations, Israel is God's only betrothed. Even if Israel is unfaithful with other gods, God remains faithful to Israel. Israel will be punished but is never divorced (Isa. 50:1). As Paul affirms: "For the gifts and the call of God are irrevocable" (Rom. 11:29). The unique bond between God and Israel is mutual in the sense that Israel must have no other God and God will never have another people.

One final rabbinic text about God's intimacy and love for the people Israel. We read:

> Said R. Yohanan in the name of R. Yose, How do we know that the Holy One, blessed be he, says prayers? Since it is said 'Even them will I bring to my holy mountain and make them joyful in my house of prayer' (Isa. 56:7). 'Their house of prayer' is not stated, but rather 'my house of prayer.' On the basis of that usage we see that the Holy One, blessed be he, says prayers. What prayers does he say? Said R. Zutra bar Tobia said Rab, 'May it be my will that my mercy overcome my anger, and that my mercy prevail over my attributes, so that I may treat my children in accord with the trait of mercy and in their regard go beyond the strict measure of the law.' (b. Ber. 7a)

God, it seems, prays to himself about the welfare of his children which is dependent on whether God's attribute of law or mercy — in Christian terminology, law or gospel — gains the upper hand. In a calm moment, it seems, God prays that he will be able to control his anger and exercise mercy. For Christians, it seems to me, the invocation of Jesus in faith guarantees divine mercy. Jews have no such guarantee. At times, God's justice conquers his mercy and then Israel suffers. Ultimately, mercy must prevail because God's promises cannot be annulled even if, in the short run, justice can prevail when the God of Israel acts as a wrathful though just God. God prays that these interludes be few if not totally absent.

To summarize: I have approached the topic of incarnation from the vantage point of God's proximity to Israel as his point of contact with humanity. The people of Israel and the Temple in Jerusalem are God's dwelling places in the world. When the Temple is out of commission, God's presence on the Temple Mount is reduced though not absent. But then his presence in the people Israel is increased.

As the nation in whom God dwells, Israel is in grave danger, a danger inherent in the strategy of election that God has chosen as his way of relating to humanity. At first, God did not envisage the election of a particular people for particular proximity to God. All of humanity created in the image of God would be the elect of the creation. But the string of failures recorded in the first eleven chapters of Genesis causes God to change course. The welfare of all humanity remains God's ultimate goal as evidenced by his remark to Abraham that "by you all the families of the earth shall bless themselves" (Gen. 12:3). But it is worth noting that the first half of the verse just quoted reads "I will bless those who bless you, and him who curses you I will curse." However much the election of Abraham is intended to serve the welfare of all, God seems aware that the very act of election, even if this involves imposing a higher standard of conduct on the elect, will generate resentment and there will be those who will curse Israel. On the other hand, there will be those who will accept God's sovereign choice in love and obedience and they will be blessed.

These two tendencies co-exist in Christian consciousness. There are those Christians who stress Israel's transgressions and its remoteness from God. There are those who stress the Jewish "no" to Jesus and Jewish secularism and materialism. And there are those who — without overlooking Israel's failures — sense the overwhelming love with which God relates to this people and who find it possible to participate in that love. Those who do, become adopted sons and daughters in the house of Israel. The others practice a Christianity that dwells in a house no longer shared with Israel.

There remains the question of the relationship of God to matter or, more specifically, flesh. We are told (John 1:14): "And the Word became flesh and dwelt among us, full of grace and truth; we have beheld his glory, glory as of the only Son of the Father." By now, we should not be surprised at the notion of God's indwelling, that he dwells in the Temple and among or in the people Israel. While the glory of God can dwell in the Temple, God does not become one with the stones of his dwelling place. They undoubtedly become holy but being holy is not the same as being God. And the same is true if God dwells not only in the midst of Israel but in it. By God's indwelling in the people, it becomes a holy people, "a kingdom of priests and a holy nation" (Exod. 19:6). But does this mean that God has become flesh? I do not think so.

The distinction I wish to draw is between God's dwelling in the midst of or even in the flesh of Israel and God becoming flesh. Here is where the Christian creeds are so helpful because they insist on a high level of clarity in this matter. We learn in the definition of Chalcedon (451 c.e.) that Jesus Christ

> is perfect both in deity and also in human-ness; this selfsame one is also actually God and actually man, with a rational soul and a body. He is of the same reality as God as far as his deity is concerned and of the same reality as we are ourselves as far as his human-ness is concerned; thus like us in all respects, sin only excepted.

Here it is not a question of God indwelling in a Tabernacle or a people, with the Tabernacle or the people retaining its material or human identity and God retaining his divine identity with the latter dwelling in the former. The authors of the definition of Chalcedon were very clear in wishing to avoid such a formulation. Instead, they wished to depict a person who was both human and divine while retaining his identity as one person. As this person walked the earth, believers could point to him and say: "Here is God walking the earth as a physical human being and as God." This is my understanding of Christian incarnation and I do not find anything like that in Jewish sources.

Curiously enough, it is Judaism that has often been characterized as a carnal religion and contrasted with Christianity that has been described as a religion of faith rather than works, with works understood as another dimension of Jewish materialism. And yet, when it came to the final unification of God with flesh, it was Christianity that took that leap and Judaism that rejected it. It is as if the carnality of Jewish existence, the understanding of Israel as the seed of Abraham obligated to obey the commandments that mainly regulate the physical conduct of the Jew, enabled Judaism to keep God in the incarnational sense out of the material order. If the Torah of God penetrated the material world, God would not have to do the same. Christianity, on the other hand, with its reservations with respect to the carnal Mosaic law and its understanding of the church as a community of faith rather than a natural human family, balanced its preference for the spiritual by a God who became human flesh. Both faiths thus struggle with God's relationship to the material order; one, by a Torah that regulates the material order but keeps God out of that order; the other, by preaching salvation through faith and not by works of the law but depicting a God who has become man.

The thesis of one person with two natures and one God with three persons generated an immense discussion in which Jews played almost no role. It has frequently been pointed out that the early creeds and the discussion surrounding them proceeded on the basis of Greek metaphysical categories that may not be as convincing today as they were in the ancient world. While there probably is some merit in this determination, it is not one that can play a decisive role in the context of the Jewish-Christian dialogue which must focus on a common scripture — the Hebrew Bible — rather than on alleged metaphysical shortcomings of Christian articles of faith. It is for this reason that in the definition of Chalcedon cited above, my attention is drawn to the following sentence: "He [Jesus Christ] is of the same reality as God as far as his deity is concerned and of the same reality as we are ourselves as far as his human-ness is concerned; thus like us in all respects, *sin only excepted* [emphasis not in original]." But how seriously can the human-ness of Jesus be taken if he is not capable of sin? This is the ultimate test of the incarnation of God. The temptation and the ability to sin is a defining characteristic of humanity. Perfection and therefore the inability to sin is a defining characteristic of God. How can these two natures co-exist?

By rejecting the Nestorian heresy — that Jesus had two persons, one human and the other divine — the church insisted on the unity of the person of Jesus even if this one person had two natures, one human and the other divine. It would therefore be wrong to speak of the flesh of Jesus as pertaining to his human but not his divine nature. "For it should be considered," asserted the Synod of Constantinople (753 c.e.), "that that flesh was also the flesh of God the Word, without any separation, perfectly assumed by the divine nature and made wholly divine." The flesh of Jesus was therefore divine flesh because there is no ontological separation in Jesus between his human and divine natures. That is why Mary can be spoken of as the mother of God and not just the mother of the human aspect of Jesus. Jesus is one person and whoever is the mother of his physical body is also the mother of God.

So sin cannot be ascribed to Jesus the human being and withheld from Jesus as God. Either Jesus as a whole is capable of sin — and, if so, then God is capable of sin — or Jesus as a whole is not capable of sin. Faced with these two options, Chalcedon opts for a Jesus who is not capable of sin. In so doing, it seems to me, it endangers the full humanity of Jesus. Leviticus 16 deals with the sacrificial order of the Day of Atonement. We read (v. 16):

Thus he shall make atonement for the holy place, because of the uncleanness of the people of Israel, and because of their transgressions, all their sins; and so he shall do for the tent of meeting, which abides with them in the midst of their uncleanness.

Commenting on this verse, the *Sifra* writes:

Even though the [Jews] are unclean, the Divine Presence is among them.

To believe that God became incarnate in Jesus the Jew is to encounter the Divine Presence in the people Israel. The alternative is to contend that the Jewishness of Jesus was purely contingent, as was the color of his hair or his precise weight. I know of no Christian author who has made this claim. But if the Jewishness of Jesus is not contingent, then it is — for Christians — the climax of the process that began with the election of Abraham. My claim is that the Christian teaching of the incarnation of God in Jesus is the intensification of the teaching of the indwelling of God in Israel by concentrating that indwelling in one Jew rather than leaving it diffused in the people of Jesus as a whole. From my perspective, such a severing of any Jew from his people is a mistake because, biblically, God's covenant partner is always the people of Israel and not an individual Jew. While a mistake, the severing in question was not as thorough as it could have been. Against Marcion, the scripture that was sacred to Jesus remained part of the church's scripture and the salvation history that began with Abraham remained part of the salvation history of the church.

The doctrine of the incarnation thus separates Jews and Christians but, properly understood, also sheds light on incarnational elements in Judaism which are more diffuse than the Christian version but nevertheless very real. If the Christian move was a mistake — and I believe it was — it was a mistake that has helped me better understand a dimension of Judaism — God's indwelling in the people Israel — that I would probably not have understood as clearly without the Christian mistake.

# Israel, the Church, and Election

The Second Vatican Council did not propose a detailed account of the Church's relationship to the Jewish people, and most of what it did say on the topic was ultimately located in the declaration entitled "On the Relationship of the Church to Non-Christian Religions" (*Nostra Aetate*, issued October 28, 1965). Despite this arguably inauspicious location (since it seems to overlook the special character of the Church's relation to the Jewish people), the declaration marked an important milestone in the history of the Church's teaching about Judaism. It repudiated anti-Semitism, rejected the idea that Jews bear collective responsibility for the death of Christ, and called for "mutual understanding and appreciation" between Christians and Jews. In its crucial theological affirmation, the declaration stated, "It is true that the church is the new people of God, yet the Jews should not be spoken of as rejected or accursed, as if this followed from Holy Scriptures." In this essay occasioned by *Nostra Aetate*, Wyschogrod does not respond to the declaration point by point. Instead, he briefly expounds a Jewish theology of "non-Jewish religions," within which he then locates the Church, emphasizing in particular the theological dangers that threaten the Church when it is tempted to adopt a supersessionist posture toward the Jewish people. Originally published in *Brothers in Hope*, ed. John M. Oesterreicher (New York: Herder and Herder, 1970), pp. 79-87.

—◊◊◊—

In the Council's "Declaration on the Relationship of the Church to Non-Christian Religions," the Catholic Church addresses and instructs her faithful. In this document, the non-Christian religions are spoken *about*, not spoken *to*. In a strict sense, therefore, it is not a document that requires a response from those thus spoken of. But those about whom we speak can also speak about us; indeed, it is to be expected that they will do so. In this age of instantaneous communication, we must be aware that he about whom we are talking hears us and that we are therefore talking to him as well as about him. Yet, the distinction between being talked about and being talked to is not thereby obliterated. To overhear a conversation about oneself remains not an altogether painless experience. Parallel talks about each other may, however, be the prelude to the truly reconciling act of one addressing the other. It is in this spirit that I wish my comments understood.

# I

The people of Israel pursues its course in history in the faith that it is the people of God. Because God loved Abraham, he chose him and his seed as the people of his Covenant. Because this people is a human family with all the frailties and failings of humankind, the people of Israel has never ceased to prove unworthy of its election, rebelling against the mission laid upon it by God, more often than is seemly to say. God, in his infinite mercy, nevertheless continues to love this people above all others. To it, he has given his name so that he is known to all the families of the earth as the God of Israel.

Although God is both the creator and ruler of the universe, he reveals himself to humankind, not as the conclusion of the cosmological or teleological proofs, but as the God of Abraham who took the people of Israel out of the land of Egypt and whose people this nation remains to the end of time. He thus remains inaccessible to all those who wish to reach him and, at the same time, to circumvent this people. Because he said, "I will bless those who bless you, and curse him that curses you; in you shall all the families of the earth be blessed" (Gen. 12:3), he has tied his saving and redemptive concern for the welfare of all humankind to his love for the people of Israel. Only those who love the people of Israel can love the God of Israel. Israel is thus God's first-born, most precious in his eyes.

From this, two great dangers follow, both of which have come to pass. The first is Israel's vain pride in its own election and the second is the nations' jealousy at that same election. This twofold drama is prefigured in the tale of Joseph and his brothers, but so is the reconciliation that awaits us at the end of time.

Many times, Israel has found it hard to believe that its election is not the fruit of its virtue, that the endless love God bestows on this people is not richly deserved. Uncannily expert in the failings of the nations, often remembering only its faithfulness and rarely its unfaithfulness, turned inward by the hostility of the peoples among whom it lives, Israel tends to forget that its election is for service, that it is a sign of the infinite and unwarranted gift of God rather than any inherent superiority of the people.

Hated on all sides by those who contest its election, Israel looks at times with contempt at a humanity that is not only unwilling to grant its claims but insists on expressing hatred for the God of Israel through the crucifixion of Israel's body. Thus the two reinforce each other: The more Israel is hated, the less it lives up to its divine calling; the less it lives up to its divine calling, the more ludicrous and offensive its claims of divine election become. All this is not to say that had Israel proved more worthy of its election it would not have incurred the hatred of those whom God did not elect. Israel must, nevertheless, come to terms with its failure, with the misuse to which it has put its election. While the role assigned by God to Israel, that of the favorite son, was indeed a difficult one, it could have been fulfilled because election — God's favor — is not a temptation at which humans must fail.

# II

The unfaithfulness of Israel is, however, only part of the truth, though it is the part Israel likes to forget and the nations like to remember. The other part of the truth is Israel's faithfulness:

> I remember the affection of your youth.
> Your bridal love:
> How you followed me through the wilderness,
> Through a land unsown.

> (Jer. 2:2)

If it is true that Israel is not worthy of its election, it is also true that God's election is not in vain. Not only has he transformed Israel's resistance into an occasion for the glorification of his name, but he has also chosen a people that, side by side with its resistance, acts as the willing servant of God, traversing a wilderness populated by those not willing to acquiesce in the exercise of sovereignty that is God's election of Israel. The prophet tells us:

181

Israel is the Lord's hallowed portion,
His first fruit of the harvest;
All that devour him shall be held guilty.
Evil shall come upon them,
Says the Lord.

(Jer. 2:3)

Israel's record is thus not all negative. Starting with Abraham's love for his God which was so great that he was willing to sacrifice his only son, and not ending with those Jews who, holding their children by their hands, walked into Hitler's gas chambers, grateful for the opportunity to sanctify God's name, Israel has shown that obedience is also a genuine possibility, that the image of God in humankind makes humanity not only the descendant of Cain but also of Abel.

Just as Israel's record is mixed, so is that of the nations. Instead of accepting Israel's election with humility, they rail against it, mocking the God of the Jews, gleefully pointing out the shortcomings of the people he chose, and crucifying it whenever an opportunity presents itself. Israel's presence is a constant reminder to them that they were not chosen but that this people was, and that this people remains in their midst as a thorn in the flesh. Minute by minute, the existence of Israel mocks the pagan gods, the divine beings who rise out of the consciousness of all peoples but which are gentile gods because they are deifications of humanity and the forces of nature rather than the true, living God of Abraham.

The pagan mind knows very well that the God of Israel demands compassion for the lowly and the suffering, and that this attitude is incompatible with the honor of the warrior and the pleasure of victory, the stuff of which gentile history is made. The eros of the gentiles is threatened by the existence of Israel because this people, living in exile and lacking all the outward manifestations of the state, the normal instrument of national existence, survives the mightiest nation-states, many of which have long disappeared from history, while Israel, against all human calculation, endures. Israel is thus a living witness that the God who chose it is the Lord of history and that his purpose will be achieved. Refusing to cherish gratefully the blessing that is promised to all nations through the election of Israel, a blessing which according to the divine word is the purpose of Israel's election, the nations rise with the full anger of their uncircumcision against the God of the Covenant and the people of the Covenant.

## III

Gradually something emerges which is to have the profoundest effect: the Church. The Church transcends national boundaries, substituting a community of faith for one based on language and soil. In the Church, the vocabulary of Israel is used — covenant, election, suffering servant, and redemption — and the book that Israel hears as the word of God is for the first time heard by a people that is not of the seed of Abraham. Can anything but joy fill the heart of Israel as it observes the mysterious way in which the God of Israel begins to be heard by the nations? Is it not the faith of Israel that, in the fullness of time, the God of the patriarchs will become the God of all peoples and, if this is not just an idle dream, must Israel not be ready to perceive signs of this even in the travail of history? Maimonides pointed out that Christianity and Islam "served to clear the way for King Messiah to prepare the whole world to worship God with one accord," since through them "the messianic hope, the Torah, and the commandments have become familiar topics — topics of conversation (among the inhabitants) of the far isles and many peoples, uncircumcised of heart and flesh."[1] There is, then, at least, a segment of the nations that collaborates with Israel in its mission.

But the Church claims to be the new people of God, Abraham's sons according to faith. Where the old Israel was an elected community, according to the flesh, the new Israel is a community of faith open to all people, whatever their ancestry. From the point of view of the Church, it appears, the election of Israel is thus superseded in God's plan by a new election. Does this mean that the old Israel, the sons of Abraham according to the flesh, ought to disappear from the stage of history? This is not clear. It would seem that the answer is "Yes" because the Church, with the exception perhaps of the very first decades, did not insist that Jews who embraced Christianity retain their identity as Abraham's offspring. Instead, Jews who entered the Church intermarried and their descendants quickly lost knowledge of their origins.

## IV

Had the Church believed that it was God's will that the seed of Abraham not disappear from the world, she would have insisted on Jews retaining their separateness, even in the Church. The fact that Paul asserts that in Christ

---

1. *The Code of Maimonides: The Book of Judges*, trans. Abraham M. Hershman (New Haven: Yale University Press, 1949), p. xxiii.

"there is neither Jew nor Greek, neither slave nor freeman, neither male nor female" (Gal. 3:28) does not rule out such a special role for the children of ancient Israel in the Church, just as the abolition in Christ of the difference between man and woman does not prevent Paul from insisting that women remain silent in the assembly. Even in Christ, men are men and women are women; only in an ultimate, perhaps eschatological, sense are they one. The Church could have asserted the same of the difference between Jew and gentile. Since the Church did not assign to the Jew who became a Christian such special status, it can be inferred that — quotations from Paul (Rom. 11:28-29) to the effect that God does not repent of the gifts he makes notwithstanding — the Church seriously holds that its election superseded that of the old Israel. The existence of the Jewish people as the seed of Abraham seems, therefore, to her no longer a demand of God.

Israel must, of course, reject this view. All attempts to transform its election into a universal election of all people in faith can be interpreted by Israel only as the beginning of that movement toward the universal which, fully developed, culminates to the universal truth of a philosophy antithetical to the concreteness of the God of Abraham. The philosophical component in Christianity, its deep involvement with Platonic and Aristotelian philosophy and the myriad problems brought about by this involvement, is thus not merely an accident of intellectual history, but rooted in the Christian kerygma itself.

The substitution of a universal election of faith for the national election of the seed of Abraham lays the groundwork for a universalization that must, in due course, look to philosophy with its even more universal structures. In a sense, the Christian doctrine of election is a demythologization of the Jewish doctrine of election, which Christianity interprets as the concrete symbol of a possibility open to all people. For this reason, the Christian mind was driven to an ever greater concern with philosophy, a tendency that, while not totally absent in the history of Judaism, never reaches the proportions it does in Christianity.

V

The Church's claim of being the new people of God — a claim the Vatican II declaration under discussion specifically reiterates — is, from the Jewish point of view, another example of the nations' protest against the election of the stock of Abraham. Just as Joseph's brothers rebelled against the favor shown by their father toward this one child of his, so the nations refuse to accept the election of Israel. And just as Joseph was not guiltless in the matter in that he did not accept his election as he should have, in humility, in fear and trembling, so Israel has not often made it easy for the nations to accept its election. Just as Joseph suffered for his deeds, so has Israel; just as Joseph retained the election, proving worthy of it, so has Israel. The question that remains is this: What is Israel to make of the Church's claim that it is the new people of God?

We have already dealt with the negative moment of the answer to this question: Israel cannot fail to see in this claim an act of rebellion against the word of God, however much guilt Israel shares in this rebellion. But that is not all Israel must see. To be envious of the election of Israel, the Church must seek the God of Israel; the Church must love that God. This, from the Jewish viewpoint, is the overwhelming significance of the Church's claim to be the new people of God. The nations, as represented by the Church, seek the God of Abraham. This is a fact that has never impressed itself into the Jewish consciousness. Persecuted throughout its history, surrounded by paganism on all sides, a paganism that had nothing but contempt for the God of Abraham, Israel has never grasped that there is a segment of the gentile world into which the word of the God of Abraham has penetrated.

Because the Christian is a human being and, like the Jew, not sinless, he often falls short of that ultimate humility which accepts the will of God in love even where God's will is the election of someone other than himself. Short of that ultimate perfection, a perfection that almost surpasses the human, the Christian is addressed by the God of Jesus who is the God of Abraham. This God is a God of covenant: he relates himself to a people through a covenant that makes that people his people and him their God. Access to this God is only through a covenant by means of which a people becomes the people of God; once this is perceived, the Church arises as the people of a new covenant. Christianity, therefore, expresses the longing of those not included in the Covenant with Israel for election by the God of Israel.

# VI

Hence Israel must ask itself how it envisages the relation of the nations to its God. Traditionally, this has been answered in terms of the Noachide laws. They, in turn, were sometimes interpreted in terms of natural law: All that is required of the nations is that they obey the moral law as dictated by human reason. If this is all that is required of the nations (though, from another point of view, this is more than humans are capable of when not aided by

God), it would follow that God's relationship is only with Israel and that the nations cannot have their own covenant with him. This, however, is a biblical theology altogether unacceptable: It ignores the promise to Abraham that through his election the nations, too, will be blessed; it further ignores the covenant with Noah, which is not natural law but a covenant in its own right. Maimonides insists that non-Jews fulfill their obligations under the Noachide laws only when they receive them as commanded by God. To be commanded by God is to be addressed by him, and it is therefore incumbent upon Israel to welcome the covenant of the nations with the God of Israel.

From the human point of view, it is not difficult to understand why a people as uniquely related to God as Israel is, cherishing its election in spite of, or because of, the suffering this election has entailed, is reluctant to entertain the possibility that God may be willing to address other nations and be their Father as well. Because the relation between Israel and God has been so concrete, the mechanisms of human jealousy come into play. God's faithfulness to Israel is thus often thought to imply unconcern with other peoples. But God's willingness to address others and to love them in no way diminishes his love for Israel. Israel must therefore work, hope, and expect the day when many peoples shall go and say:

> Come! Let us go up to the mountain of the Lord,
> To the house of the God of Jacob,
> That He may teach us His ways
> And that we may walk in His paths.

(Isa. 2:3)

# VII

For their part, the nations who seek the God of Israel must meditate on the mystery of their non-election. Surely non-election does not equal rejection. Ishmael and Esau, the sons of non-election, are suffused in the divine word with a compassion in some respects more powerful than the love of the sons of election. Is it not possible that those who love God so much that, even in their non-election, they submit with love and serenity to the destiny chosen for them by God, are very dear to him indeed? Not to be the favorite son of a human father is a painful experience, but the non-election of God is never a finality, only one way of being touched by the finger of God. If, in the election of Israel, there is also chastisement of a sinful Israel, in the non-election of the nations there is also the father's love for all of his children. In the end of days, there will be a reconciliation of all the families of the earth without division. To foreshadow that day, the Jew must speak humbly of his election, the gentile with love of his non-election, both waiting together for the final redemption of creation.

# Paul, Jews, and Gentiles

Modern Jewish thinkers have sometimes drawn a sharp distinction between Jesus and Paul, arguing that while Jesus remained rooted in his Jewish context, Paul departed from it drastically and became the founder of a foreign religion. In contrast, Wyschogrod approaches Paul as a Jewish thinker whose views demand to be understood in Jewish terms. In this previously unpublished essay, Wyschogrod offers an extensive discussion of major issues central to Paul's apostolate, including the significance of the Christ event, the status of Torah obedience among Jesus' followers, and justification by faith. In each case, Wyschogrod holds that a proper understanding of Paul's thought demands taking into account the relevance of the distinction between Jew and gentile, which the Christ event modifies but does not erase.

WHAT WAS the significance of the Christ event for Paul? What had changed as a result of this event and what had remained the same?

There is no question that Paul's decisive message is contained in just this sense of newness, of something having happened which has drastically altered the human condition as it had never been altered before and as it will never be altered again. But what precisely is the nature of this alteration?

A preliminary and probably quite accurate answer to this question is this: Because of the crucifixion and resurrection of Jesus who was the son of God, humanity's sins were forgiven and it was therefore saved from the eternal death which was the fate that had previously awaited it. Before Christ, the human creature stood guilty before God for not fulfilling the demands of the Law, the obligation God had transmitted to Israel through Moses. Being a sinner, the individual was subject to the penalties prescribed by the Law, penalties very vividly detailed in Deuteronomy 28:15 through the end of the chapter. Because of the Christ event these penalties were no longer applicable. When Paul says in Galatians 3:13, "Christ bought us freedom from the curse of the Law by becoming for our sake an accursed thing," he does not mean that the Law is a curse, a thought that is pure madness and contradicts Paul's clear statement in Romans 7:12: "therefore the Law is in itself holy, and the commandment is holy and just and good." He does mean that there is a curse attached to disobeying the holy Law. "Curse of the Law" should perhaps even be translated as "the curse attached to disobeying the Law," which is undoubtedly more faithful to the meaning of the text than "Curse of the Law" which seems to imply that the Law is itself a curse rather than disobedience to it, a misinterpretation with wide currency.

Immediately, a number of questions present themselves. If the meaning of the Christ event is that the penalty attached to the Law is no longer in effect, how is this to be understood? Does it mean that indiscriminate transgression of the Law is no longer to be avoided since there is nothing to fear anymore? This would be one way in which the curse attached to disobeying the Law could be understood as having been lifted, but it is clearly not Paul's understanding in view of his extensive objections to antinomian and libertarian manifestations. Does it mean that the curse attached to disobeying the Law is lifted by the Christ event in quite another sense, namely, those who died and are reborn in Christ escape the curse attached to disobeying the Law by having obtained a power with the help of which they simply never disobey the Law and thereby escape the punishment that awaits those who do disobey it? This is a more likely interpretation in view of Paul's comments about the virtuous life led by those with faith in Jesus as the Messiah. But it is nevertheless not satisfactory because it would seem to imply that Christians never sin, a theme that runs counter to the forgiveness of sin motif that is also powerful in Paul. Finally, Paul must have been aware that the Law of Moses was never thought of as obligatory for non-Jews. As Apostle to the Gentiles, what possible significance could the message that the curse attached to disobeying the Law of Moses had been lifted have for Paul's gentile listeners who had never come under the jurisdiction of this Law in the first place? Obviously, there is something we are not grasping properly.

Central as the Christ event is in the thinking of Paul, it is incorrect to think of it as having the same effect for Jews and gentiles. The Christ event does narrow the gap between Jews and gentiles, perhaps very much so, as we will see. But it does not erase it. We will therefore examine the effect of the coming of Christ on gentiles and then on Jews, moving then to an examination of what these two segments of the Church have in common and what distinguishes them.

Before we can understand the significance of the coming of Christ for gentiles, we must understand the attitude toward gentiles in the Judaism of the period. Gentiles were under no obligation to obey the commandments of the Torah, an obligation which was the result of God's covenant with Israel and which did not apply to those outside of the covenant. Nevertheless, God was by no means indifferent to the conduct of gentiles. This conduct had to conform to the so-called Noachide commandments which bore Noah's name because, in rabbinic thinking, they were rooted in God's covenant with Noah and his descendants reported in the ninth chapter of Genesis. As understood by the rabbis, this covenant covered the basic moral law including such transgressions as incest, murder, robbery, and so on. Curiously enough, included among these was the prohibition against amputating a limb of a living animal for the purpose of eating it, while leaving the crippled animal alive, a practice the rabbis referred to as "a limb from the living." There is reason to believe that this practice was widespread in the ancient world with its absence of means of refrigeration so that a whole animal would go to waste if it was killed without all of it being eaten fairly quickly. Mutilation of the animal was therefore a commonly used method of preserving the unused portion of the animal for future use. The prohibition against this practice is included in the Noachide Commandments by the rabbis because of Genesis 9:4: "But you must not eat the flesh with the life, which is the blood, still in it," a verse which appears in the context of the covenant with Noah and which becomes the only prohibition that cannot perhaps be classified too easily as belonging to the basic moral law though, as a prohibition of cruelty to animals, it has a clearly moral dimension.

The Noachide Law is, then, the Torah of the gentiles. They are under obligation to obey it as the Jews are under obligation to obey all of the Torah. A gentile who obeys the Noachide Law pleases God and has a portion in the world to come. For this reason, it is not advisable for gentiles to convert to Judaism since, once circumcised, the gentile becomes a Jew and is under obligation to obey the whole Torah as are all Jews. Since the rabbis understood that obedience to the Torah is a difficult thing, so difficult that Israel has often failed to measure up to its demands and suffered grievously for it, they were of the opinion that gentiles were well advised to live a righteous life under the Noachide Commandments rather than to expose themselves to a much more difficult challenge. Nevertheless, even for the rabbis, gentiles who persisted in their desire to become Jews and place themselves under the demands of the Torah were permitted to do so, as long as the implications of their contemplated course of action were fully understood. For the vast majority of righteous gentiles, however, the absence of circumcision and the need to accept the full Torah meant that they did not become members of the house of Israel, of the people elected by God, "a nation of priests and a holy people." The term used by the rabbis to describe such a righteous gentile was *Ger Toshav,* the indwelling stranger, to differentiate that individual from the *Ger Tzedek,* the righteous stranger, who had fully become a Jew. There is reason to believe that both in Palestine and the exile, fairly large numbers of *Gere Toshav* followers of the Noachide Commandments were at various times attached to the Jewish communities as sympathizers with the faith of Israel who had not fully embraced Judaism. In fact, there is reason to believe that it was precisely from this group that most of Paul's converts originated. As persons familiar with Jewish concepts and sympathetic to them, they were a natural audience for a message that would have been very difficult to grasp for persons totally unfamiliar with Jewish ideas.

We are now in a position to understand Paul's view of what the Christ event had done for gentiles. With the coming of Christ, a gentile who was willing to obey the Noachide Laws and who had faith in Jesus as the Messiah became an associate member of the house of Israel. I use the phrase "associate member" because it is the only expression I can think of to characterize the new standing of the gentile Christian. He was more than a *Ger Toshav.* A *Ger Toshav* was a righteous person who pleased God and had a portion in the world to come but he was not a Jew. A *Ger Tzedek* was no longer a gentile: as a result of circumcision and willingness to accept the Torah, he has become a Jew, a new birth to all intents and purposes. Prior to Paul there were therefore full members *(Ger Tzedek)* and non-members *(Ger Toshav).* For Paul, the Christ event had made possible a new category: gentiles who were not circumcised and not obedient to the Torah but who were still not excluded from the house of Israel. Because of their obedience to the Noachide Laws and their faith in Christ, they assumed the status of adopted sons, not to be confused with the natural sons who remained the root that sustains the branches (Rom. 11:18). But the gentiles in Christ have been grafted into the tree, even if it is as a grafting of a new branch into an old tree. They had become members of the household of Israel, something which prior to Christ could be achieved only by full conversion to Judaism.

It is further quite clear that this opinion of Paul's was not universally shared by Jewish Christians. There were those who believed that to become a Christian involved everything that had previously been necessary in becoming a Jew: circumcision and acceptance of the Torah. For those who held this opinion — we hear of them in Acts 15 and in Galatians — there was no new category of membership in Israel. The coming of Christ had been an event in Judaism. It had produced a division among Jews — those who recognized what had happened in the person of Jesus and those who had not. But it had not produced a new category of persons — those who were not Jews but had ceased being gentiles who were external to the house of Israel. Rather, for Paul's opponents, becoming a Christian meant becoming a Jew, the kind of Jew who had recognized Jesus as the Messiah. And since becoming a Jew implied, and had always implied, circumcision and obedience to the Torah, it was perfectly clear to these Jewish Christians that those who called themselves Christians but had not been circumcised and did not obey the Torah had been profoundly misled. When they came across communities that had been converted by Paul, they found to their amazement communities that profoundly believed themselves to be Christian but which were not circumcised and which obeyed only the Noachide Commandments. These Jewish Christians who disagreed with Paul lost no time in informing these uncircumcised Christians that they had been misled, that they were not Christians at all since to become a Christian involved circumcision and the Torah. It is not difficult to imagine the distress that the news must have caused the new Christians. One can only compare it to the state of mind of a contemporary of ours who had been converted to Judaism by a reform rabbi and is then told, perhaps on a visit to Israel, that he is no Jew at all since Orthodox Judaism demands circumcision and the pledge to live in accordance with the Torah. From Acts 15 we know that Paul, in order to settle once and for all whether he or his opponents were right, submitted the matter to the Jerusalem church which, after extended debate, ruled in his favor. The ruling of Acts 15 specifically refers to the Noachide Laws as binding on gentile Christians and rejects the view that they were under obligation to embrace circumcision and the Torah.

Was Paul or were his opponents more continuous with rabbinic Judaism? This is an interesting question because there is no simple answer to it. In one respect, Paul's opponents were the more traditional since they adhered to the view that people were either Jews or they were not and if they were, they had to be circumcised and obey the Torah and if they did not do these things they were not Jews, though, of course, they could be righteous gentiles. In another respect, it was Paul who was being more traditionally Jewish. The thrust of rabbinic Judaism had been to discourage conversion, as I have already explained. In rabbinic thinking, Nazirites, Jews who voluntarily imposed additional obligations on themselves, were not held in favor simply because it was not for human beings to increase their obligations, as if those that already applied to them were so easy to bear. In very much the same spirit, the gentiles, in the rabbinic view, ought not voluntarily to increase their obligations beyond the Noachide Commandments to which they were subject. Paul, in discouraging the circumcision of gentiles, was therefore acting within the traditional rabbinic framework. What was new about Paul's view, as we have already seen, was the belief that the Noachide Laws combined with faith in Jesus as the Messiah brought into being a new category of persons, associate members in the house of Israel. If this is the central achievement of Christ for gentiles, then it follows that a gentile who embraced circumcision and the Torah after the coming of Christ was in effect saying that Christ had not happened, that everything was as it had been before and that the only entrance into the house of Israel was through full conversion, i.e., circumcision and acceptance of the Torah. This is what, I think, Paul means when he says, "If you receive circumcision Christ will do you no good at all" (Gal. 4:2). He does not nor can he mean that Christ is not efficacious for those who are circumcised. He does mean that for those who are not circumcised, to travel the route of full conversion is to overlook the new route that Christ had opened to membership, albeit associate membership, in the elect people. Paul's mind on the circumcision question is therefore shaped by two considerations: the new route to associate membership in Israel opened by Christ and the traditional Jewish opposition to and discouragement of gentile conversion to Judaism. Paul's opponents, on the other hand, reject the new possibility of associate membership. To the extent that they advocate gentile circumcision as the only route to Christ, they are being untraditional in not discouraging gentile circumcision. We can therefore see that both Paul and his opponents are continuous with but also modify the traditional rabbinic approach to the problem of gentile conversion.

If gentiles needed Christ to achieve a kind of membership in Israel, surely this was of no great relevance to Jews who already were members of the people of election. The contribution of Christ for Jews lies in another direction: it has to do with Israel and its obligation — under the Torah, or *nomos*, the Law, in the Greek translation.

It is first necessary to clear up a view that I consider a misinterpretation: the view that it was Paul's opinion that because of Christ, the Torah was no longer obligatory for Jews because it had been superseded by a new Law, the Law of love which was the Law of Christ rather than of Moses. There is no denying that there are seemingly good reasons for holding this view. Paul says many negative things about the Law. We have already spoken of his reference to the Deuteronomic curse associated with disobedience to the Law. The charge "that you teach all the Jews in the Gentile world to turn their backs on

Moses, telling them to give up circumcising their children and following our way of life" is reported in Acts 21:21. Galatians, to which we have already referred, is a sustained polemic against a backsliding community which, after having embraced Christ, is attracted to circumcision and the Law. These are some of the reasons for the firm establishment of the view that Paul broke with the Law of Moses. And yet it is an incorrect view, if we understand the matter correctly.

Acts 15 is decisive in this respect. We are told about a dispute occasioned by "certain persons who had come down from Judaea" (Acts 15:1) who taught "that those who were not circumcised in accordance with Mosaic practice could not be saved." Since this teaching, as we have already seen, conflicted with that of Paul, who believed that circumcision (and obedience to the Law, since these always go together — see Gal. 5:3) was not necessary for gentiles, it was arranged that the matter be brought to the attention of the Jerusalem church for adjudication. After *lengthy* debate (Acts 15:7) the decision is reached, and communicated in a letter, that no further burden beyond the Noachide Laws is to be placed on gentiles. In so doing, Paul's position on the matter is fully vindicated by the authoritative Jerusalem church. It is not difficult to infer from this episode that for Jews the Torah obviously was thought of as remaining obligatory in the view of the Jerusalem church. Had the thought that with the coming of Christ the Law had been abolished entered anyone's mind in Jerusalem, there could clearly not have ensued a long discussion, settled with some difficulty, as to whether circumcision and the Law ought to be made obligatory for gentiles. If it was no longer obligatory for Jews, how could it possibly become so for others? The only possible explanation dictated by the facts is that the possibility of the Torah not remaining binding for Jews never occurred to anyone in Jerusalem. With this as the basic background fact, we can understand how a debate could have arisen and apparently did arise about whether the Torah was obligatory for gentiles. And we can, furthermore, also understand how the mistaken impression that Paul considered the Law abrogated for Jews was generated. We have already referred to Acts 21:21 in which the Jerusalem church cautions Paul that this slander against him is abroad and suggests a method, accepted by Paul, to lay the slander to rest. It is worth noting, parenthetically, that the Jerusalem church prefaces its report of the slander against Paul by a remark about how "many thousands of converts we have among the Jews, all of them staunch upholders of the Law" (Acts 21:20). In any case, because Paul preached against circumcision and the Law for gentiles and clearly came into conflict with Jewish Christians who believed that circumcision and the Law was essential for gentiles also, it is easy to imagine how this position could have generated the mistaken or perhaps willful misinterpretation that Paul was preaching against circumcision for Jews as well as gentiles. But the fact remains that this is not what he believed or preached.

With this in mind, we can also better understand Paul's comments on the Law, particularly his emphasis on the Deuteronomic curse (Deut. 28:15-68). To the Jewish reader of Paul, the most immediate question is why Paul emphasizes the Deuteronomic curse and totally ignores the blessing which precedes the curse (Deut. 28:1-14). Chapter 28 of Deuteronomy consists of a blessing and a curse: a blessing if Israel obeys the commandments contained in the Torah and a curse if it does not. Must not both be spoken of if Paul's readers are to get a complete picture of the Law, of the implications of being subject to the Law, as Israel is? The answer is simple, though, I believe, most significant. Paul is writing to gentiles. He is attempting to discourage them from circumcision and acceptance of the yoke of the Law. In so doing, he is continuing the rabbinic tradition of discouraging gentiles from conversion to Judaism and accepting and putting themselves under the judgment of a set of demands considerably more stringent than the Noachide Laws. When doing this, it is necessary to stress the negative aspect of coming under the Law, the danger of punishment when the Law is violated. It is perhaps even permissible to exaggerate the negative so as to dissuade the gentiles. At the very least, it is necessary not to discuss the positive aspects of coming under the jurisdiction of the Law. If the gentiles persist in spite of all the discouragement, if they embrace the faith of Israel in spite of everything they have heard, then the time has come to tell them of the blessing which flows from the Law, from obedience to it and the love of it. Prior to that point, however, the note to be struck is one of discouragement, not as a falsehood but because there are grave dangers associated with being bound by the Torah, dangers which Israel has experienced firsthand, again and again, because of its disobedience. This is exactly what Paul is doing. He is pointing out the disadvantages of being bound by the Law, so as to discourage gentiles from coming under its jurisdiction. He is not — though this is how he was understood for many centuries — giving a total picture of the Law. Here and there, in spite of this, as a Jew raised in and respectful of the Law, he cannot help but say some good things about it. Basically, however, Paul is the Apostle to the Gentiles and therefore the negative side of the Law, the side that must be displayed to the potential gentile convert, predominates.

Having cleared away this misunderstanding, we must now ask: what has Christ done for Jews? We know what he has done for gentiles. He has made it possible for them to receive a kind of membership in the house of Israel. But what has he done for Jews? They obviously don't need to be added to the family that is Israel since they already are that family. For a long time, it was thought that with the coming of Christ, the Law had ceased to be relevant to Jews. We now know that this is not so. What difference had Jesus then made to Jews?

The answer is that he had brought them out from under the curse of the Law, the threat of punishment that, according to the Hebrew Bible, hangs over every Jew who tries to fulfill the demands of the Law but who is in constant danger of punishment when he transgresses it, as he will more or less inevitably do. To understand this properly, we must approach it from the rabbinical framework in which God's dimension as the giver of Law stands in tension with God as the father of mercy.

The rabbis noticed that in the Hebrew Bible God was sometimes referred to by J and sometimes by E. Modern biblical scholarship explains this by positing different traditions or texts which were woven into a more or less continuous narrative which nevertheless retains the marks of its composite origins. The rabbis knew nothing of this explanation. They saw in J and E two aspects of God: J was the aspect of mercy, E of Law. The world was created by E, God in his aspect of Law. His original intention was to create human beings, lay down a Law to govern their conduct, and then to judge them in justice in accordance with the Law, dealing out to them what they deserve in accordance with their actions. God found that this course led to the flood because humankind transgressed the Law and brought disaster on itself. God then decided that justice must be tempered with mercy if the experiment that was humankind was to continue. We therefore hear of J, God in his aspect of mercy who acquits humans when justice would dictate their conviction. And for the rest of the Bible, J and E appear together, sometimes actually joined and sometimes alternating. At times, God metes out justice. At other times, his mercy gains the upper hand and humans receive more than they deserve; life when they deserve death, acquittal when they deserve condemnation. Jewish existence is thus a very insecure one. There is no way of knowing whether, in any given situation, the justice or the mercy of God will predominate. Israel always beseeches God to be dealt with in mercy, not to be held accountable by the strict application of the criterion of justice. But there is no way of assuring that this will be the case. At times, God permits mercy to triumph and the judgment is averted. At other times, often after repeated exercises of mercy, justice is permitted to exact its demands and then it goes hard with Israel. When Israel begs for mercy, most characteristically the patriarchs are invoked, because God loved them especially and sometimes, for their sake, tempers his justice with mercy. Because mercy is something undeserved, Israel cannot demand it but only beg for it and be grateful when it is dispensed.

It is this situation that is radically changed by Christ, in Paul's view. For Paul, Jesus means *Midas Horachamim*, God's aspect of mercy. Where previously the aspects of justice and mercy alternated, with Israel sometimes receiving what it deserved and at other times the recipient of God's mercy, with the Christ event and with faith in Christ, God's aspect of mercy becomes the permanent and exclusive mode of his relationship to Israel. There is no longer any alternation between mercy and justice. Now only mercy is applicable and therefore the curse that is attached to disobedience to the Torah becomes inoperative because the curse, as punishment, is possible only when the justice of God is active. Jesus on the cross was the lightning rod which drew all punishment to itself, thereby protecting all others (Gal. 3:13). Once and for all, the terrible danger of living under the Law is lifted because God's *Midas Hadin*, his aspect of justice, has permanently yielded to his mercy.

This, then, is the significance of the Christ event for Jews, in Paul's theology. Gentiles are brought into the house of Israel by Christ, which previously they could only achieve by circumcision. Jews are freed from the danger of punishment if they disobey the Torah because God is all mercy now. It must be added that in one respect God's justice remains operative. Those who are outside Christ (however "outside" is to be defined) are not assured of God's mercy. "There is no condemnation for those who are united with Christ Jesus," writes Paul in Romans (8:1) but the same may not be the case for those not so united. God as mercy is therefore true only within the Church, that island of redemption established by Christ but surrounded by a world in which the wrath of God is still operative. Nevertheless, since access to Christ is open to all, in a significant way the justice of God can be escaped for his mercy.

It is therefore true that in one sense Paul sees the Law as abrogated to the Jews, if by "abrogated" we mean that it is no longer demanded of the Jews that they be obedient to it. Now it might be argued, and Paul is well aware of this possibility, that if God's mercy is assured, if there is no danger of punishment, why should sin be resisted? Is sin then not merely an opportunity for God to exercise his guaranteed mercy? Paul rejects this line of reasoning vigorously (i.e. Rom. 6:1-23). Christians are assured of God's mercy but they must also be sinless. I dare say that early Jewish Christians were particularly devout followers of the Law. We need only remind ourselves again of Acts 21:20 where the Jerusalem church speaks proudly of its "many thousands of converts we have among the Jews, all of them staunch upholders of the Law."

Two more points before our concluding comments. As I read it, Paul thought of the church as made up of two complementary portions. One portion of the church was to consist of former gentiles who were bound by the

Noachide Laws and believed in Jesus as the Christ. The other portion was to consist of Jews bound by the Torah and believing that Jesus was the Christ. These two segments of the church had their faith in Jesus in common and, for Paul, this was the decisive factor. But there was also a difference in that Jews in the church remained loyal to the Torah. They were the original household to which the gentiles had, through Christ, been admitted. This was their blessing in Christ. The blessing that Christ conferred on Jews was that he freed them from the dire dangers that resulted from violation of the Torah. Once and for all, Jewish Christians knew that God's mercy and not his justice would be meted out to them. It might be interesting to speculate which of the blessings, that of the gentiles or the Jews, was the more overwhelming. I rather think that for Paul they were both approximately equal.

It follows that if this analysis is correct and if Paul remains authoritative for the church, Jews who embrace Christ must be persuaded by the church to retain their identity as the seed of Abraham, as Jews always have, by rejecting intermarriage. They must also remain loyal to the Torah and its command-ments, with their faith in Jesus as the Christ as the only characteristic differ-entiating them from other Jews. It might be thought that such a retaining of Jewish identity in the church contradicts Paul's assertion (Gal. 3:28) that in the church "there is no such thing as Jew and Greek, slave and freeman, male and female." This passage, important as it is, must not be read to introduce a rigid uniformity into the church. Elsewhere, Paul identifies the role of women in the church and it is not the same as that of men. Similarly, Paul advises Christian slaves to be good slaves and Christian masters to be good masters. In the ultimate sense, the most important sense, all people are the same for Paul in Christ. But in any sense other than the most ultimate, differences re-main with the difference between Jews and gentiles certainly not qualifying, for Paul, as an ultimate difference but neither as no difference at all.

And now for the second of my pre-concluding remarks. One of Paul's most telling arguments against those who insist that circumcision and the Law are a prerequisite of salvation is that a human being is not justified by the Law but only by faith. It has been traditional to think of Judaism as preaching that humans are justified by the merits accruing from doing good deeds in ac-cordance with the commandments of the Torah while Christianity clings to faith rather than good deeds as the way to salvation. There is some truth in this but also much misunderstanding.

What does justification by works of the Law mean? What would some-one be believing who believed that a person is justified by works of the Law? We must turn once again to the difference between *Midas Hadin* and *Midas Horachamim*, God's aspect of justice and of mercy. A person who believed that he was justified by works of the Law alone would, in effect, be saying to God: "Judge me in accordance with my deeds, give me what is coming to me, but I do not ask for mercy, for anything more than what I deserve." I suppose that from time to time there have been such proud defendants who have refused to beg for mercy, whatever their reason may have been, be it confidence in the unassailability of their case or plain pride that made begging for mercy an intolerable option for them. Whatever the case may have been in such situations, it is unthinkable for Judaism or a Jew to strike such a pose before God. Judaism has always understood that if judged by the strict demands of the Law, no Jew can prevail. We are all sinners who must beg for the mercy of God; without it, we are lost. In the morning liturgy, we find the following: "Master of all worlds! It is not on account of our own righteousness that we offer our supplications before thee, but on account of thy great mercy." When Paul says that humans are not justified by works of the Law, this is exactly what he means. He is saying nothing that is in any way different from common rabbinic opinion. It must be added, of course, that this does not mean that we may therefore discontinue obeying the Law and fulfilling its demands. We must do the best we can, striving in every way possible to fulfill the Law, even while we know that we will fall short of its demands and therefore have to beg for God's mercy. It is true that Judaism has cherished the mitzvah, the deed done in accordance with God's command. But this has not meant that it has therefore felt it unnecessary to appeal for God's mercy. To the best of their ability Jews must strive to fulfill the mitzvoth; but it is also most advisable for them to beseech God's mercy.

Until now, I have been trying to penetrate the mind of Paul, attempting to understand him from within the framework of Judaism which was, after all, his framework. We have learned that the Christ event was for Paul a very crucial event, having decisive significance for Jews and Gentiles, though in somewhat different ways. Because Christ is so central for Paul, it is easy to forget the effects of the Christ event and, instead, concentrate exclusively on Jesus as the Christ. Judaism is in little danger of this temptation because it does not share Paul's evaluation of Jesus as the Christ. For this very reason, it becomes particularly important for Judaism to examine what Christ is alleged to have accomplished, even if Judaism maintains its dissent that it is he who accomplished it. Just as Judaism, as I have argued elsewhere,[1] cannot claim on *a priori* grounds that God could not have become incarnated in a Nazarene carpenter since to do so would be to make of Judaism a philosophic system

1. Cf. "Why Was and Is the Theology of Karl Barth of Interest to a Jewish Theologian?" pp. 211-224.

rather than the story of the free acts of God, so, it seems to me, Christianity cannot argue on *a priori* grounds that God could have admitted the gentiles to the house of Israel and suspended the wages of sin only by means of an incarnation and crucifixion. It is for this reason that I will restrict myself to the consequences of the Christ event, as Paul conceived them.

Judaism has rarely understood the depth of the gentiles' feeling of exclusion. Because Jews have experienced persecution and rejection for so long, it has been difficult for them to understand that there are gentiles, and not a few, who wish to become members of the family that is the Jewish people, the seed of Abraham elected by God for his service. Judaism has never elaborated the Noachide covenant as a form of election, not unrelated to the election of Israel. It has not, for example, found a place in the synagogue for the Noachide converts, not as Jews, but as gentiles who love and are obedient to the God of Israel who is also the God of all humankind. I must reiterate that this has not been due to any real theological objections to such a course, but to a kind of disbelief that Jews have of the concept that there are gentiles who deeply desire to enter into Israel's relation with God. While there have always been converts received by Judaism, they have been few and scattered. The thought that there might be such a movement toward its God by large numbers who are not prepared nor required to become Jews has not seemed real to Judaism. This is what we can learn from Paul. We can learn from him that Israel has a responsibility to enable gentiles to obey its God and live in covenant with him. For Paul, this possibility centers on and is inconceivable without Christ. But it must also become a possibility for Judaism within its own framework. The God of Israel is a God who chooses the least likely: Moses the stutterer; Saul of the tribe of Benjamin, the smallest of the tribes of Israel and of the least important family in that tribe; and David, the youngest of eight brothers. If the gentiles today are the non-elect, then that is the more reason for Israel to pay special attention to them since the God of Israel has so often made the first last and the last first. I say this with the full belief that Israel's election is eternal. But the election of Israel was so that "in thee shall all the families of the earth be blessed" (Gen. 12:3). The non-election of the gentiles cannot be as deep and permanent as Judaism has often assumed. This is the truth of Paul.

And now, let us look again at the thesis that the God of mercy has permanently displaced God in the aspect of justice and that therefore the curse of the Law, the punishment for transgressing the Law, is abolished. Israel does not believe this because it knows in its flesh that the God of Abraham, Isaac, and Jacob punishes and punishes terribly. We live in the light of the terrible seriousness of the Torah. Our transgressing it is not a small matter; our lives and the lives of our children depend on it. The God of Israel is not a permissive grandfather who no longer knows what is right and wrong and who is, in any case, too busy to punish his children. Israel pleads for mercy because it knows the alternative as a real possibility. History has proven this beyond doubt.

It may be asked: how can Israel live with this, with the knowledge that the wrath of God may erupt at any moment, that there is no knowing when his mercy will suspend the requirements of justice or when, God forbid, he will exact what the Law requires in full measure? The answer is this: Israel can live with this because it feels itself so deeply loved that the wrath of God is never experienced as total. However terrible it may be, it is a passing fury while his love is forever. Had Israel not known this in its bones, it could not have survived, it would have turned against itself in the fury of God, hating itself as children who are not loved hate themselves. And here and there, there have been manifestations of such Jewish self-hatred. But basically, the Jewish people has loved itself, and its individual members each other, because it felt itself loved by God irrevocably, eternally, and absolutely. It is understandable that children by adoption are somewhat less certain of this love and are therefore much more frightened by the wrath and must therefore believe that the wrath is gone forever. Perhaps as they come to feel more at home, they will more easily accept the wrath which is the other side of God's love.

Nevertheless, Paul is right in one way. God's wrath and mercy are not equal. Mercy is deeper than Law, more final, destined to triumph and to redeem Israel and humankind. Humanity will be redeemed, preferably in accordance with their merit, because they will deserve it. But if not, God will redeem them in his mercy anyway. We do, therefore, have a guarantee of mercy, even if only finally, as the last act. That is how Judaism understands it.

# A Letter to Cardinal Lustiger

The following remarkable letter was sent by Michael Wyschogrod to Cardinal Jean-Marie Lustiger, archbishop of Paris. The son of Polish Jewish migrants, Cardinal Lustiger was born in Paris in 1926 and converted to Catholicism in 1940. Down through the centuries, church and synagogue have tacitly agreed that no one can be both a Jew and a Christian at the same time. Despite this, Cardinal Lustiger has never ceased to identify publicly with his Jewish background and experience. In this letter, Wyschogrod holds that orthodox Jewish teaching supports the cardinal's self-identification as a Jew. But by the same token, Wyschogrod argues, Lustiger also remains obligated to live in a manner consistent with Torah. Moreover, while such a manner of life would be out of step with traditional Christian thinking, it would mark an important and clarifying return to the theology and practice of the early church. The letter dramatically illustrates the depth of Wyschogrod's commitment to the unity of the Jewish people, as well as his belief that the question of Christian supersessionism turns finally on the church's posture toward Jewish followers of Jesus. A version of the letter that did not identify its recipient was published, together with Jewish and Christian responses, in Modern Theology 11:2 (April 1995): 165-171. Cardinal Lustiger did not reply to Wyschogrod's letter.

—◦◦◦—

*A Letter to Cardinal Lustiger*

July 28, 1989
His Eminence
Jean-Marie Cardinal Lustiger Archeveque de Paris
32, rue Barbet de Jouy 75007 Paris
France

Your Eminence:

It is now several years that we have met, first in Paris in your office and then in May of 1986 during your visit to the American Jewish Congress when our dialogue advanced a bit. Since then I have been thinking about some of the things we spoke about and I now feel a need to put on paper some ideas that have been going through my mind. In doing so, I speak for no one other than myself. I am not acting as a representative of any organization or institution. As an individual, I simply feel the need to address you. I hope you will find the time and the inclination to answer my letter since such matters are best dealt with in the context of a dialogue. But even if you do not reply (which itself would be a sort of reply), I still feel impelled to tell you what I think because I am convinced that the issues involved are very important indeed for believing Jews and Christians. In fact, I think that your position, the role you play in the Roman Catholic Church and in the dialogue between Judaism and Christianity, is of historic importance — if properly understood and correctly interpreted.

## 1. A Jewish Cardinal?

You are a Jew who became a Catholic and rose in the Church to become the bishop of Paris and a cardinal. While this is remarkable enough, it is, of course, not unprecedented. I do not know whether any baptized Jew has ever reached a position comparable to yours in the Church. But that is not the point. The point is that there have been many Jews who, in the course of the centuries, entered the Church. From a spiritual point of view, the rank in the Church reached by such persons is not terribly important.

What is important is that, in the past, when a Jew accepted baptism, he severed his bonds with the Jewish people and with Judaism. Being a Jew and a Christian were thought to be incompatible by the adherents of both religions. While everyone knew that Judaism and Christianity had some beliefs in common, most Jews and Christians focused on the differences and these were important enough to convince everybody that a choice had to be made: one was either a Jew or a Christian but one could not be both.

From the Jewish point of view — and probably also from the Christian point of view — this state of affairs had its advantages. Both faith communities required clear identities. Because there was a time — albeit long ago — when the two communities were one, both have been anxious over the centuries to define their identities in contrast to the other community. This effort would be ill served by any degree of toleration of dual citizenship. One had to be one or the other; one could not be both.

But you did not look at things that way. You wrote that,

> in becoming a Christian, I did not intend to cease being the Jew I was then. I was not running away from the Jewish condition. I have that from my parents and I can never lose it. I have it from God and he will never let me lose it.[1]

When you decided to be baptized, you said to your parents:

> "I am not leaving you. I'm not going over to the enemy. I am becoming what I am. I am not ceasing to be a Jew; on the contrary, I am discovering another way of being a Jew."[2]

And you added:

> "I certainly do feel very much a Jew."[3]

Here we have something relatively new: a Jewish cardinal archbishop of Paris. Not a cardinal archbishop of Paris who had once been a Jew but ceased being one when he became a Christian, but one who is a Jew while he is the cardinal archbishop of Paris. In short, we have a Jewish cardinal archbishop of Paris. This is a situation that deserves thought.

## 2. An Ethnic or Religious Jew?

The question that arises, of course, is the sense in which you consider yourself a Jew. The question of what and who is a Jew is a notoriously complicated one and there is at least one sense of being a Jew — the ethnic or national one —

---

1. Jean Marie Lustiger, *Dare to Believe: Addresses, Sermons, Interviews, 1981-1989* (New York: Crossroads, 1986), p. 91.
2. Lustiger, *Dare to Believe*, p. 91.
3. Lustiger, *Dare to Believe*, p. 51.

in which being a Jew and a Christian are compatible. But I do not think that is the sense in which you consider yourself a Jew.

Someone might reason as follows: Being a Jew has two components, a national and a religious one. Most Jews who are ethnically or nationally Jewish also happen to be adherents of the religion known as Judaism or, at the very least, they have not adopted another religion. But this is a purely accidental correlation. In principle, the ethnic or national component can be separated from the religious one and it is therefore eminently possible for a national or ethnic Jew to become the adherent of another religion, as it is possible for a Frenchman to stop being a Catholic and become a Muslim or a Buddhist.

Your position would then amount to saying that you consider yourself an ethnic or national Jew who has adopted another religion. Your ethnic or national identity has no essential connection with your religion. The statement that you are a Jew would then have no religious content. I cannot believe that this is what you mean when you say you are a Jew.

As a believing Christian, you cannot interpret Jewish identity in purely national-ethnic terms. While it is true that being a Jew involves belonging to a nation, the nation in question is a very special one. It is a nation chosen by God to stand in covenantal relationship with him. In the past, many Christians believed that the chosenness of the Jewish people had come to an end with its rejection of Jesus of Nazareth as its redeemer. But this view has been widely repudiated, based on St. Paul's teaching that "the gifts of God are irrevocable" (Rom. 11:29). So being a Jew remains, from the Christian point of view, a theologically significant fact even today and even with respect to Jews who do not share the Christian faith.

So I return to your claim that you remain a Jew in spite of being a bishop and a cardinal of the Roman Catholic Church. Is this a claim that I can accept?

Of course, I can. Anyone born of a Jewish mother or anyone properly converted to Judaism is, according to rabbinic law, a Jew. You were born of a Jewish mother, therefore you are a Jew. In the eyes of God, as you say, there is nothing anyone can do about that.

That does not mean that, from the point of view of rabbinic Judaism, you are a good Jew. From the Jewish point of view, converting to another faith is a very serious matter. This is particularly true when the faith to which a Jew converts believes in the teaching of the Trinity. As you well know, this teaching is particularly objectionable to Jews, who see it as compromising monotheism.

So it is clear that from the Jewish point of view accepting trinitarian

Christianity is not a good thing to do. In fact, it is so bad that a Christian Jew loses all sorts of privileges in the community of Israel, such as being an acceptable witness in a rabbinic court or being counted in a prayer quorum of ten. But all this in no way changes the fact that a Christian Jew remains a Jew.

To be a Jew means to labor under the yoke of the commandments. Jews are required by God to live in accordance with the commandments of the Torah while gentiles are required by God to obey the Noachide commandments based on Genesis 9:1-17. The Noachide commandments resemble the natural moral law though they do not coincide with it. It therefore follows that a gentile who eats leavened bread during the Passover season (to choose but one example) is in no way displeasing God while a Jew who does so is, from the Jewish point of view, displeasing God because God has forbidden Jews to eat leavened bread during Passover (see Lev. 23:6).

The only operative test, therefore, for whether someone is a Jew is whether he sins when he eats leavened bread on Passover, does not inhabit a *Succah* (booth) during Tabernacles, or violates any of the other positive or negative commandments of the Torah. A gentile does not sin in any of these instances (except when he violates the Noachide commandments) and a Jew does.

Now the point is that once someone is a Jew, he always remains a Jew. Once someone has come under the yoke of the commandments, there is no escaping this yoke. So baptism, from the Jewish point of view, does not make eating pork into a neutral act. In fact, nothing that a Jew can do enables him to escape from the yoke of the commandments. This proves like nothing else that a Jew who has converted to Christianity remains a Jew, albeit one who has done something he should not have done.

So I have no difficulty agreeing with you that you are a Jew, religiously speaking.

There are Jews who probably do not agree with me. Their first priority is to keep Judaism and Christianity distinct. They fear that if one can be a Christian Jew or a Jewish Christian, then the lines between the two religions will have been blurred and this will make it easier for Jews to become Christians. Many Jews, they think, refrain from baptism because they do not relish declaring themselves disloyal to their Jewish heritage. But if it is made possible for them to enter the Church and somehow still remain Jews, then the reluctance to enter the Church will be much diminished.

I do not think that there is much merit in this argument. Most Jews who wish to become Christians will do so irrespective of whether other Jews will continue to consider them Jews or not. And even if this is not so, the truth remains the truth. According to authentic Jewish teaching as I understand it, a

Jew remains a Jew no matter what religion he adopts and this basic truth cannot be changed for political or prudential reasons.

## 3. Implications

Having established that we agree that you are a Jew, we must now ask what significance this fact has for the situation in which you find yourself.

Let us start by attempting to answer this question from a Jewish point of view. Because you are a Jew, you are obligated, like all Jews, to obey the mitzvoth (e.g., tefilin [phylacteries] in the morning, kashrut, sabbath, etc.). Like all other Jews, you are not perfect. You have violated some of the commandments of the Torah and you should repent of these violations. If, in your conscience, your conversion to Christianity is in accordance with God's wishes and therefore not a sin, then you have no reason to repent of that particular act. But in any case, from the Jewish point of view you are obligated to live in accordance with the mitzvoth just like any other Jew.

But the more interesting question concerns what significance the fact has, from a Christian point of view, that you are a Christian who is also a Jew. Even if you still consider yourself a Jew, you also consider yourself a Christian, and the question then arises, what is the practical significance of the fact that you are a Christian Jew or a Jewish Christian.

In the past, this question would not have been difficult to answer. Jews who became Catholics were supposed to act like all other Catholics. The fact that they had once been Jews had no current significance. The Church was guided by the words of Paul (Gal. 3:28): "There is neither Jew nor Greek, there is neither slave nor free, there is neither male nor female: for you are all one in Christ Jesus." In Christ, all distinctions fall away and the obligations of Christians who had been Jews is no different than the obligations of Christians who had been gentiles.

In fact, throughout the centuries, Jews who entered the Church very quickly lost their Jewish identity. Within several generations they intermarried and the Jewish traces disappeared. The only exceptions to this rule were Jewish converts in Spain and Portugal, the sincerity of whose conversions was questioned and who retained a Catholic identity tinged with some Jewish elements. But this was never sanctioned by the Church.

In short, if all Jews in past ages had followed the advice of the Church to become Christians, there would be no more Jews in the world today. The question we must ask is: Does the Church really want a world without Jews? Does the Church believe that such a world is in accordance with the will of

God? Or does the Church believe that it is God's will, even after the coming of Jesus, that there be a Jewish people in the world?

As I have already said, the answer of the old theology to this question was clear. The Church was the new Israel and there was no further need for the old Israel. If the old Israel insisted on surviving, it was only because it did not recognize its redeemer and continued to wait for him who had already appeared. Were all Jews to recognize the truth, they would cease their stubborn insistence on continuing to exist as an identifiable people and become an integral part of the new Israel — the Church — which is God's new covenant partner in the world. The disappearance of the Jews from the world would be no theological loss because their place would have been taken by the new people of God.

## 4. An Alternative Theology

An increasing number of Christians are no longer comfortable with the old theology. If "the gracious gifts of God and his calling are irrevocable" (Rom. 11:29), then it would seem that God's election of Israel is not just an historical curiosity but a contemporary reality. According to Pope John XXIII, God's covenant with the Jewish people has never been revoked. However the Catholic Church today interprets its identity as the new Israel, it no longer seems possible to view the election of Israel as having been superseded by that of the Church, leaving Israel out in the cold. But if, from the Christian point of view, Israel's election remains a contemporary reality, then the disappearance of the Jewish people from the world cannot be an acceptable development.

Closely related to the survival of the Jewish people is the question of the Mosaic Law. Until now, the Christian view has been that Jesus abolished the ceremonial law while he confirmed the moral part of the Mosaic Law. It was therefore no longer necessary for Jewish Christians to obey ceremonial mitzvoth. This was largely based on Paul who wrote (Gal. 5:2) that "if you receive circumcision Christ will do you no good at all." Based on this, Thomas Aquinas concluded that to continue obeying the ceremonial Law after Christ was a mortal sin since "the ceremonies of the Old Law signified Christ as to be born and to suffer, whereas ours signify him as having been born and having suffered" (*Summa Theologiae*, 1a 2ae, q. 103, art. 4, reply). In short, the purpose of the Mosaic ceremonial law was to foretell the coming of Christ but to continue obeying it after the coming of Christ was a mortal sin because it constituted a denial that he had come.

But the traditional Christian view of the Mosaic Law has a number of problems. First, the distinction between the ceremonial and moral parts of the Law is not intrinsic to the Hebrew Bible which knows only of God's commandments to Israel. Second, it must be remembered that Paul's negative statements about the Law are made to gentile Christians with the purpose of discouraging them from circumcision and the Law. Paul himself (Acts 21:20-26) participates in the Temple service in order to lay to rest rumors "that you teach all the Jews in the gentile world to turn their backs on Moses, telling them to give up circumcising their children and following our way of life." We must also remember the passages in the Gospels (e.g., Matt. 5:17-19; Luke 16:16-18) where Jesus speaks with great reverence about the Law. In short, neither Jesus nor Paul taught that any portion of the Law of Moses had become outmoded for Jews.

This is most clearly to be seen in Acts 15. There we are told about a community of gentile Jesus believers who are visited by some Jewish Jesus believers who claim "that those who were not circumcised in accordance with Mosaic practice could not be saved." It can be assumed that the issue here is not only circumcision but Torah observance in general, which is made obligatory by circumcision. Paul disagrees and causes the problem to be brought to the attention of the Jerusalem community. "After a long debate," the decision is reached not to require circumcision and Torah obedience of the gentile Jesus believers but only acceptance of commandments that correspond to a large degree with the Noachide commandments (vv. 20 and 28).

From this episode, a clear conclusion can be drawn. The Jerusalem community harbored two parties. There were those who believed that gentile believers in Jesus had to be circumcised and accept full Torah obedience as part of their conversion to Jesus. Others in the Jerusalem community of Jesus believers believed that gentiles did not have to be circumcised but their faith in Jesus together with a version of the Noachide commandments was sufficient. *But it is clear that both parties agreed that circumcision and Torah obedience remained obligatory for Jewish Jesus believers since, if this were not the case, one could hardly debate whether circumcision and Torah obedience was obligatory for gentiles. Such a debate could only arise if both parties agreed on the lasting significance of the Mosaic Law for Jews. Where they differed was its applicability to gentiles. But both sides agreed that Jewish believers in Jesus remained obligated to circumcision and the Mosaic Law.*

The verdict of the first Jerusalem Council, then, is that the Church is to consist of two segments, united by their faith in Jesus. However, with respect to the Mosaic Law, Jewish Christians would remain under it while gentile Christians would come under the Noachide commandments.

## 5. Conclusion

I now respectfully turn to you, Your Eminence, for a reaction. Am I right or wrong? If I am wrong, where is the flaw in my argument? But if I am right, are you not, from the Christian point of view, obligated to lead a Torah-observant life because you are a Jew? Are you not obligated to obey the dietary laws, the sabbath, the Jewish festivals, etc.?

It is clear that such a decision would cause problems both for the Church and for Jews. But that cannot be the decisive issue. If you, in your conscience, become convinced that as a Jew you are obligated to lead a life in accordance with the Torah, then you must do so, no matter what the consequences.

In fact, were there to be a Jewish cardinal of the Roman Catholic Church who leads a life in accordance with Torah prescriptions, a profound clarification of the Church's attitude to the Hebrew Bible and its Jewish roots will have taken place.

Respectfully,
*Michael Wyschogrod*

# Why Was and Is the Theology of Karl Barth of Interest to a Jewish Theologian?

Wyschogrod recounts the following anecdote about the Swiss Reformed theologian Karl Barth: "On a sunny morning in August 1966 I visited Barth in his modest home on the Bruderholzallee in Basel. He had been told that I was a 'Jewish Barthian,' and this amused him to no end. We spoke about various things and at one point he said: 'You Jews have the promise but not the fulfillment; we Christians have both promise and fulfillment.' Influenced by the banking atmosphere of Basel, I replied: 'With human promises, one can have the promise but not the fulfillment. The one who promises can die, or change his mind, or not fulfill his promise for any number of reasons. But a promise of God is like money in the bank. If we have his promise, we have its fulfillment and if we do not have the fulfillment we do not have the promise.' There was a period of silence and then he said, 'You know, I never thought of it that way.' I will never forget that meeting." What follows is Wyschogrod's most complete account of the significance of Karl Barth for his own theology. The essay was originally published in *Footnotes to a Theology: The Karl Barth Colloquium of 1972*, ed. Martin Rumscheidt (SR Supplement, 1974), pp. 95-111.

—◈◈◈—

I HAVE BEEN asked to explain why a Jewish theologian is interested in the work of Karl Barth. Implied in that question is a more generic one: why is a Jewish theologian interested in Christianity and Christian theology? Let us therefore start with the genus and then turn to the species.

Since every question proceeds from a frame of reference and is based on some assumptions, it is reasonable to assume that the asking of this question proceeds from some degree of wonder that a Jewish theologian should be interested in Christianity. It has been argued, and there are those who continue to maintain, that while an interest in Judaism is necessary and inevitable for the Christian theologian, a corresponding interest in Christianity is neither necessary nor inevitable for the Jewish theologian. Christianity, we are reminded, presupposes Judaism from which it originated and whose promises it claims to have fulfilled. As such, a knowledge of Judaism is essential for a Christian who wishes to understand his faith. Judaism, the argument continues, does not presuppose Christianity and can therefore pursue its path without much interest in Christianity. While it is, of course, a fact of life that Judaism has, for much of its history, existed in a Christian world and, therefore, been forced into contact with Christian civilization, those who believe that an interest in Christianity is not essential to Judaism consider this relationship a relatively external one, not reaching into the religious center of Jewish faith. It is on such ground that the mild wonder aroused by a Jewish theologian who nevertheless is interested in Christian theology can perhaps be explained. Furthermore, there is the degree of strain that has obtained between the two faiths for some time, a strain that you probably have heard of, and that, too, enters the calculation when this question is considered. In the light of all this, why is a Jewish theologian interested in Christianity? What explains this mystery?

It is, of course, not possible to deny the validity of the point concerning the asymmetry between Judaism and Christianity as regarding their origins. Christianity is rooted in Judaism in a way that Judaism is not rooted in Christianity and there seems to be no way of escaping this fact. I cannot, however, conclude from this that a Jewish theologian, therefore, ought or perhaps even must remain uninterested in Christianity. I base this opinion on two considerations, both of which, I think, bear attention by Jewish theology.

First, there is the Divine promise to Abraham that through his election, or in him, there shall be blessed the families of the earth (Gen. 12:3). This makes quite clear that the election of Abraham and his seed, while in many ways separating the history of Israel from those of the nations, cannot rest with such a separation. However appropriate such a separation may be on the way, in a fundamental sense the destinies of the families of the earth and that of Israel are intertwined because it is the Divine intention that the blessing, which is initially Abraham's, in time redound to the benefit of the nations. Israel cannot therefore be ultimately isolationist, however vital it be that it be so penultimately. As it pursues its path through history, it expects the redemption of the nations and watches with great interest those developments which give indication of such a future. Because this is so, the Jewish theologian can and must maintain a vital interest in the spiritual life of the nations with whom it is, in a sense, jointly embarked on the path to redemption. It is not to detract from the centrality assigned to Israel in this process to emphasize this point. Not to emphasize it is too often symptomatic of a misunderstanding of Israel's election, as if the redemption of Israel could be accomplished alongside the non-redemption of the nations.

But if the Jewish theologian is therefore necessarily interested in the religious life of all peoples, how much more must he be interested in Christianity, which has mediated the vocabulary of Israel to all parts of the earth. At times, I find myself driving on a Sunday morning in some rural area of the United States. At this time, as one plays with the dial on the car radio, just about the only reception available consists of church services from this or that local church. And as one switches from station to station, what names does one hear? David, Solomon, Ezekiel, Jeremiah, Isaiah, Jesus, Paul, and so on, Jews one and all. And what concepts does one hear? Sin and redemption, the Messiah, sacrifice, the Passover, Jerusalem, and so on, Jewish concepts one and all. And this Jewish vocabulary, this imagination, these Jewish hopes and expectations issue from gentile seed, from stock that is not of Abraham, from people whose forefathers had not been brought out of Egypt and for whom God did not split the Red Sea. How can a Jewish theologian not be interested in this? True, to the Jewish ear there are at times notes that are not fully harmonious with his consciousness, notes often disturbing and even strange. But it is not this that is the wonder. The wonder is that nations not of the stock of Abraham have come within the orbit of the faith of Israel, experiencing humankind and history with Jewish categories deeply rooted in Jewish experience and sensibility. How can a Jewish theologian not perceive that something wonderful is at work here, something that must in some way be connected with the love of the God of Israel for all his children, Isaac as well as Ishmael, Jacob as well as Esau? It is this that Maimonides perceived about Christianity when he wrote that Jesus "only served to clear the way for King Messiah, to prepare the whole world to worship God with one accord, as it is written 'For then will I turn to the people a pure language, that they may all call upon the name of the Lord to serve him with one consent' (Zeph. 3:9). Thus the messianic hope, the Torah, and the commandments have become familiar topics — topics of conversation (among the inhabitants) of the far isles and many peoples. . . ."[1] Because

1. *The Code of Maimonides*, Book 14, trans. Abraham M. Hershman (New Haven: Yale University Press, 1949), p. xxiii.

Christianity has and continues to play this crucial role related to Israel's mission, Jewish theology cannot fail to be interested in Christian developments.

My second reason for believing that Judaism should cultivate an interest in Christian theology is perhaps less central than the first but nevertheless important. Christianity is heir to an exceedingly rich theological tradition. For various reasons, Judaism has not generally invested its most active energies in the theological enterprise. In order to interpret this fact correctly, considerable acquaintance with Christian theology is required. In the process, the Jewish theologian learns better to understand the framework of his faith because he compares it with an alternate strategy, one that was not taken by his tradition. The result is that dialogue with a theology as sophisticated as that of Christianity advances Judaism theologically and compels it to examine problems it might not otherwise have done. The danger in all this is that Judaism, by being forced into a theological mold perhaps partially foreign to it, is moved toward a self-understanding that is defective in proportion to its exchange of immediacy for mediacy, of being for doctrine, of life for thought, and of the scriptural for the philosophic. But no advance is possible without risk and it should be possible for a responsible Jewish theology to benefit from the experience of Christian theology and avoid those pitfalls so clearly marked out by Barth.

Having made these points in defense of a Jewish theologian's interest in Christian theology generally, it is now necessary to focus on Karl Barth and to ask why he, in particular, attracts the attention of a Jewish theologian. The answer can be stated very simply. Karl Barth is the Christian theologian of our time who is oriented toward scripture, who does not substitute the Word of man for that of God, and who does not find himself helpless before the mighty technology of "scientific" biblical scholarship — an enterprise often replete with all sorts of hidden agendas not obvious at first sight. And because Barth is scriptural, his attention turns to Israel in a rather unique way which the Jewish theologian reads with avid interest if for no other reason than the feeling that it was not written to be read by a Jew, to be commented on by a Jew, to be challenged by a Jew. It cannot, of course, be maintained that this is unique with Barth. Bultmann, to mention but one other example, is at least equally oblivious to the possibility of falling into Jewish hands. But then he is so thoroughly gentile, so Heideggerian, so little humbled by the so largely Jewish Word of God, that one would not expect much from him. Barth is different. Because he is so biblical he is, in some sense, a member of the family whom Israel cannot ignore.

The first and basic point, then, that impresses a Jewish reader of Barth is that his faith is not grounded in some alleged eternal verities of reason or on some noble and profound religious sensibility that is shared by all people or by a spiritual elite, but on a movement of God toward humankind as witnessed in scripture. It is of course true that in this formulation we have omitted the christological center without which any summation of Barth's position is incomplete, to say the very least. For him, God's movement toward humanity is inconceivable without Jesus and it is he who is witnessed in scripture. The Jewish reader, however, while fully realizing the centrality of the christological in Barth, can understand Barth's appreciation of God's movement toward humanity in the light of the Word of God which, after all, is also central for Barth, even if not fully equal to the event of Jesus. The two concepts that emerge as crucial are therefore the theology of divine initiative and the theology of the Word, both of which are deeply Barthian.

Both of these points are Jewish points. It is Israel that speaks of its God as he who has brought it out of Egypt and entered into covenant with this people. It is not inaccurate to say that Israel's definition of God is derived from the saving acts experienced by Israel at the hands of this God. The God of Israel is therefore the God of Abraham, Isaac, and Jacob from which it follows that the God spoken of without the explicit or implicit invocation of the patriarchs is, to Israel, a foreign God who does not simply automatically coincide with its God. Barth's refusal to substitute ontological constructions, whether in the form of the "ground of being" or any other similar deflection of the God known by Israel, for the God who acts in Jewish history, cannot fail to meet with instinctive recognition by the Jewish reader that he has before him a biblically attuned thinker whose focus is on the God of Israel, even if, at a certain point, the Jewish story diverges from the Christian. I am convinced that it is necessary to formulate the matter in these terms, to speak of stories that diverge, because too often rationalistically minded Jewish theologians have made it appear that Judaism resists incarnation on some *a priori* grounds as if the Jewish philosopher can somehow determine ahead of time just what God can or cannot do, what is or is not possible for him, what his dignity does or does not allow. The truth is, of course, that it would be difficult to imagine anything further removed from authentic Jewish faith which does not prescribe for God from some alien frame of reference but listens obediently to God's free decisions, none of which can be prescribed or even anticipated by humanity. If Judaism cannot accept incarnation it is because it does not hear this story, because the Word of God as it hears it does not tell it and because Jewish faith does not testify to it. And if the Church does accept incarnation, it is not because it somehow discovered that such an event had to occur given the nature of God, or of being, reality, or anything else, but because it hears that this was God's free and gracious decision, a decision not predictable by humankind. Strangely enough, the disagreement between Judaism and Christianity, when understood in this light, while not reconcilable, can be brought into the context within which it is a difference of faith regarding the free and sovereign act of the God of Israel.

Barth's relation to scripture is the second point at which the Jewish reader senses a kinship that is crucial. Barthian theology is obedient listening to the Word of God. Barth develops his theology of scripture in the early volumes of the *Dogmatics* and while it can hardly be maintained that scripture diminishes in significance in the later volumes, it nevertheless seems that after the initial discussion Barth does not reopen this basic issue. In any case, Barth knows what scriptural authority is, and is constitutionally incapable of imposing on the Word of God hermeneutic devices derived from alien loyalties which so often, in other cases, turn out to be Greek or other gentile sensibilities. The loyalty to the scriptural is therefore a spiritual conversion to Israel's mind, a matter of decisive significance. That Barth is the first Christian theologian to look to scripture for his foundation would be impossible to maintain. Luther and Calvin were also, of course, scriptural in a very fundamental way. And yet, there is a difference. Strangely enough, perhaps it is the historical perspective that any writer in the twentieth century, even one as resistant to historical relativization as Barth, brings to his work. For Luther and Calvin it was probably not altogether clear that the Bible was an ancient document which must be read by means of an attempt to penetrate the minds of the ancient Jews to whom the Word of God was addressed. Barth is not primarily a historian; Bible-centered as he is, he is not a Hebrew scholar (his Greek and Latin are clearly superior to his Hebrew, unfortunately) and he does not capitalize on the latest advances in "scientific" biblical scholarship. Nevertheless, there is a very clear recognition of the distance in space and time between Jerusalem and Basel and the result of this is that Barth does not carry as much of his Swiss identity into his work as might otherwise have been the case. Consciousness of the historical alone is not sufficient for the achievement of this attachment to a God who has, as it were, hyphenated his name to that of Israel so that the two move through history together. This is proven by Bultmann who, historian that he is, also remains splendidly gentile to an amazing extent. But Barth, I think, does not remain a gentile, which is to say, he becomes a Christian.

All of this must not, however, be taken to mean that Barth's relation to the written Word of God is the same as that of Judaism. Because he is, in a sense, so close to it his distance from it is so apparent. I know of no better way of illustrating this than by reference to the so-called Law, the commandments of the Pentateuch which are the foundations of Judaism. It is not necessary here to review the Law-Gospel problem in Luther, Calvin, and its appropriation by Barth. After all the complexity of this issue is taken into account, after we survey the fulfillment of the Law in Gospel, which is so central to Christianity, the fact still remains that the commandments of the Pentateuch remain standing, the "moral" as well as the "ritual," and Israel is told time and again that they are to remain "unto all your generations." Because Israel hears the Word of God in Scripture it is simply not capable of dismissing these commandments, whether they make sense or whether they do not, whether they are in the domain of morality or even conflict with human morality. Immanuel Kant, in commentating on Psalm 79:11-14, in which he finds "a prayer for revenge which goes to terrifying extremes," can dismiss with contempt a writer who comments, "The Psalms are inspired; if in them punishment is prayed for, it cannot be wrong, and we must have no morality holier than the Bible," and instead hurl the following rhetorical question which, for Kant, obviously settles the issue: "I raise the question as to whether morality should be expounded according to the Bible or whether the Bible should not rather be expounded according to morality."[2] Expounding the Bible according to morality, the choice of Kant, is surely the antithesis of everything Barth believes, a form of natural ethics corresponding to that other error, natural theology. The Jewish reader therefore dreams of a Barth who would understand Israel's refusal to discard its commandments, its stubborn clinging to practices which make no sense other than that they are written in the Bible which is all we know or need to know. I have not found in Barth such an understanding of Israel's biblical obedience. Upon more sober reflection, however, that too is understandable.

We must return to Christology. Barth is profoundly right when he emphasizes so often that the glory of his God is his making himself humble enough to enter into intercourse with humankind. This is the most amazing proclamation of the Hebrew Bible, the decisive difference that separates it from the Platonic and the Aristotelian Godhead. As such, the Christian proclamation that God became flesh in the person of Jesus of Nazareth is but a development of the basic thrust of the Hebrew Bible, God's movement toward humankind. And if all this is true, then at least in this respect, the difference between Judaism and Christianity is one of degree rather than kind. Nevertheless, even here a difference remains. Without the incarnation, however much movement towards humanity there is on the part of God, there remains a separation between them which is decisive. If God became human, the gulf is really bridged, the natures joined if not fused, the incommensura-

2. Immanuel Kant, *Religion within the Limits of Reason Alone*, trans. T. M. Greene and H. H. Hudson (New York, Harper and Row, 1960), p. 101.

ble made commensurable. And if this is so, there can be no demand made on humanity which is alien to its nature, in which God's demand cuts into the flesh of humankind because it comes from him who is other than human, who, while graciously having entered into relation with humanity, is nevertheless not human but God. The God who became human commands a being who at least once was fused with God, which destroyed once and for all the abyss between them. Israel can therefore tolerate a command which it cannot understand just because it comes from God who is not one with the human. From Israel's vantage point, the divine command must both reverberate in humanity's being and appear strange because God has turned to the human being but is also different from him. It is therefore almost necessary, if I may be permitted a forbidden word, that the divine commandments on the one hand fulfill Israel's deepest moral being and on the other also shatter it, because God is not flesh. To the Jewish reader, it is difficult to escape the feeling that in Christianity there is a tendency toward the rationalization of the commandments, though the word "rationalization" might not be the best possible. In any case, it is a tendency to make the commandments spiritually comprehensible as in Jesus' contention that (Mark 2:27) "The sabbath was made for man, and not man for the sabbath," a remark which directs attention to the recipient of the sabbath rather than to its originator. For the Jew, while the sabbath was given to Israel, it is commanded by God who is not commensurable with humanity and whose demands need not always "make sense" to humankind. In fact, any system of demands which fully made sense to humanity might likely be the work of his hands rather than the Word of God. It seems to me, therefore, that in this respect Judaism is more Barthian than Barth — a possibility that, I hope, will not strike you as just too funny.

The proximity and distance between Israel and God is expressed most forcefully in rabbinic literature in the duality of God's attributes of Law *(Din)* and Mercy *(Rachamim)*. At times God acts in accordance with law, as the judge who metes out to each what he deserves. At other times he acts in accordance with mercy, canceling deserved condemnation and awarding undeserved rewards. The Jew is fully aware that no man can pass muster before God if he rests his case on law, on what he deserves, rather than the unmerited mercy of God. "Not because of our righteousness," explains the daily morning liturgy, "do we lay our supplication before thee, but because of thine abundant mercies." Paul's polemic against justification by law is therefore hardly an attack on Judaism, as if the Jew felt no need for the mercy of God but rested his case on what was coming to him under the law! No thought could be more alien to Israel. Without God's mercy a person is hopelessly lost in his sin, in his guilt before God. But while God's mercy can be beseeched, it

# Why Is the Theology of Karl Barth of Interest?

cannot be guaranteed because, however terrible for humans to contemplate, at times God does mete out justice. If mercy corresponds to God's proximity and law to his remoteness, then Judaism sees alternation which it cannot control. True, in some ultimate sense God's mercy exceeds his justice, his reconciliation with Israel will be forever while his remoteness is only temporary. But in the pre-redeemed time the wrath of God is felt by Israel as the deserved chastisement of the people whom God loves above all others.

For Christianity, things are otherwise. Before Christ, Paul seems to think, there was law and mercy and one could never know which would rule at any given moment. If anything, it was law that predominated. With the coming of Christ, there is a permanent and fundamental change. Jesus is equated with the divine attribute of mercy so that those who believe in him permanently escape the danger of standing in the relationship of law to God. In Christ, the attribute of mercy (Midas Horachamim) has once and for all triumphed which means that the believer has now escaped the possibility of encountering the justice of God, of being judged according to the law, according to what he deserves. The christological event is therefore the final drawing together of God and humanity, their final reconciliation.

In the later volumes of the Dogmatics, this reconciliation also triumphs in the theology of Barth. His divergence from Calvin in the rigors of predestination is rooted in the reconciliation that is the event of Jesus Christ. And just as the proximity to God erased those features of the law that were incommensurable with human understanding, so the proximity to God, the incarnation, makes possible the triumph of mercy and the permanent calming of the fear of those who, while praying for the mercy of God, know that God is sovereign, that his love cannot be fathomed by humans and that therefore his wrath, his deserved wrath, cannot be excluded as a possibility. I have often wondered why the house of Israel whose intimacy with the God of Abraham cannot, after all, be paralleled by any other people, can live with this proximity and remoteness, this possibility of wrath together with the certainty of love, while the gentiles who draw near to the God of Abraham cannot bear his wrath, only his more fundamental love. Perhaps the answer is that toward the natural son, the father can afford to lose his temper because there is a security that cannot be shaken. The adopted son must be dealt with more carefully, with greater love, because there is less security, less certainty of the love of the father, a lingering remoteness that must be fought by a greater proximity. If this is so, then the wrath of God is Israel's sign of sonship, of its being the first-born, the caressed son of election. But the gentiles in Christ are also loved and in time will also be worthy of his wrath.

It is now possible to turn to the final topic that requires discussion if

you are to understand at all why a Jew is interested in Karl Barth. I am referring to his doctrine of Israel, a topic dealt with at some length by Marquardt
in his recent study.[3] Given Barth's attention to scripture, given his refusal to
substitute human theorizing for the Word of God, it is inevitable that the
Jewish people and Judaism play a significant role in his theology because they
do in scripture, both in the Old and New Testaments. But this, of course, is
hardly unexpected or new. Christian authors from the very first have been interested in Judaism. What is decisive about Barth is his insight into the status
of the Jewish people after the decisive event of their rejection of the
messiahship of Jesus of Nazareth. Very often, the view explicitly or implicitly
held was that, while the Jews had been the chosen people up until Christ once
they rejected the messiah who had been sent to them, they lost their election,
and their place was taken by the Church which thus became the "new Israel,"
a phrase used as recently as Vatican II to describe the Church. This view Barth
apparently rejected decisively. In 1949 he wrote:

> Without any doubt the Jews are to this very day the chosen people of God
> in the same sense as they have been so from the beginning, according to
> the Old and New Testaments. They have the promise of God; and if we
> Christians from among the gentiles have it too, then it is only as those
> chosen with them; as guests in their house, as new wood grafted onto
> their old tree.[4]

In 1942, while the Jews of Europe were being murdered by the millions in Europe, he wrote: "A Church that becomes antisemitic or even only a-semitic
sooner or later suffers the loss of its faith by losing the object of it."[5] And
again, speaking of Israel, he writes:

> For it is incontestable that this people as such is the holy people of God:
> the people with whom God has dealt in his grace and in his wrath; in the
> midst of whom he has blessed and judged, enlightened and hardened, ac-
> cepted and rejected; whose cause either way he has made his own, and has
> not ceased to make His own, and will not cease to make his own. They are
> all of them by nature sanctified by him, sanctified as ancestors and kins-
> men of the Holy One in Israel, in a sense that gentiles are not by nature,

---

3. Friedrich Wilhelm Marquardt, *Die Entdeckung des Judentums für die christliche
Theologie: Israel im Denken Karl Barths* (Munich: Kaiser Verlag, 1967).

4. Karl Barth, "The Jewish Problem and the Christian Answer," in *Against the Stream*
(London: SCM Press, 1954), p. 200.

5. Karl Barth, *Church Dogmatics* II/2, trans. T. F. Torrance, G. W. Bromiley (Edinburgh:
T&T Clark, 1957), p. 234.

not even the best of gentiles, not even the gentile Christians, not even the best of gentile Christians, in spite of their membership in the Church, — in spite of the fact that they too are now sanctified by the Holy One of Israel and have become Israel.[6]

It may be an exaggeration to assert that statements such as these cannot be found in the writings of any other contemporary Christian theologians. But if they exist, they cannot easily be found and, in any case, are probably not as clear as those of Barth. Barth is thus perfectly clear about the election of the Jewish people, especially their continuing election after the crucifixion. It will hardly surprise you to learn that this is pleasing to a Jewish reader who sees in this a Christian return to its roots in the faith of Israel.

But this, of course, is not the whole story. Together with statements such as those just referred to, are others more conventionally Christian and less pleasing to the Jewish reader. Marquardt draws some of those phrases together from the exposition in paragraph #34 of the *Dogmatics* in a sentence all of whose operative phrases are quotations from Barth's discussion of Jews and Judaism in this key portion. Barth refers to the Synagogue as "that dark and monstrous side of Israel's history," "the disobedient, idolatrous Israel of every age," "the whole of Israel on the left hand, sanctified only by God's wrath"; he says that the Synagogue is "the Synagogue of death" which, yes, "hears the Word and yet for and in all its hearing is still unbelieving," is "the tragic, terribly painful figure with covered eyes," the "living petrifaction of the Old Testament in itself and in abstraction," an "organization of a humanity which again and again hastens toward an empty future." That organization, Barth states, is "the phenomenon of the unbelieving, the refractory Synagogue," which is characterized by a "vaunting lie" and its "nationalistic-legalistic Messiah-dream," it stands there like a "spectral form," its members are "wretched members of the Synagogue"; "the Synagogue Jews are not numbered among the obedient." Rather, the Synagogue is "the debased Israel of the Synagogue," it is seen as "an enemy of God," which has "no . . . part now in the fulfillment of the promise given to it," going by a "cheerless chronology," living a "carnal hope," taking a stand on "a carnal loyalty to itself," and practicing "Jewish obduracy, melancholy, caprice and phantasy," in short, the Synagogue cuts the figure of "a half-venerable, half gruesome relic, of a miraculously preserved antique," the figure of "human whimsicality" (*Church Dogmatics* II/2, pp. 195ff.).[7] While

6. Barth, *Church Dogmatics* II/2, p. 287.

7. Marquardt, *Die Entdeckung*, p. 335. "Barth sagt von den Synagoge in #34, sie sei die 'ungeheure Schattenseite den Geschichte Israels,' das 'ungehorsame, götzendienerische Israel aller Zeiten,' das 'nun durch Gottes Zorn geheiligte Israel zur Linken,' sei die 'Synagoge des

it is true, as Marquardt himself admits, that the very drawing together of all these expressions in one sentence lifts them from their context and conveys a somewhat more negative picture than is warranted, the fact remains Barth uses every one of these expressions in that paragraph and that no account of Barth's position on Judaism can be even provisionally complete without taking this fact into account. What is to be made of it?

The truth is that Barth's position towards Jews is ambivalent. Because of the authenticity of his Christianity, because he reads scripture obediently, he becomes aware of the centrality of Israel in God's relation with humanity and in the very message that Christianity proclaims to the world. There is little doubt that Barth's experience with Nazism taught him just how equivalent the anti-Christ is to anti-Semitism, how necessary the destruction of the Jewish people is to those who make war on the God of Israel and his commandments. But there is also in Barth an anti-Semitism made up of two parts: the traditional anti-Semitism of European Christendom (whether the Swiss suffer from this more or less than others I cannot say) and the anti-Semitism of Christian theology. As far as the first sort of anti-Semitism is concerned, it may surprise some that a man of Barth's stature is not completely immune to it. We must never forget that Barth is also a human being subject to human frailties. In this connection, I wondered for years how a man, whom I admire as much as I do Karl Barth, with near-perfection of his grasp of the evil of Nazism, could have had less than a perfect grasp of the evil of that other great war on the God of Israel, Communism. The only answer I have been able to come up with is that it was God's way of reminding us that Karl Barth, after all, was only a human being. The rabbis claim that the reason that the burial place of Moses was not made known was the fear that, were it known, it might have become a focus of worship, with the concomitant danger that divine attributes would have been attached to Moses. With Karl Barth, too, in the ab-

---

Todes,' die zwar 'hörende, aber bei allem ihrem Hören immer noch glaubenslose Synagoge'; sie sei die 'tragische, unheimlich schmerzliche Gestalt mit verbundenen Augen,' sei 'leibhaftig das in Erstarrung stehen gebliebene Alte Testament an sich und in abstracto,' sei die 'Organisation einer noch und noch in eine leere Zukunft eilenden Menschheit'; sie biete das 'Phänomen der ungläubigen,' das 'Phänomen der renitenten Synagoge,' sei charakterisiert von 'hochmütiger Lüge' and ihrem 'nationalistisch-gesetzlichen Messiastraum'; sie biete schlechthin eine 'gespensterhafte Gestalt'; ihre Mitglieder seien 'unselige Mitglieder der Synagoge' and 'die Synagogenjuden gehören nicht zu den Gehorsamen'; es sei die Synagoge 'das unecht gewordene Israel,' sie stehe da 'als Feind Gottes,' habe 'an den Erfühlung der ihr gegebenen Verheissung zunächst keinen Anteil,' habe eine 'trostlose Zeitrechnung,' lebe eine 'fleischliche Hoffnung,' realisiere eine 'fleischliche Treue gegen sich selbst,' praktiziere 'judischen Starrsinn, Schrulle, Phantasterei' — kurz: sie biete das Bild einer 'halb ehrwürdigen, halb grausigen Reliquie, einer wunderlich konservativen Antiquität,' das Bild 'menschlicher Schrulle.'"

sence of one relatively major flaw, there is no knowing what people would have made of him. It is perhaps for this reason that the vision in his left eye was not permitted to be equal to that in his right.

Putting aside the less prominent portion of Barth's defective attitude to Judaism, the conventionally European one, we must turn to the far more important aspect, the theological one. Here the crux of the matter is, of course, Israel's rejection of the messiahship of him who is the Lord of the Church. This is a decisive matter and it would be ludicrous to minimize the significance of this rejection. In fact, I find it interesting that the Church concluded that, in spite of the fact that a minority of Jews accepted Jesus as the Christ, it was not this minority that represented the Jewish people, but the non-accepting majority that did so. Barth, in close conformity to the tradition, detects a pattern here. Israel, the elect people, is also from the very first a rebellious people who kills its prophets, etc. The rejection of Jesus is therefore very much in character for the Jews who are established experts in returning disobedience for the unmerited gifts that God bestows on this people. Again and again we are told that the record of Israel is consistent: to return evil for the good of God, disobedience for love, rebellion for faithfulness.

We have reached a point where I have one confession and one comment to make. The confession is simply this: there is nothing more important that I have learned from Barth than the sinfulness of Israel. There is no question that the history of the Jewish people is a history of obduracy and of unfaithfulness. It is a people that, time and again, has returned evil for God's good and has suffered grievously for it. I do not know that this point would be as clear in my mind were it not for my reading of Barth (and of course, Paul). It might be surprising that this should require a reading of Barth when this point is so clear in the Bible. Nevertheless, it is not a point which is naturally in the forefront of Jewish consciousness and I am deeply grateful to Barth for teaching it to me.

But, to turn from confession to comment, it is not the whole truth. Reading Barth one would gain the impression that there is nothing but faithfulness on God's part and unfaithfulness on Israel's. This is not so. "Go and cry in the ears of Jerusalem," proclaims Jeremiah (2:23), "saying, Thus saith the Lord: I remember thee, the kindness of thy youth, the love of thine espousals, when thou wentest after me in the wilderness, in a land that was not sown. Israel is holiness unto the Lord, and the first fruits of his increase, all that devour him shall offend; evil shall come upon them, saith the Lord." There is nothing but faithfulness on God's part but it is not the case that there is nothing but unfaithfulness on Israel's part. Along with the unfaithfulness, there is also Israel's faithfulness, its obedience and trust in God, its clinging to its election, identity, and mission against all the odds. True, all of Israel's obedience is tinged with its disobedience but all of its disobedience is also tinged with its obedience. It is true that Israel does not deserve its election but it is also true that its election is not in vain, that this people, with its sin, has never ceased to love its God and that it has responded to God's wrath, to his unspeakable wrath, to his unthinkable wrath, by shouldering its mission again, again searing circumcision into its flesh and, while hoping for the best, prepared for what it knows can happen again. Perhaps it is not seemly to speak thus, to praise Israel when it should be criticized. But he who knows the God of Israel knows how he loves his people and that he loves those who love it.

To see Barth struggling toward the sign that is Israel, to see him fighting against his gentile nature that demands antipathy to the people of election, to see this nature yield to the Word of God and to Barth's love for that Jew whom he loves above all others, is to see the miraculous work of God. The work is incomplete. There remains a dark side, an emphasis on Israel's disobedience which, as we have said, is not the whole truth. But even more important is this final point. Whatever Israel's problems with its God may be, however great Israel's sin and God's wrath may be, the quarrel is a family one, between Israel and its God, its father. For strangers to intervene, to point out the shortcomings of the son, to revel in them, to make a theology of them, to feel superior because of them, is a very, very dangerous strategy. However terrible the anger of a father toward his son may be, it is an anger that he can afford because underneath it is a love that is a father's. When others are stimulated by this anger, something totally different enters the picture and the father can only be appalled. It is very dangerous to get mixed up in such family quarrels. He who does will incur the wrath of both sides.

I will therefore be frank. It is not for gentiles to see the sins of Israel. It is not for gentiles to call Israel to its mission, to feel morally superior to it and to play the prophet's role towards it. It is for gentiles to love this people if need be blindly, staunchly, not impartially but partially and to trust the instincts of this people whom God has chosen as his own. If they need be chastised they will be, by their father who is not fooled. But woe unto those gentiles who become the rod of God's chastisement of Israel, the instrument of this anger, the satisfied bystanders of the punishment. It were better had they not been born rather than witness this lovers' quarrel.

I have said that it is for gentiles to love Israel. This, of course, is wrong, it cannot be asked of gentiles. But it can be asked of Christians.

# The Impact of Dialogue with Christianity on My Self-Understanding as a Jew

In the concluding essay of this volume, Wyschogrod takes an inventory of some of the central features of his understanding of Judaism and explores the extent to which dialogue with Christianity has contributed to the formation of his views. Originally published in *Die Hebraeische Bibel und ihre zweifache Nachgeschichte*, ed. Erhard Blum, Christian Macholz, and Ekkehard W. Stegemann (Neukirchen-Vluyn: Neukirchener Verlag, 1990), pp. 725-736.

—◦◦◦—

AFTER MORE than thirty years of involvement in Jewish-Christian dialogue, the time has come to ask myself what influence the dialogue has had on my self-understanding as a Jew. To admit that it has had an influence is not without danger because there is probably no more efficient method of committing Orthodox Jewish suicide than admitting that any part of my interpretation of Judaism is the result of contact with Christianity. Such claims are usually charges against which one is supposed to defend oneself. And even the claim that the charge is not true is not a perfect defense.

The story is told of a yeshiva student in Eastern Europe who was summoned by the head of the yeshiva who informed the student that rumors were circulating that he was seeing a married woman. The student threw himself on the floor and moaned: "Rebbe, I swear it is not true." The rabbi, more incensed than ever, hit the student in the face and screamed: "Villain, outcast, true it should also be!" Such rumors, it seems, need not be true to be damning. If one is a decent yeshiva student, such rumors do not arise and if they do, even if they are not true, things are in pretty bad shape.

225

Since I therefore cannot escape my predicament by denying that I have been influenced by Jewish-Christian dialogue, I will, in desperation, plead guilty to the charge with an explanation.

Judaism and Christianity are both continuous and discontinuous. I believe that the dialogue with Christianity has helped me see these continuities and discontinuities with much greater clarity than had there been no dialogue. The obvious temptation is to stress the continuities and to ignore the discontinuities or to stress the discontinuities and to ignore the continuities. Both of these strategies are erroneous. It is necessary not to ignore the discontinuities because they are there. But it is also necessary not to ignore the continuities because they are also there. On the whole, Judaism, for understandable reasons, has tended to stress the discontinuities and underplay the continuities. But this also distorts Judaism because any interpretation of Judaism that aims to maximize its differences with Christianity imposes as much of a foreign agenda on Judaism as the reverse. So I will enumerate some of the features of my understanding of Judaism and speculate with you about the extent to which my dialogue with Christianity has influenced my adopting these interpretations. In each case, my defense will be that whether or not the dialogue with Christianity has, positively or negatively, influenced my thinking, the interpretations are Jewishly licit.

# I

My Judaism is biblical. This means that the Hebrew Bible is the most important source of my religious self-definition. I have been criticized in some Orthodox Jewish circles for being insufficiently rabbinic. Many Orthodox Jews equate Judaism with rabbinic Judaism. The study of the Bible is neglected and nothing important is ever settled by reference to any biblical text. The biblical text, in a sense, does not even exist independently of the rabbinic commentary. The Oral Torah is seen as the real Torah with the Written Torah as an almost unnecessary historical appendage. The Written Torah is seen as a book sealed with seven seals until its meaning is revealed by the rabbis. These are attitudes that I do not share, at least not completely.

I am not a Karaite (the medieval Jewish sect that rejected rabbinic Judaism as inauthentic and placed all its faith in the Hebrew Bible). I see the vast body of rabbinic literature as transmitting supplementary revelation to that found in scripture. In addition, rabbinic literature contains the record of the human enterprise of interpretation which is an ongoing process without which no living faith can adjust to ever changing conditions. I therefore have the deepest reverence for the Torah of the rabbis in which I was trained and by which I try to live. It is the rabbis, after all, who formulated the canon and who determined what did and did not go into it.

But having said all of that, the Written Torah still remains for me the highest source of religious authority. It is in scripture that primary revelation takes place, that the word of God is delivered. It is in scripture that the formula "Thus sayeth the Lord" is heard. The rabbis understand themselves as functioning at a time when that formula is no longer heard. The rabbis live in a world in which prophecy has ceased. They are transmitters and interpreters but not direct spokespersons for God. I do not believe that the rabbis saw themselves as sovereign over scripture. There are those who believe that the rabbis rode roughshod over scripture, that they invented a new religion that has only the most tenuous of connections with the faith of biblical Israel, a faith that is largely discontinuous with the Judaism of the rabbis. I do not believe this to be true. The logical foundation of rabbinic Judaism is scripture.

Since there is no revelation as such in the literature of the rabbis and since the rabbinic system understands itself as resting on a foundation of revelation, that revelation must come from somewhere and that somewhere cannot be anything but scripture.

But there is also a kind of empirical proof of this. Suppose we asked a visitor from another planet to study the Pentateuch carefully and then to visit the religious communities of our planet to determine which of them adhered most closely to the teachings of the Pentateuch. If our extraterrestrial visitor were any intelligent and fair observer, I think he would have to conclude that it is Orthodox Jews who follow the way of life of the Pentateuch most closely. They obey the festivals of the Pentateuch, the dietary laws, the menstrual laws, the law forbidding the mixing of wool and linen in clothing, and many other commandments. I omit mention of the commandment to love one's fellow human being as oneself because it is more difficult to judge an individual's or group's adherence to that commandment merely by brief external observation. In the total scale of things, such inner commandments are probably more important than those dealing with external conduct, adherence to which can be more readily evaluated by observing people's behavior.

If what I have said is true, then it follows that the Judaism of the rabbis is not fundamentally discontinuous with biblical Judaism. Our extraterrestrial observer would, of course, not fail to observe practices for which he would be hard-pressed to find a Pentateuchal source. But overall, he would have little difficulty in identifying the life of contemporary Orthodox Jews as rooted in the Pentateuch. And that proves to me that the rabbis were essentially obedient to the voice of scripture.

The question now arises whether my biblical orientation has anything to do with my experience in Jewish-Christian dialogue. I suppose it does, to some extent. It is, after all, the Hebrew Bible, the Old Testament of Christians, that Jews and Christians have in common. Adin Steinsalz, the Israeli Talmudist, recently pointed out that Judaism and Islam have far fewer theological differences than Judaism and Christianity. And yet, over the centuries, there has been much less theological interaction between Judaism and Islam than between Judaism and Christianity. He explains this, and I think correctly, by the fact that Judaism and Christianity share a scripture while Judaism and Islam do not. Whatever differences two groups may have, as long as they share a scripture they have something to talk about. But if they do not share such a book, the possibility of dialogue is far more limited. There is simply no common point of departure which can be appealed to.

It is for this reason that Maimonides ruled that a Jew may teach Torah to a Christian but not a Muslim. Christians, argues Maimonides, accept the Hebrew Bible but they interpret it incorrectly. Such an error can be cleared up in the course of Jewish-Christian interaction. But since a Muslim does not accept the inspiration of Hebrew scripture, there is no basis on which to proceed and a Jew should therefore not engage in a hopeless task. Naturally, in the Jewish-Christian dialogue of the past thirty years in which I have participated, the Hebrew Bible has played a central role. Scripture is binding for Christians and rabbinic texts are not, so a Jew who wants to score with Christians must think biblically. This may have played a role in pushing my thinking in the biblical direction. Be that as it may psychologically, there are a sufficient number of inner-Jewish considerations to justify such an orientation to convince me that I have not embarked on an un-Jewish path.

# II

I am also a theological Jew. Now we all know about the claim that Judaism has no theology, that theology is a Christian enterprise and that anyone who traffics in "Jewish theology" is in the import business since there is no domestically produced item that can be called Jewish theology.

Like all partial truths, this partial truth has some truth in it. There is certainly a sense in which theology is more central to Christianity than to Judaism. From its inception, or at least very close to its origins, Christianity was permeated by Greek thinking which is, of course, philosophical. The most fundamental book of Christianity is a Greek book although no one has ever accused Jesus of being a Greek speaker. Greek philosophy is present at the beginning of Christianity, which is not so in Judaism. Judaism makes contact with philosophy in its adulthood rather than in its childhood. So Judaism's bond with philosophy is not as intimate as is Christianity's.

Theology is the offspring of biblical faith and philosophical investigation. At the outset of my career I was far more interested in the philosophy of religion than I am now. By the philosophy of religion I understand the philosophical enterprise that investigates a broad range of religious issues from a philosophical perspective without tying the investigation to any particular tradition of revelation. In the course of the years I have developed considerable skepticism toward this enterprise because I have come to see it as lacking an anchor in the soil of faith. What God does the philosophy of religion deal with? If it is the biblical God, then it is doing biblical theology and not the philosophy of religion. And if the God it deals with is not the biblical God, then what is it, in which philosophical laboratory was it created?

So I now find theology much more interesting. Theology has a philosophic side to it but its point of departure and ultimate validation are scripture and history. And this enterprise is not at all foreign to Judaism. The tradition of Philo and Saadia, culminating in Maimonides, is not a minor strain in Judaism, even if it is less major than its counterpart in the Christian camp. But Jewish theology is practiced in various styles, of which the methods of the Jewish philosophers are not the only ones. The classic rabbinic midrashic texts are often theological if by theology we mean the attempt to understand somewhat systematically the basic teachings of the Bible about God and his interrelationship with humanity and the universe. To do theology, whether Jewish or Christian, requires a stepping back from the immediacy of the biblical text in order to see the forest and not only the trees. This is particularly important in a tradition that specializes in commentary as a literary genre. The virtue of commentary is that it does not lose sight of the authoritative text and therefore does not find itself without moorings. But the drawback is that certain kinds of questions which are not easily connected with any particular text but which pertain to the whole worldview of the text are neglected. It is here that Jewish theology has its work cut out for it.

Again I ask, has my contact with Christianity sharpened my theological appetite? I cannot truthfully deny it. But I must insist that the enterprise is essential and legitimate for strictly inner-Jewish reasons and if my interest in it has been heightened by contact with Christianity, then the contact with Christianity has enriched rather than impoverished my Judaism.

## III

The Jewish-Christian dialogue has taught me that there is no Judaism without the law. It is perhaps not wise to translate Torah as "law." Torah is more than law. The Pentateuch is not a code of law, not even as the Mishnah is and certainly not as Maimonides' *Mishneh Torah* is. The laws of the Pentateuch are interspersed among narratives and poems and, taken as a whole, the Pentateuch is probably more a book of narration and poetry than it is a manual of law. And yet, there is no Judaism without law. I am not saying that law is the most important feature of Judaism. But I am saying that it is the most characteristic feature of Judaism.

If I must determine whether I am dealing with a Jew whose Judaism is in relatively good shape, I observe his or her behavior. If he or she observes the sabbath, eats kosher, attends a synagogue fairly often, refrains from eating leavened bread during Passover, etc., I come away feeling fairly secure about that person's Judaism. It may turn out that I was fooled, that behind the pious façade there is a hypocrite, a thief, a liar, or worse. But if that happens I am surprised and, I think, so would you be. You do not expect an observant Jew to be a thief and liar though, I very much regret to say, there are some who are.

My point is that there is no Judaism without Torah observance. And I want to take this opportunity to put in a good word for the ritual law. The division of the law into the ritual and the ethical is not biblical. For the Bible there is only the command of God and I do not find any deep distinction drawn between ritual and ethical commandments. In fact, there are a number of commandments that I could not easily classify as one or the other (the sexual prohibitions, for example). Nevertheless, the distinction between the ritual and the ethical commandments is with us and probably unavoidable.

The temptation to stress the ethical commandments and to downgrade the ritual ones is great, probably as old as the Prophets and certainly to be observed in Reform Judaism of modern times. But I am inclined to try to resist the temptation. I do not know why God wants us to do certain things and not to do other things. In a certain sense, I suppose, I have a better understanding of why God wants me not to murder than of why he wants me not to eat pork. But, then again, I sometimes wonder. Do I really understand why God wants me not to murder? I know that he does not want me to do it and that should be enough. The moment I refrain from murder on other grounds than that God forbids it, I have embarked on a slippery slope. So if I really don't know the rationale of the ethical commandments, then the lack of an obvious rationale for the ritual commandments becomes a bit more palatable.

So I am committed to a fairly strict adherence to the commandments, ritual and ethical. I have never really understood the reasoning of the non-Orthodox branches of Judaism that pick and choose among the commandments they feel like obeying. It seems to me that if one does that, the whole system collapses. On what basis does one make such a selection? The Karaites accepted the Bible and rejected rabbinic commandments which did not have a clear biblical mandate. But that does not yield a Judaism that appeals to the modern mind because some of the least "rational" commandments are biblical and some of the most rational ones rabbinic. So modern reformers of Judaism did not draw the line on the basis of the biblical/rabbinic distinction but some other basis which they failed to make clear to me.

What role did my contact with Christianity play in the formulation of these attitudes? I think a rather important role. There is no doubt that Christianity, ever since Paul, represents an extremely sustained and fundamental critique of the Jewish law. Christians claim that Judaism is a religion of legalism while Christianity is a religion of the spirit. Judaism is stuck in the letter of the law while Christianity has penetrated to its spirit. And once one operates on the level of the spirit, adherence to the externals of the law is no longer necessary and might even be forbidden. Thomas Aquinas, we need to be reminded, taught that to adhere to the Mosaic Law after Christ is to commit a mortal sin.

Early in my career as a student of Paul, I was deeply perplexed by his attitude to the law. To be quite frank about it, I could not understand how a religiously sensitive Jew such as Paul could speak about the law as he did. I could understand, to an extent, his fascination with Jesus but I could not understand, and to a degree still cannot understand, why the fascination with Jesus had to lead to such hostility to the Law of Moses, to the law of the Pentateuch. I was particularly annoyed by the idea that Jews think they are saved by deeds while Christians know they are saved by faith and only by faith. The idea that merely believing something saved a person always sounded far too easy to me. In addition, it was simply not true that Jews thought they were saved by deeds or works.

If a Jew thought this, he would, in effect, be saying to God: Don't do me any favors, don't give me more than I deserve but also don't give me less than I deserve, give me exactly what's coming to me and then I have nothing to fear. I doubt that any Jew in the history of Judaism has thought this. Every Jew knows, or should know, that if God were to pay him what he deserves, neither more nor less, he would be lost. His only chance depends on the mercy of God. If God decides to overlook his sorry record and to bestow mercy rather than justice on him, then he has a chance. But certainly not otherwise.

So the Jew does not claim to be "justified" by the works of the law but rather by the mercy of God. At the same time, this does not mean that he can do whatever he wishes. The commandments of the Torah are binding and it is the obligation of every Jew to obey them to the best of his or her ability. But chances are very good, almost certain, that he will fall short of the mark and that is where the mercy of God comes in. So it does not follow that if one takes the law seriously one sees oneself as justified by the law. Only God justifies and he justifies far more on the basis of mercy than on the basis of rewards earned by good deeds.

This being so, how could Paul have so misunderstood things? Part of the answer is his fixation on Jesus. The Jesus event so absorbed his theological attention that nothing could be permitted to compete with Jesus including the Torah, which had the deep loyalty of most Jews. Reverence for the Torah was so great that, in the mind of Paul, it was a threat to the proper appreciation of Jesus. Nothing was to be permitted to compete with Jesus as the path to salvation and the inadequacies of the Torah therefore had to be exposed in no uncertain terms so that only Jesus would remain as the basis for hope.

But there is more to it than that. The question for Paul is not mainly the significance of Torah for Jews but its significance for Jesus-believing gentiles. Paul was the apostle to the gentiles and his problem was whether gentiles who came to faith in Jesus needed circumcision and the law in addition to their faith in Jesus. From Acts 15 and elsewhere we learn that a segment of the Jerusalem church believed that gentiles who wished to belong to the Jesus fellowship had to be circumcised and had to accept all the commandments. Paul disagreed and believed that Jesus-believing gentiles did not first have to become Jews and only then could they consider themselves followers of Jesus. Had this view prevailed, Jesus-believing Jews would have remained a small Jewish sect and Christianity would probably not have conquered the Western world.

Paul's polemic against the law is therefore to be seen as a polemic against gentiles obeying the law. Raymond Brown expresses this as the problem of Paul's son: had Paul had a son, would he have had him circumcised? Brown answers affirmatively which means that, in Paul's view, Jews were obligated to observe the commandments of the Torah even after the coming of Jesus.

That this is so can be inferred from Acts 15. There this issue is brought to the Jerusalem church and after long debate it is decided that Jesus-believing gentiles need not undergo circumcision. Instead, they must obey the basic moral law, known in rabbinic terminology as the Noachide laws, because they are based on the covenant made by God with Noah when the latter emerged from the ark after the flood (Gen. 9:1-13). But the very question of whether

Jesus-believing gentiles needed to obey the whole Torah implies that both parties in the debate took it for granted that Jewish Jesus-believers would remain under the Torah even after their faith in Jesus. The difference of opinion began only when the question of gentiles was raised. Some of Jesus' followers in Jerusalem believed that gentiles could become proper Jesus-believers only if they had themselves circumcised and accepted the yoke of the commandments. Others — and this group prevails at the Jerusalem council — thought it was sufficient for gentiles to embrace the Noachide law. But this difference of opinion about gentiles who are drawn to Jesus could hardly have arisen if anyone thought that the law was abolished for Jews with the coming of Christ. If the law was no longer binding for Jews because of Jesus, then it certainly could not be binding for gentiles. We must therefore conclude that for both parties in Jerusalem the assumption was that the law remained in full force for Jews. The difference of opinion was restricted to the case of gentiles who wished to join the Jesus community.

If this is so, then all the nasty things Paul says about the law are intended to discourage gentiles from embracing the law and are thoroughly misunderstood if they are read as expressions of Paul's opinion about the value of the law for Jews.

There was a time when I was convinced that this was the solution to the problem of Paul. I still think so in large measure but perhaps with a bit less conviction than in the past. When Paul says (Gal. 3:19) that the law was a temporary measure promulgated through angels, it is difficult to maintain that this is true for gentiles but not for Jews. On the other hand, it is possible that Paul is so eager to deflect gentiles from circumcision and the law that he dumps on the law in a way that he does not really mean as if the end (persuading gentiles not to take the path of the law) justifies negative statements about the law that he does not really mean, at least not with respect to Jews.

In short, I am a bit confused at this point. But my confusion pertains to what Paul thought about the law, it does not pertain to what I think about the law. I believe that an attack on Torah law as it applies to Jews is a lethal attack on Judaism, whether it emanates from Christian sources or from Reform or Conservative Judaism.

We must remember that, according to Acts 21:21-26, the Jerusalem church tells Paul that "it is said that you teach all the Jews in the gentile world to turn their backs on Moses, telling them to give up circumcising their children and following our way of life. What is the position, then?" Paul is advised to go with some men to undergo the ritual of purification in the Temple. "Then everyone will know that there is nothing in the stories they were told about you, but that you are a practicing Jew and keep the Law yourself"

233

(Acts 21:24). Paul accepts James's advice and visits the Temple for the rite of purification. Could it be that Paul was, after all, an Orthodox Jew?

## IV

The contact with Christianity has therefore strengthened — if it needed strengthening — my appreciation of the centrality of law in Judaism. But it has also influenced my understanding of the law.

As I have already said, the law is certainly central to Judaism. It is indispensable. But it is not the whole of Judaism nor is it possibly the most important part of Judaism. The law can be a necessary and indispensable aspect of Judaism without being its most important aspect.

1. The law is revealed at Sinai. But by the time the Jewish people reaches Sinai it is a fully developed people with a fully developed relationship to God. God could have begun his relationship with Abraham by bestowing the law on him. But he did not do this. There is a whole complex relationship between God and the patriarchs, Joseph, and Moses and the whole people before Sinai is reached. The law is embedded in this relationship. It presupposes the stories of this relationship. The biblical text intertwines the law with these stories. In short, the law is not a self-contained entity. It is not the deepest layer of God's relationship with the Jewish people. It is an essential part of that relationship but not its foundation.

2. There is no relationship between God and man and God and Israel without command. The relationship with Adam is sealed by the commandment not to eat of one of the trees of the Garden. With Abraham, by the commandment to leave his natural home to go to the country that he will be shown. God commanding and the necessity for man to obey those commands is absent on very few pages of the Hebrew Bible.

But what is the relationship between God's commandments and the law? I do not think they are identical. Ideally, there should be a separate divine commandment for each situation in which a human being finds himself. No two situations are exactly alike and if I extrapolate God's will in one situation from knowledge of God's will in another situation — which may be similar to the current situation but is not identical with it — I am guessing and I may be wrong.

The really important question that I must answer is what is God's will for me here and now. To attempt to answer that question by means of legal reasoning is the only way we can attempt to answer that question at a time when there is no direct revelation. But legal reasoning is a second best. When the daughters of Zelophehad (Num. 27:1-11) presented Moses with a novel case, Moses does not engage in legal reasoning but (Num. 27:5) brings the case before God.

While we cannot do that in our time, it is essential for us to remember that God is the ultimate judge, even today, and that a relationship to the law that makes the law autonomous as if God had gone into retirement after he revealed the law is unacceptable. There is no place in Judaism for halachic deism and this is so in spite of the rabbinic texts which reject divine intervention in deciding matters of law. This is not the time or the place to examine those texts in detail. All I can say is that I do not read them to be saying that, having given the Torah, God has given the rabbis a blank check to interpret it as they see fit.

My conviction of the centrality of law in Judaism is therefore combined with a God-centered Judaism. Martin Buber, who was not a halachically observant Jew, once told me that he had an Abrahamic and pre-Sinaitic soul. Unlike Buber, I did not completely miss Sinai. But like Buber, my Judaism did not begin at Sinai but rather with Abraham, whom I have always felt a bit closer to than I do to Moses.

## V

One final influence of Jewish-Christian dialogue on my self-understanding as a Jew. This refers to my attitude to gentiles. In a 1967 letter, Karl Barth wrote:

I am decidedly not a philosemite, in that in personal encounters with living Jews (even Jewish Christians) I have always, so long as I can remember, had to suppress a totally irrational aversion, naturally suppressing it at once on the basis of all my presuppositions, and concealing it totally in my statements, yet still having to suppress and conceal it. Pfui! is all I can say to this in some sense allergic reaction of mine. But this is how it was and is.[1]

The aversion to Jews to which Barth confesses in this letter is not without its counterpart on the Jewish side. There are Jews who have just such an aversion to gentiles. This is the flip side of the election of Israel. By means of this election or the consciousness of this election, a powerful religious and family community has evolved among Jews. Jews are proud of their having

1. Karl Barth, *Letters: 1961-1968*, ed. J. Fangmeier and H. Stoevesandt, trans. and ed. G. W. Bromiley (London: T&T Clark, 1981), p. 262.

been chosen by God. They are proud of their loyalty to the covenant, of their determination to retain their identity against all the odds. They are proud of their achievements, intellectual, artistic, political, and financial. They are proud of their intelligence which they believe is nurtured by their culture. And they feel very close to other Jews even across all kinds of linguistic and social barriers which might seem insurmountable. Covenantal Judaism creates a powerful sense of community.

A natural concomitant of this is the exclusion of gentiles. They are outside the family. They are different. They probably dislike Jews who must be wary of them because they are just about capable of anything. In any case, numerous as they are, they play a very insignificant role in the overall scheme of things because it is the destiny of the Jewish people in the context of its relationship to God around which the drama of human history revolves.

I have never disliked gentiles. Our deepest solidarity is with our fellow human beings because they are created in the image of God (Gen. 1:26). This statement, to my mind the single most powerful in the Bible, is made about the human being as such, not about Jews. If the result of the election in Abraham is an alienation of Israel from the rest of humanity, then the election has achieved the opposite of its intended result. The purpose of Abraham's election was that "in you shall all the families of the earth be blessed." If Israel withdraws into its own identity and loses interest in the ties that bind it to the rest of humanity and that make it a surrogate of that humanity, then Israel will have tragically misunderstood its true identity.

There is a form of Christianity that does not intend to replace Israel as the people of God but join it as adopted sons and daughters in the household of God. The existence of this Christianity has helped me shape a Jewish identity that can live in deep appreciation of this new Christianity.

# Works by Michael Wyschogrod

## Books

*Parable and Story in Judaism and Christianity.* Co-edited with Clemens Thoma. New York: Paulist Press, 1989.

*Understanding Scripture: Explorations of Jewish and Christian Traditions of Interpretation.* Co-edited with Clemens Thoma. New York: Paulist Press, 1987.

*Das Reden von einen Gott bei Juden und Christen.* Co-edited with Clemens Thoma. Bern: Peter Lang, 1984.

*The Body of Faith: Judaism as Corporeal Election.* Minneapolis: Seabury-Winston, 1983. Paperback edition as *The Body of Faith: God in the People Israel.* San Francisco: Harper & Row, 1989. Second Edition as *The Body of Faith: God and the People Israel.* Northvale, N.J.: Jason Aronson, 1996. German translation as *Gott und Volk Israel: Dimensionen jüdischen Glaubens.* Stuttgart: Kohlhammer, 2001.

*Jews and "Jewish Christianity."* With David Berger. New York: Ktav, 1978.

*Kierkegaard and Heidegger: The Ontology of Existence.* London: Routledge and Kegan Paul; New York: Humanities Press, 1954. Reprinted 1970.

## Essays

"Democracy, Judaism and the Church." *Lesarten des jüdisch-christlichen Dialogs: Festschrift zum 70. Geburtstag von Clemens Thoma.* Edited by Silvia Kaeppeli. Bern: Peter Lang, 2002: 343-350.

"Determining the Will of God." *"Die Gemeinde als Ort von Theologie": Festschrift für Jürgen Seim zum 70. Geburtstag.* Edited by Katja Kriener, Marion Obitz, Johann Schmidt. Bonn: Verlag Dr. Rudolf Habelt GmbH, 2002: 189-194.

"The Revenge of the Animals." *Hören und Lernen in der Schule des Namens: Mit der Tradition zum Aufbruch: Festschrift für Bertold Klappert zum 60.*

*Geburtstag.* Edited by Jochen Denker, Jonas Marquardt, Borgi Winkler-Rohlfink. Neukirchen-Vluyn: Neukirchener, 1999: 23-25.

"Incarnation and God's In-Dwelling in Israel." *Incarnation.* Edited by M. M. Olivetti. Cedam, Biblioteca dell 'Archivio di Filosofia,' 1999: 147-157.

Participant in "The Sea Change in American Orthodox Judaism: A Symposium." *Tradition* 32:4 (Summer 1998): 139-142.

"Auferstehung Jesu im jüdisch-christlichen Dialog: Ein Briefwechsel." Michael Wyschogrod/Peter von der Osten-Sacken. *Evangelische Theologie* 57:3 (1997): 196-209.

"Seen and Heard Commands: Ethics and the Metaphysics of Time." *Philosophie de la religion entre ethique et ontologie.* Edited by M. M. Olivetti. Milan: Cedam, 1996: 475-481.

"The Torah as Law in Judaism." *Seeds of Reconciliation: Essays on Jewish-Christian Understanding.* Edited by Katharine T. Hargrove. Bibal Press, 1996: 117-128.

"A Jewish Perspective on Incarnation." *Modern Theology* 12:2 (April 1996): 195-209.

"Letter to a Friend" and "Response to the Respondents." *Modern Theology* 11:2 (April 1995): 165-171, 229-241.

"Inkarnation aus jüdischer Sicht." *Evangelische Theologie* 1/95: 13-28.

"Die Botschaft der Bibel" (in dialogue with Klaus Wengst). *Deutscher Evangelischer Kirchentag Muenchen 1993.* Edited by Konrad von Bonin. Gütersloher Verlagshaus, 1993: 138-149.

"Christianity and Mosaic Law." *Pro Ecclesia* 2:4 (Fall 1993): 451-459.

"Incarnation." *Pro Ecclesia* 2:2 (Spring 1993): 208-215.

"Resurrection." *Pro Ecclesia* 1:1 (Winter 1992): 104-112.

"A View from the Take-Off." *Sh'ma* 23:455 (May 28, 1993): 117-118.

"'Was sollen wir nun dazu sagen?' Ein jüdischer Beitrag zum Gespräch von Wolfgang Schweitzer mit Paul van Buren." *Der Jude Jesus und die Völker der Welt: Ein Gespräch mit Paul M. van Buren* by Wolfgang Schweitzer. Berlin: Institut Kirche und Judentum, 1993: 215-221.

"Unfinished Business in Interfaith Dialogue." *Sh'ma* 23:448 (Feb. 19, 1993): 57-59.

Contribution to "Symposium: Reflections on the Six-Day War after a Quarter Century." *Tradition* 26:4 (Summer 1992): 24-25.

"Some Reflections on Jewish Biblical Ethics in the Contemporary Context." *Reverence, Righteousness, and Rahamanut: Essays in Memory of Rabbi Dr. Leo Jung.* Edited by Jacob J. Schacter. Jason Aronson, 1992: 315-324.

"A Jewish View of Christianity." *Toward a Theological Encounter: Jewish Understandings of Christianity.* Edited by Leon Klenicki. New York: Paulist Press, 1991: 104-119.

"Jewish Survival in the Context of Jewish-Christian Dialogue." *Christians and Jews Together: Voices from the Conversation.* Edited by Donald G. Dawe and

# Works by Michael Wyschogrod

Aurelia T. Fule. Theology and Worship Ministry Unit, Presbyterian Church (U.S.A.), 1991: 118-128.

"Judaism and the Sanctification of Nature." *Melton Journal,* no. 24 (Spring 1991): 5, 7.

"Two Germanies into One." *Hadassah Magazine* (May 1990): 14-15.

"The Impact of Dialogue with Christianity on My Self-Understanding as a Jew." *Die Hebraeische Bibel und ihre zweifache Nachgeschichte.* Edited by Erhard Blum, Christian Macholz, and Ekkehard W. Stegemann. Neukirchen-Vluyn: Neukirchener Verlag, 1990: 725-736. German translation as "Die Auswirkung des Dialogs mit dem Christentum auf mein Selbstverständniss als Jude." *Kirche und Israel* (Feb. 1990): 135-147.

"Genius and Bigotry: The Odd Coupling." *Moment* 15:4 (August 1990): 36-39, 58-60.

"The Bishops and the Middle East." *First Things* 2 (April 1990): 15-16.

"When Christianity Speaks of Judaism: The Old Theology and the New." *Congress Monthly* 56:7 (Nov.-Dec. 1989): 1, 23.

"Was This Fight Necessary?" *Sh'ma* 19:380 (Oct. 27, 1989): 146-147.

"Jüdische Identität." *und ich will bei euch wohnen: Texte Ev. Kirchentag Berlin '87.* Berlin: Evangelischer Kirchentag, 1988: 9-25.

"This One — and No Other." *Ehad: The Many Meanings of God.* Edited by Eugene B. Borowitz. *Sh'ma* 1988: 95-98.

"Verbunden für alle Zeit: die jüdische und die deutsche Geschichte." *Deutsches Allgemeines Sonntagsblatt* (Oct. 23, 1988): 20.

"Zum gegenwärtigen Stand des jüdisch-christlichen Gesprächs." *Das jüdisch-christliche Religionsgespräch.* Edited by Heinz Kremers and Julius H. Schoeps. Stuttgart and Bonn: Burg Verlag, 1988: 210-212.

"A Jewish Postscript." *Encountering Jesus: A Debate on Christology.* Edited by Stephen T. Davis. John Knox Press, 1988: 179-187.

Participant in "Podiumsgespräch: Seht, welch ein Mensch . . . und wo bleibt das Reich Gottes?" *Kirche und Israel,* vol. 2 (1987): 109-124.

Participant in symposium "Seht, welch ein Mensch — und wo bleibt das Reich Gottes?" *Deutscher Evangelischer Kirchentag Frankfurt 1987.* Edited by Konrad von Bonin. Stuttgart: Kreuz Verlag, 1987: 292-318.

"Thomas von Aquin und das mosaische Gesetz: ein jüdischer Kommentar." *Chronik der Ludwig-Maximilians-Universität, München, 1984-1986:* 109-120.

"A Jewish Reading of St. Thomas Aquinas on the Old Law." *Understanding Scripture: Explorations of Jewish and Christian Traditions of Interpretation.* Edited by Clemens Thoma and Michael Wyschogrod. New York: Paulist Press: 125-138.

"Christology: The Immovable Object." *Religion and Intellectual Life* 3:4 (Summer 1986): 77-80.

"La Loi dans le Judaisme." *La Revue Sidic* 19:3: 10-16.

"A Theology of Jewish Unity." *L'Eylah Journal* 21 (1986): 26-30.

"Sin and Atonement in Judaism." *The Human Condition in the Jewish and Christian Traditions.* Edited by Frederick E. Greenspahn. New York: Ktav, 1986: 103-128.

"Torah as Law." *SIDIC Review* 19:3 (1986): 8-13.

"A Jewish Perspective on Karl Barth." *How Karl Barth Changed My Mind.* Edited by Donald M. McKim. Grand Rapids: William B. Eerdmans Publishing Co., 1986: 156-66.

Foreword to *The Unfinished Dialogue: Martin Buber and the Christian Way.* John M. Oesterreicher. New York: Philosophical Library, 1986: 13-16.

"Dialog ist notwendig." *Gottes Augapfel: Beiträge zur Erneuerung des Verhältnisses von Christen und Juden.* Edited by Edna Brocke and Jürgen Seim. Neukirchener Verlag, 1986: 173-179.

"Zugang zu einer biblischen Ethik im gegenwärtigen Judentum." *Damit die Erde menschlich bleibt.* Edited by Wilhelm Brenning and Hanspeter Heinz. Herder, 1985: 71-85.

"Is the Holy Person a Contemporary Possibility?" *New Traditions,* no. 3 (Summer 1986): 47.

"After Fifteen Years — My World." *Sh'ma* 15 (Nov. 1, 1985): 153-154.

"Reconciliation in Munich." *Congress Monthly* 52:5 (July-August 1985): 3-5.

"Comment on Arthur Berk." *Quaker Religious Thought* 21:2 (Summer 1985): 16-18.

"Comments on the Paper of Hans-Hermann Henrix." *Defining a Discipline: The Aims and Objectives of Judaeo-Christian Studies.* Edited by Jakob J. Petuchowski. Hebrew Union College — Jewish Institute of Religion, 1984: 83-87.

"Der eine Gott Abrahams und die Einheit des Gottes der jüdischen Philosophie." *Das Reden vom einen Gott bei Juden und Christen.* Edited by Clemens Thoma and Michael Wyschogrod. Peter Bern, 1984: 29-48.

"The 'Shema Israel' in Judaism and the New Testament." *The Roots of Our Common Faith.* Edited by Hans-Georg Link. Geneva: World Council of Churches, 1983: 23-32. German translation as "Das 'Shema Israel' im Judentum und im Neuen Testament." *Wurzeln unseres Glaubens: Glaube in der Bibel und in der Alten Kirche.* Edited by Hans-Georg Link. Frankfurt am Main: Verlag Otto Lembeck, 1985: 31-43.

"Islam and Christianity in the Perspective of Judaism." *Trialogue of the Abrahamic Faiths.* Edited by Isma'il Razi al Faruqi (International Institute of Islamic Thought). 1982: 13-18.

"Lebanon: A Loss of Confidence." *Sh'ma* 13:250 (March 18, 1983): 72-73.

"Eine Theologie der Jüdischen Einheit." *Judaica* 39:2 (June 1983): 75-84. Reprinted in *Welches Judentum steht welchem gegenüber?* Arnoldshainer Texte, Band

36. Edited by Hans-Hermann Henrix and Werner Licharz. Haag und Herchen Verlag, 1985: 45-50.

"A New Stage in Jewish-Christian Dialogue." *Judaism* 31:3 (Summer 1982): 355-365. German translation as: "Ein Neues Stadium im Jüdisch-Christlichen Dialog." *Freiburger Rundbrief,* vol. 34 (1982): 22-26

"Symposium: The State of Orthodoxy." *Tradition* 20:1 (Spring 1982): 80-83.

"Heidegger: The Limits of Philosophy." *Sh'ma* 12:231 (April 2, 1982): 83-85.

"Buber's Evaluation of Christianity: A Jewish Perspective." *Martin Buber: A Centenary Volume.* Edited by Jochanan Bloch. Tel-Aviv: Kibutz Hameuchad, 1981: 403-417 (Hebrew). English: "Buber's Evaluation of Christianity: A Jewish Perspective." *Martin Buber: A Centenary Volume.* Edited by Haim Gordon and Jochanan Bloch. New York: Ktav, 1984: 457-472. "Bubers Beurteilung des Christentums aus Jüdischer Sicht." *Martin Buber: Bilanz seines Denkens.* Hrsg. Jochanan Bloch und Haim Gordon. Herder, 1983: 470-486.

"Judaism and Conscience." *Standing before God: Studies on Prayer in Scriptures and in Tradition with Essays in Honor of John M. Oesterreicher.* Edited by Asher Finkel and Lawrence Frizzell. New York: Ktav, 1981: 313-328.

"Religion and International Human Rights: A Jewish Perspective." *Formations of Social Policy in the Catholic and Jewish Traditions.* Edited by Eugene J. Fisher and Daniel F. Polish. University of Notre Dame Press, 1980: 123-141.

"Judaism and Evangelical Christianity." *Evangelicals and Jews in Conversation on Scripture, Theology, and History.* Edited by Marc H. Tanenbaum, Marvin R. Wilson, and A. James Rudin. Grand Rapids: Baker Book House, 1978: 34-52.

"'Auschwitz' Beginning of a New Era? Reflections on the Holocaust." *Tradition* 16:5 (Fall 1977): 63-78.

"Why Was and Is the Theology of Karl Barth of Interest to a Jewish Theologian?" *Footnotes to a Theology: The Karl Barth Colloquium of 1972.* Edited by Martin Rumscheidt (SR Supplements 1974): 95-111. German translation as "Warum war und ist Karl Barths Theologie für einen jüdischen Theologen von Interesse?" *Evangelische Theologie* 34:3 (March 1974): 222-236.

"Some Theological Reflections on the Holocaust." *Response,* no. 25 (Spring 1975): 65-68.

"God's Mercy Is Beyond Our Searching Out." *Sh'ma* 2:39 (Oct. 13, 1972): 148-149.

"The Mitzvoth Are More Than Ethics." *Sh'ma* 2:31 (April 21, 1972): 83-84.

"Faith and the Holocaust." *Judaism* 20:3 (Summer 1971): 286-294.

"Leningrad: Essence or Accident?" *Sh'ma* 1:6 (Jan. 22, 1971): 41-42.

"Angela Davis and American Philosophy." *Sh'ma* 1:1 (Nov. 9, 1970): 1-2.

"Reason on the College Campus." *Sh'ma* Trial issue 2 (June 9, 1970).

"Israel, the Church and Election." *Brothers in Hope.* Edited by John M. Oesterreicher. New York: Herder and Herder, 1970: 79-87.

"The Law, Jews and Gentiles: A Jewish Perspective." *Lutheran Quarterly* 21:4 (Nov. 1969): 405-415.

"Reform Reformed." *Tradition* 10:4 (Fall 1969): 88-91.

"Symposium: Jewish Youth and the Sexual Revolution." *Dimensions in American Judaism* 3:2 (Winter 1968-1969): 28.

Participant in "The Religious Meaning of the Six Day War: A Symposium." *Tradition* 10:1 (Summer 1968): 5-20.

"My *Commentary* Problem and Ours." *Judaism* 17:2 (Spring 1968): 148-161.

"Psychedelics and Religion: A Symposium." *Humanist* 27:5 & 6 (Sept. and Dec. 1967): 153-156 and 190-191.

"Jewish Religious Unity." *Congress Bi-Weekly* 34:16 (Nov. 20, 1967): 8.

"Art Therapy: Pros and Cons" (Abstact). *Psychiatric Spectator* 4:6: 16-18.

"The Voices of Orthodoxy." *Congress Bi-Weekly* (Dec. 19, 1966): 9-21.

"*Commentary* and the Rabbis." *Congress Bi-Weekly* (Oct. 24, 1966): 6.

"The Cult of Creativity." Columbia University's *Teachers College Record*, May 1966: 618-622. Same article also appeared in *Review of Existential Psychology and Psychiatry*, 7:1: 30-35.

"Peace: The Real Imperative." *Congress Bi-Weekly* (April 4, 1966): 7-8.

Articles on "Martin Buber" and "Yehudah Halevi." *Encyclopedia of Philosophy*. Macmillan, 1968.

Article on "Will in Psychology and Philosophy." *Encyclopedia Americana*. New York, 1962, vol. 28: 770-772.

"Second Thoughts on America." *Tradition* 5:1: 29-30.

Comment on Aharon Lichtenstein's "Brother Daniel and the Jewish Fraternity." *Judaism* 13:1 (Winter 1964): 107-110.

Comment on Paul Weiss's "The Religious Turn." *Judaism* 12:1 (Winter 1963): 26-27.

"The Problem of the Intellectual." *Jewish Life* 30:2 (January 1963): 11-14.

"Rejoinder to 'Red or Dead.'" *Tradition* 4:2 (Spring 1962): 206-209.

"Agenda for Jewish Philosophy." *Judaism* 11:5 (Summer 1962): 195-199.

"Israel: Secular State." *Jewish Horizon* 25:4: 9.

"Sartre, Freedom and the Unconscious." *Review of Existential Psychology and Psychiatry* 1:3 (Fall 1961): 179-186.

"Divine Election and Commandments." *Judaism* 10:4 (Fall 1961): 350-352.

"Belief and Action." *Religious Experience and Truth: A Symposium*. Edited by Sidney Hook. New York University Press, 1961: 180-186.

"Heidegger's Ontology and Human Existence." *Diseases of the Nervous System* 22:4 (April 1961): 540-556.

Introduction and translation, with Jacob L. Halberstam, of selections from *Pirke Aboth*. *Commentary* (March 1953): 292-294.

## Works by Michael Wyschogrod

Introduction to selections from Rashi's commentary to the Song of Songs. *Commentary* (Feb. 1953): 187-188.

Introduction and translation of excerpts from Rabbi Hayim Volozhin's *Nefesh Hachayim*. *Commentary* (Dec. 1952): 595-597.

## Book Reviews

*Consciousness and the Mind of God* by Charles Taliaferro (Cambridge: Cambridge University Press, 1994). *International Studies in Philosophy* 31/4: 133-134.

*The Coming of God: Christian Eschatology* by Juergen Moltmann, trans. Margaret Kohl (Minneapolis: Fortress Press, 1996), and *The Future of Theology: Essays in Honor of Jürgen Moltmann*. Edited by Miroslav Volf, Carmen Krieg, and Thomas Kucharz (Grand Rapids: William B. Eerdmans Publishing Co.). *Journal of Ecumenical Studies* 35:2 (Spring 1998): 295-296.

*Jew and Philosopher: The Return to Maimonides in the Jewish Thought of Leo Strauss* by Kenneth Hart Green (Albany: State University of New York Press, 1993). *Jewish Political Studies Review* 9:3-4 (Fall 1997): 87-90.

"Reflections on Eva Hoffman's *Shtetl: The Life and Death of a Small Town and the World of Polish Jews*." *Sarmatian Review* 18:2 (April 1998): 537-539.

*Christologie "nach Auschwitz": Kritische Bilanz für die Religionsdidaktik aus dem christlich-jüdischen Dialog* by Gabriele Niekamp (Friburg: Herder, 1994). *Journal of Ecumenical Studies* 34:1 (Winter 1997): 142-143.

*Verbindliches Zeugnis I: Kanon — Schrift — Tradition*. Dialog der Kirchen 7. Edited by Wolfhart Pannenberg and Theodor Schneider (Göttingen: Vandenhoeck & Ruprecht, 1992). *Journal of Ecumenical Studies* 33:1 (Winter 1996): 103.

*Metaphysical Drift: Love and Judaism* by Jerome Eckstein (New York: Peter Lang, 1991). *International Studies in Philosophy* 26:4: 123-124.

*The Moral Core of Judaism and Christianity: Reclaiming the Revolution* by Daniel C. Maguire (Minneapolis: Fortress Press, 1993). *Journal of Ecumenical Studies* 31:1/2 (Winter/Spring 1994): 169-170.

*Interpreting Maimonides: Studies in Methodology, Metaphysics, and Moral Philosophy* by Marvin Fox (Chicago: University of Chicago Press, 1990). *Tradition* 28:2 (Winter 1994): 69-74.

*That Jesus Christ Was Born a Jew: Karl Barth's "Doctrine of Israel"* by Katherine Sonderegger (University Park, Pa: Pennsylvania State University Press, 1992). *Modern Theology* 9:3 (July 1993): 306-307.

*Judaism: Between Yesterday and Tomorrow* by Hans Küng (New York: Crossroad, 1992). *Journal of Ecumenical Studies* 30:2 (Spring 1993): 287-288.

*Das christliche Bekenntnis zu Jesus, dem Juden. Eine Christologie 1.* by Friedrich-Wilhelm Marquardt (Munich: Chr. Kaiser Verlag, 1990) and *Das christliche*

*Bekenntnis zu Jesus, dem Juden. Eine Christologie 2.* by Friedrich-Wilhelm Marquardt (Munich: Chr. Kaiser Verlag: 1991). *Journal of Ecumenical Studies* 29:2 (Spring 1992): 275-276.

*The Lonely Man of Faith* by Joseph B. Soloveitchik (New York: Doubleday, 1992). *Commonweal* (Jan. 15, 1993): 26.

*After the Absolute: The Dialogical Future of Religious Reflection* by Leonard Swidler (Minneapolis: Fortress Press, 1990). *Journal of Ecumenical Studies* 28:1 (Winter 1990): 175.

*"Geh in das Land, das ich Dir zeigen werde. . . ." Das Land Israel in den frühen rabbinischen Tradition und im Neuen Testament* by Katherine Elena Wolff (New York: Peter Lang, 1989). *Journal of Ecumenical Studies* 27:1 (Fall 1990): 787.

*The Emergence of Jewish Theology in America* by Robert G. Goldy (Bloomington: Indiana University Press, 1990). *American Jewish History* 80:2 (Winter 1990-1991): 311-312.

*Judaica: Kleine Schriften I.* Wissentschaftliche Untersuchungen zum Neuen Testament 37 (Tübingen: J. C. B. Mohr, 1986). *Journal of Ecumenical Studies* 27:3 (Summer 1990): 606.

*The Lamp of God: A Jewish Book of Light* by Freema Gottlieb (Northvale, N.J.: Jason Aronson, 1989). *Judaism* 40:3 (Summer 1991): 382-384.

*Holocaust Testimonies: The Ruins of Memory* by Lawrence Langer (New Haven: Yale, 1990). *Sh'ma* 21:411 (April 5, 1991): 84-85.

*Die Kraft der Wurzel: Judentum-Jesus-Kirche* by Franz Mussner (Freiburg: Herder, 1987). *Journal of Ecumenical Studies* 27:1 (Winter 1990): 129-130.

*The Theology of the Churches and the Jewish People: Statements by the World Council of Churches and Its Member Churches* (Geneva: WCC Publications, 1988), and *Pope John Paul II on Jews and Judaism, 1979-1986,* edited by Eugene J. Fisher and Leon Klenicki (Washington, 1987), and *Die Kirche und das Judentum: Dokumente von 1945 bis 1985,* edited by Rolf Rendtorff and Hans Hermann Henrix (Munich: Chr. Kaiser Verlag, 1988). *Journal of Ecumenical Studies* 26:4 (Fall 1986): 682-683.

*Spinoza and Other Heretics, Vol. 1: The Marranos of Reason, Vol. 2, The Adventure of Immanence* by Yirmiyahu Yovel (Princeton: Princeton University Press, 1989). *Commonweal* 117:7 (April 6, 1990): 227-228.

*God at the Center: Meditations on Jewish Spirituality* by David Blumenthal (San Francisco: Harper, 1988). *Tradition* 24:4 (Summer 1989): 99-101.

*Angst and the Abyss: The Hermeneutics of Nothingness* by David K. Coe (Chico, Calif.: Scholars Press, 1985). *International Studies in Philosophy* 21:1 (1989): 73-74.

*Zum Thema: "Diaspora und Oekumene" Handreichung für Erwachsenenbildung, Religionsunterricht und Seelsorge,* edited by Lothar Rupert, Lother Ullrich,

# Works by Michael Wyschogrod

Hans Joerg Urban, and Franz Georg Untergassmair (Paderborn: Verlag Bonifatius, 1986), and *Zionismus: Befreiungsbewegung des jüdischen Volkes,* 2nd enlarged edition, Veroeffentlichungen aus dem Institut Kirche und Judentum (Berlin, 1986). *Journal of Ecumenical Studies* 25:4 (Fall 1988): 631-632.

*Where Are We? The Inner Life of America's Jews* by Leonard Fein (New York: Harper & Row, 1988). *Commonweal* 116:7 (April 7, 1989): 218-219.

*Targumic Approaches to the Gospels: Essays in the Mutual Definition of Judaism and Christianity* by Bruce Chilton (Lanham, Md.: University Press of America, 1986) and *Die Bergpredikt: Jüdisches und Christliches Glaubensdokument: Eine Sympose.* Edited by Guenter Ginzel (Verlag Lambert Schneider). *Journal of Ecumenical Studies* 25:1 (Winter 1988): 106-107.

*The People Called: The Growth of Community in the Bible* by Paul D. Hanson (San Francisco: Harper & Row, 1986). *Journal of Ecumenical Studies* 24:3 (Summer 1987): 450-451.

*Kierkegaard's Fear and Trembling: Critical Appraisals.* Edited by Robert L. Perkins (Tuscaloosa, Ala.: University of Alabama Press, 1981). *International Studies in Philosophy* 19:3: 108-109.

*Paulus — Wegbereiter des Christentums: Zur Aktualität des Völkerapostels in oekumenischer Sicht* by Eugene Biser, Claus-Hunne Hunziger, Anastasios Kallis, and Schalom Ben-Chorin (Verlag J. Pfeiffer), and *Jesus der Jude und das Jüdische in Christentum* by Laurenz Volken (Patmos Verlag). *Journal of Ecumenical Studies* 24:1 (Winter 1987): 131.

*Das Blut Christi und die Juden: Mt. 27, 25 bei den lateinisch sprachigen christlichen Autoren bis zu Leo dem Grossen* by Rainer Kampling. Neutestamentliche Abhandlungen, Band 16 (Aschendorff Muenster, 1984). *Journal of Ecumenical Studies* 23:4 (Fall 1986): 682-683.

*Mutuality: The Vision of Martin Buber* by Donald L. Berry (Albany: State University of New York Press, 1986). *Canadian Philosophical Reviews* 6:9 (November 1986): 421-422.

*Post-Holocaust Dialogues: Critical Studies in Modern Jewish Thought* by Steven T. Katz (New York: New York University Press, 1985). *Journal for the Association of Jewish Studies* 11:1 (Spring 1986): 121-126.

*Questioning Back: The Overcoming of Metaphysics in Christian Tradition* by Joseph S. O'Leary (Minneapolis: Winston, 1985). *Journal of Ecumenical Studies* 23:2 (Spring 1986): 318-319.

*Unter den Bogen des Bundes: Beiträge aus jüdischer und christlicher Existenz.* Edited by Hans Herman Henrix (Aachen, Einhard Verlag), and *Heil für die Christen — Unheil für die Juden? Von der Notwendigkeit des Gesprächs und der gemeinsamen Zeugnisses.* Edited by Werner Licharz (Frankfurt a. M.:

Haag und Herchen Verlag). *Journal of Ecumenical Studies* 22:4 (Fall 1985): 789-790.

*A Certain People: American Jews and Their Lives Today* by Charles E. Silberman (New York: Summit, 1985) and *Israel in America: A Too Comfortable Exile?* by Jacob Neusner (Boston: Beacon, 1985). *Commonweal* (Nov. 15, 1985): 649-650.

*Die Gegenwart des Auferstandenen bei seinem Volk Israel: Ein dogmatisches Experiment* by Friedrich Wilhelm Marquardt (Chr. Kaiser Verlag). *Journal of Ecumenical Studies* 21:3 (Summer 1948): 566-567.

*Myth and Metaphysics* by William A. Luijpen (The Hague: Nijhoff, 1976). *International Studies in Philosophy*, vol. 10, 1978: 179-180.

Contribution to "Religious Book Week: Critics Choices." *Commonweal* (Feb. 22, 1985): 122.

*The Age of Triage: Fear and Hope in an Overcrowded World* by Richard R. Rubinstein (Boston: Beacon, 1983). *Journal of Reform Judaism* (Fall 1984): 76-78.

*Jesus in Focus: A Life in Its Setting* by Gerard S. Sloyan (Mystic, Conn.: Twenty-Third Publications, 1983). *Judaism* 33:4 (Fall 1984): 497-498.

*The Tremendum: A Theological Interpretation of the Holocaust* by Arthur A. Cohen (New York: Crossroad, 1981). *Jewish Social Studies* 44:2 (Spring 1982): 179-180.

*Offenbarung im Jüdischen und Christlichen Gaubensverständnis*. Edited by Jakob J. Petuchowski and Walter Strolz (Herder, 1981). *Journal of Ecumenical Studies* 19:3 (Summer 1982): 61.

*Homo Quarens: The Seeker and the Sought: Method Become Ontology* by Leonard Charles Feldstein (Fordham). *International Studies in Philosophy* 15:1: 78-79.

*With God in Hell: Judaism in the Ghettoes and Deathcamps* by Eliezer Berkovits (New York: Sanhedrin, 1979). *Tradition* 19:2 (Summer 1981): 189-191.

*Maimonides: Torah and Philosophic Quest* by David Hartman (Philadelphia: Jewish Publication Society, 1976). *Tradition* 17:4 (Spring 1979): 105-111.

*The Ordeal of Civility: Freud, Marx, Levi-Strauss, and the Jewish Struggle with Modernity* by John Murray Cuddihy (New York: Basic, 1974). *Judaism* 25:4 (Fall 1976): 505-506.

*The Star of Redemption* by Franz Rosenzweig (New York: Holt, Rinehart and Winston, 1971). *Man and World* 6:1 (Feb. 1973): 100-107.

*Faith and Doubt: Studies in Traditional Jewish Thought* by Norman Lamm (New York: Ktav, 1971). *Tradition* 13:1 (Summer 1972): 161-164.

*One Man's Judaism* by Emanuel Rackman (New York: Philosophical Library, 1970). *Tradition* 12:1 (Summer 1971): 101-104.

*Athens and Jerusalem* by Lev Shestov (Athens, Ohio: Ohio University Press, 1966). *Jewish Social Studies* 30:4 (Oct. 1968): 291-292.

# Works by Michael Wyschogrod

*The End of the Jewish People?* by Georges Friedmann (London: Hutchinson, 1967). *Women's ORT Reporter* 18:1: 7, 10.

*The Artist in Society: Problems and Treatment of the Creative Personality* by Lawrence J. Hatterer (New York: Grove, 1965). *Kenyon Review,* Nov. 1966: 705-706.

*Rediscovering Tradition: Reflections on a New Theology.* Edited by Arnold Jacob Wolf. *Congress Bi-Weekly* 34:6: 18-19.

*Grundzüge der Ontologie Sartres in Ihrem Verhältnis zu Hegels Logik: Eine Untersuchung zu 'L'etre et le Neant'* by Klaus Hartmann. *Social Research* (Autumn 1966): 492-494.

*Modern Varieties of Judaism* by Joseph L. Blau (New York: Columbia, 1966). *Congress Bi-Weekly* (March 7, 1966): 17-18.

*The Code of Maimonides: The Book of Torts* (New Haven: Yale, 1955). *Commentary* (May 1955): 499-501.

*Israel Salanter: Ethical Religious Thinker* by Menahem M. Glenn (New York: Bloch, 1953). *Commentary* (February 1954): 206-208.

*Walls Are Crumbling: Seven Jewish Philosophers Discover Christ* by John M. Oesterreicher (New York: Devin Adair Co., 1952). *Judaism* 2:2 (April 1953): 189-192.

# Index

Abel, 171, 182
Abraham: blessing to all humanity through, 12-13, 175, 180-83, 186, 200, 212-13, 236; election of, 8, 11-12, 26, 30, 43-44, 47-51, 91-93, 96, 129, 140, 178, 180, 212, 234; God's love for, 8-10, 171-72; and sacrifice of Isaac, 68, 84, 182
Absolute (philosophical), 13, 30, 32, 102, 158-59
Acts, 99; Jerusalem council in, 17, 21, 163, 192, 194, 209, 232-33; on keeping of the Law, 193-94, 197, 209, 233-34
Adam, 47-48, 55-57, 61-67, 107-9, 234
Ahab. Jacob, Rabbi, 31
Akiba, Rabbi, 99
Amidah (standing prayer), 37-38
animals, 107-10, 190
anthropomorphism, 34-35, 42, 158-60, 167-68, 173-74
Aristotle, 32, 41, 184, 217
Atonement, Day of, 122, 177
atonement, Jewish understanding of, 53-54, 69-72
Augustine, 1, 97
Auschwitz: effects of, 112-15, 119-20; survivor of, 133, 144-45
autonomy, and conscience, 82, 84-88

Babel, tower of, 56, 67, 171
Babylonian Talmud: Baba Meṣi'a, 79; Berakoth, 30, 37n.10, 70n.7, 79, 173-74;

Sanhedrin, 65-66nn.4-5; Sukkah, 73n.11; Yevamoth, 108; Yoma, 71n.9
Bar Kochba, 99
Barth, Karl: on conscience, 82-84; on Jews, 20, 220-23, 235; and philosophy, 123-27; as scriptural, 5, 214-20
Bath-Sheba, 78-79
Bible, 66, 171-72, 216-18; as common bond between Judaism and Christianity, 167, 177-78; and law, 69, 209, 230-31; and sin, 55-56, 58-59, 67-68, 72; Wyschogrod on centrality of, 3, 226-28, 230-31, 236
blessing: to all families of earth through Abraham's election, 12-13, 175, 180-83, 186, 200, 212-13, 236; to Israel for obedience, 93, 195
blood: eating of prohibited, 109-10; life in, 70
body, unity of with soul, 10, 49-50, 67, 96-97, 125, 140-41
Book of Beliefs and Opinions (Saadia Gaon), 32
Borowitz, Eugene, 4n.7
Brown, Raymond, 232
Buber, Martin, 2-3, 64, 88, 122, 235
Bultmann, Rudolf, 214, 216
burial rites, Jewish, 143-46

Cain, 67, 171, 182
Calvin, John, 216-17, 219
Catholic Church, 21, 180, 207-8

248

# INDEX

Galatians, 184, 189, 192-94, 197, 198, 207-8, 233

Genesis, 56, 64, 73-74, 94, 96, 107-9, 124, 171, 175, 236; and blessing to Abraham, 91, 100, 175, 180, 200, 212; and Noachide covenant, 158, 190, 206, 232

*Genesis Rabbah*, 74n.14, 170n.2

gentiles: and Israel, 8-9, 13-14, 17-18, 21-22, 186-87, 191-94, 197, 213, 220, 224, 236; and Noachide laws, 12, 18, 50, 158, 162-63, 185-86, 190-98, 200, 206, 209, 232-33; non-election of, 8-9, 13-14, 16-17, 186-87, 200

*Ger Toshav* (indwelling stranger), 191

*Ger Tzedek* (righteous stranger), 191

Glatzer, Nahum N., 113, 121

Gnostics, 54, 67, 74, 140

God: as absolute and corporeal, 29-42, 158-60, 167-68, 171, 173-74, 184; commands of, 35-39, 54-61, 69, 230-31, 234-35; and creation, 12-13, 64, 67, 74, 108-9, 115, 170-71; and election of Israel, 6-14, 19-21, 39, 47-51, 68, 91-93, 96-100, 105, 140, 151-52, 174-75, 178, 180-85, 234; as father, 151-52, 159, 172-73, 186-87, 219, 224; freedom of, 7-9, 15, 215-16; of history, 60, 64, 66-67, 112, 119, 129, 182, 215-16; indwelling of, 13-15, 21, 101-2, 168-70, 175-78; justice of, 174, 196-201, 218-19, 231, 235; love of, 21, 49-50, 65, 151-52, 159, 170-74, 180, 201, 213, 215, 217, 224; mercy of, 174, 196-201, 218-19, 231-32; wrath of, 65, 68, 159, 171, 174, 201, 219

*God's Presence in History: Jewish Affirmations and Philosophical Reflections* (Fackenheim), 111-17

golden calf, 68

good and evil, 54-58, 61-62, 64, 73

good inclination *(yetzer hatov)*, 73

*Gottes Gegenwart in Israel* (Janowski), 168

Greek influence on Christianity, 31-33, 67, 97, 176-77, 228-29

Gush Emunim, 105

Hadrian, 113

Halivni, David Weiss, 4n.7

*haskalah* (Jewish enlightenment), 153

Hebron, 106

Hegel, G. W. F., 41, 122, 126

*Hegel und der Staat* (Rosenzweig), 122

Heidegger, Martin, 3-4, 41, 77, 82, 86-88, 127-28, 139, 141, 214

Heidelberg: Jewish death and burial in, 131-46; Theological Faculty, 133-34, 136, 145; University of, 132-33, 136, 138

Heiman, Schlomo, 25

Heschel, Abraham, 4n.7

Hitler, Adolf, 113-15, 141

Hiyya bar Abin, Rabbi, 173

Holocaust: and Christianity, 149-50, 154; and Jewish faith and identity, 60, 111-20, 150-53; survivors of, 46, 133-34, 136, 141, 143-45

Hopper, Edward, 5

Hosea, 48-49, 71, 172-73

Hoshaiah, Rabbi, 170

humanism: ethical, 82, 88; secular, 62

idolatry, 14, 99, 157-58, 166-68

image of God in man, 67, 106, 109, 170-71, 175, 236

incarnation, 14-16, 21, 97, 157-60, 166-78, 199-200, 215-19

individualism, 75, 81, 84-85

indwelling of God, 15, 168-70, 175-78

Isaac, sacrifice of, 48-49, 84, 68

Isaiah, 13, 65, 174, 186

Ishmael, 47, 186

Islam, and Judaism, 150-51, 157, 183, 228

Israel: disobedience of, 73-74, 223-24; election of, 6-14, 19-21, 49-50, 65, 68, 96-100, 119, 128, 140, 151-52, 170-74, 180-82, 184, 200-201, 224, 234; as God's dwelling place, 13, 102, 169, 175, 177-78; relationship of to the land, 10-12, 91-96, 100-103, 105; relationship of to nations, 12, 15, 17, 39, 100, 119, 185-87, 212-13; as son of God, 172-74, 180, 186-87, 219, 224; State of, 11, 26, 95, 104

Jacob, 9, 124

Janowski, Bernd, 168

Jeremiah, 68, 172, 181-82, 223

250

# Index

Jerusalem, 72, 113; church council in, 163, 192, 194, 197, 209, 232-33; as dwelling place of God, 102, 169

Jesus: death and resurrection of, 99, 128, 188; divinity and humanity of, 157-60, 166-67, 176-78, 217; and gentiles, 18, 178, 191-93, 197, 232-33; and Jews, 14-15, 18, 193-97, 199-200; and the law, 189, 196-98, 208-9, 233; as Messiah, 189, 191-93, 213, 220, 223; and salvation by faith, 67, 161, 163, 174, 198, 231

Jews: division among, 27-28, 45-46, 51-52, 67, 113-16, 119-20, 203-9; as immigrants, 76; indwelling of God among, 168-70, 175, 178; and relevance of Christ to, 193-97; and suffering, 151-52; unity of, 43-52

Job, 108

John, Gospel of, 50, 175

John the Baptist, 48

John XXIII, 20, 208

Joseph, 180, 184-85

Joshua, 100

Joshua, Rabbi, 66-67

Joshua b. Korha, Rabbi, 37

Judaism, 54, 67, 72, 160-61, 176, 198-99, 200, 214; and Christianity, 62, 67, 154-64, 203-9, 212, 225-26, 228, 231-32; in history, 105, 154; on incarnation, 168-78, 215-19; as injured, 150-53; and Islam, 157, 228; liberal, 4, 60, 71, 76, 130, 162; modern, 4, 89-90, 155, 230-33; Rosenzweig on, 124-29; on Torah observance, 81-82, 160-64, 230, 233-35; unity of secular and sacred in, 2-3, 155-56

Judges, 68

justice, 80-81; of God, 174, 196-201, 218-19, 231

Kant, Immanuel, 69, 87, 217

Kaplan, Mordecai, 28

Karaites, 226, 231

Kaufmann, Yehezkel, 30, 36

kerygma, 20, 184

Kierkegaard, Søren, 88, 123

1 Kings, 101, 168-69

Lamentations, 170

land, and Judaism, 10-12, 91-103, 105, 129, 169

law, 79, 196-98, 200-201, 230-31, 234-35; Barth on, 216-17; and Christ, 161-62, 189, 193, 196-98, 208-9, 233; and conscience, 79-80, 89-90; and Judaism, 162, 194-95, 208, 216-18, 230, 233-35; Paul on, 163, 193-97, 209

Leibniz, G. W., 126

Levenson, Jon, 4n.7

Levinas, Emmanuel, 2-3, 125

Leviticus, 58n.1, 70, 177, 206

Lichtenstein, Aharon, 19n.44

Loewe, H., 73n.10

love: of God for Israel, 6-14, 21, 68, 201; for God, 36

Luke, Gospel of, 48-49, 209

Lustiger, Jean-Marie, 17, 20-21; Wyschogrod's letter to, 202-10

Luther, Martin, 1, 76, 216-17

Maimonides, 33-34, 39, 49, 97, 159, 167-68, 173, 183, 186, 213, 228-30

Marcion, 178

Mark, Gospel of, 218

Marquardt, Friedrich Wilhelm, 220-22

Mary, as mother of God, 177

mathematical illustration of sin, 54, 57-58, 69, 82

Matthew, Gospel of, 209

Meinecke, Friedrich, 122

mercy of God, 174, 196-201, 218-19, 231-32

messianism, 11, 14, 65, 98-99, 105-6, 152

metaphysics, 31-35, 37-39, 41, 176-77

Micah, 172

*Midas Hadin* (God's aspect of justice), 197-99

*Midas Horachamim* (God's aspect of mercy), 197-99, 219

*Midrash Rabbah Lamentations,* 59n.2

Milton, John, 73

mind-body dualism, 141, 166

Mishnah, 37, 230; *Kethuboth,* 79

*Mishneh Torah* (Maimonides), 230

mitzvoth, obligation to obey, 199, 207-8

modernization, and crisis of faith, 44, 152

# Index

sin, 53-70, 72-74, 177, 189; of Adam and Eve, 55-57, 60-61, 64, 107-8, 171; atonement for, 69-70, 188; punishment for, 65, 68, 112-13, 151-52
Six Day War, 104-6
Socrates, 97, 128
Solomon's Temple, 101, 168-69
Soloveitchik, Joseph, 2, 149, 155-57
Soviet Union, 153
Spain, Jews in, 81, 207
Spinoza, Baruch, 126
Star of Redemption, The (Rosenzweig), 121, 123-30
Steinsalz, Adin, 228
Stern, David, 169-70
Strauss, Leo, 157
Summa Theologiae (Thomas Aquinas), 208
supersessionism, 17-21, 183-84
Synagogue Council of America, 157

Tabernacle, 168-69
Talmud, 37, 65
Tanna deBe Eliyahu, 74n.12
Temple: destruction of, 13, 43, 70-72, 81, 113, 161, 169-70; God's presence in, 13, 101-2, 168-70, 175
temptation, 73-74
theology: and Christianity, 214; and Judaism, 228-29; and philosophy, 165
Thomas Aquinas, 89-90, 208, 231
Torah, 25-26, 72, 90, 119, 140, 226-27; obedience in the church, 17-18, 21, 163, 192-93, 198, 232-33; obedience required of Jews, 3, 9, 37, 50, 59-60, 76, 154-55, 160-64, 190-98, 200-201, 206-7, 209, 230, 232-35
totalitarianism, 75, 153

Totalité et infini (Totality and Infinity) (Levinas), 125
Tradition (journal), 155
tree of knowledge of good and evil, 47-48, 55-57, 107
Trinity, 29, 40, 42, 157-60, 166-67, 205-6

universalization, 4, 20, 184
Untersuchungen zur Geschichtslehre der Tannaiten (Glatzer), 113
Uriah the Hittite, 78-79

Vatican II, 180, 184, 220
violence, Wyschogrod against, 11-12, 105-6

Weil, Simone, 77, 88
Wellhausen, Julius, 30
Wiesel, Emil, 112
Wittgenstein, Ludwig, 112
word of God: and conscience, 82, 84, 86, 88; and philosophy, 126-27
World War II, effect of on Judaism, 121, 150, 153
wrath of God, 201, 219

Yavneh, 26-27
yetzer hara (evil inclination), 72-74
yetzer hatov (good inclination), 73
Yiddish, 145-46
Yohanan, Rabbi, 174
Yose, Rabbi, 174

Zechariah, 38-40
Zelophehad, daughters of, 235
Zephaniah, 213
Zionism, 95, 99, 106
Zutra bar Tobia, Rabbi, 174